IMAGES
of America

ARGYLE

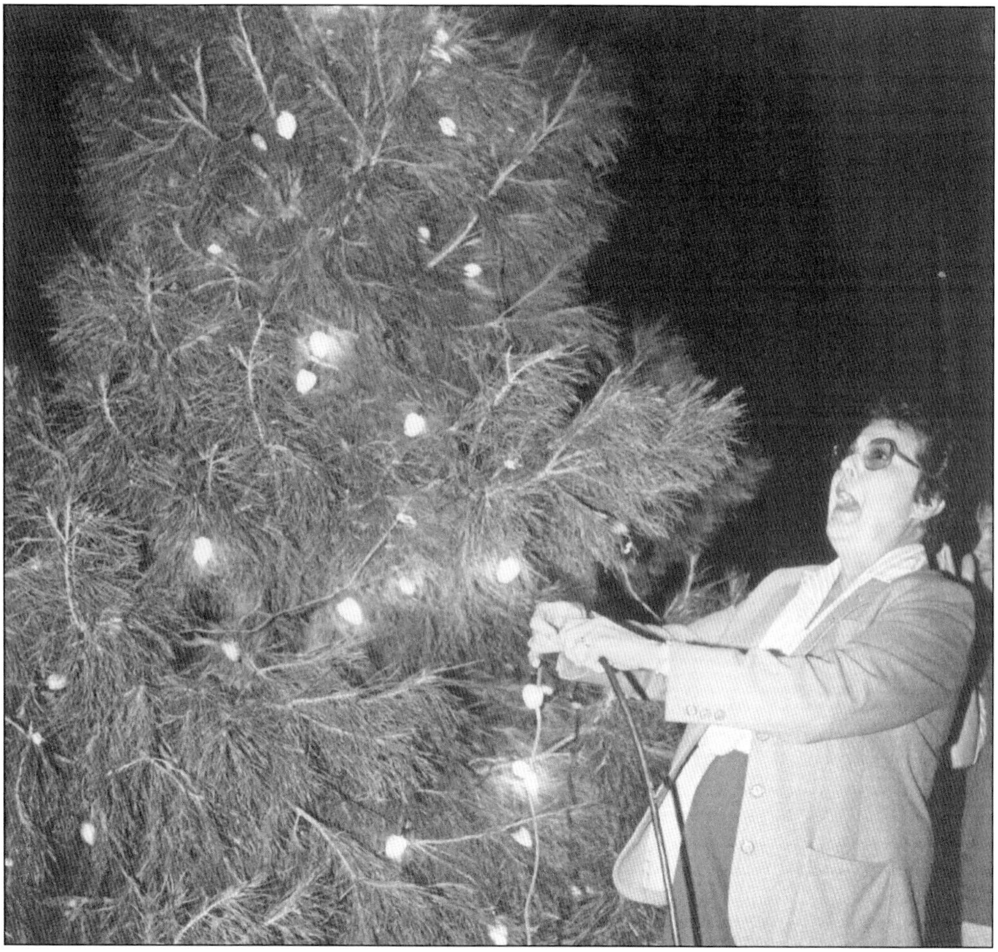

In 1981, when Mayor Yvonne A. Jenkins took office, she wanted to bring the citizens of Argyle together through community projects. In this photograph, Mayor Jenkins is seen lighting the Christmas trees at the 1984 Argyle Community Tree Lighting Ceremony that was performed at the Argyle Post Office. The Argyle United Methodist Church and the First Baptist Church of Argyle choirs sang carols followed by Santa Claus arriving on an Argyle Volunteer Fire Department fire truck. Working for the betterment of the community was nothing new to Mayor Jenkins. When she was in high school she was the caller for the Argyle Square Dance Team that traveled around the state giving demonstrations. In 1960, she was instrumental in getting Argyle incorporated; in 1962, she and her husband, Charles Jenkins, helped establish the Argyle Water Supply Corporation with Charles serving on the board of directors. In 1963, she and her husband helped organize the Argyle Volunteer Fire Department and were trained to be firefighters. In 1971, she helped form the Argyle Volunteer Fire Department Women's Auxiliary for raising funds to build a fire hall, buy a pumper truck, and purchase firefighting equipment. And, in 1976, Mayor Jenkins helped start the Argyle Volunteer Fire Department Women's Firefighting Team to fight fires when the men were at work. (Courtesy of DRC.)

On the Cover: Pictured are Tom Spencer, Red Allen, Ben Davis, and Bill Meadows in a 1920 photograph of Meadows Garage, located next to Meadows Store on US Highway 377. The highway went through downtown Argyle and ran parallel to the railroad tracks. When US Highway 377 was widened, the garage was closed to make room for the road. (Courtesy of Kay Teer.)

IMAGES
of America

ARGYLE

Lynn Sheffield Simmons

ARCADIA
PUBLISHING

ISBN 978-0-7385-8496-6

Published by Arcadia Publishing
Charleston, South Carolina

Printed in the United States of America

Library of Congress Control Number: 2011928869

For all general information, please contact Arcadia Publishing:
Telephone 843-853-2070
Fax 843-853-0044
E-mail sales@arcadiapublishing.com
For customer service and orders:
Toll-Free 1-888-313-2665

Visit us on the Internet at www.arcadiapublishing.com

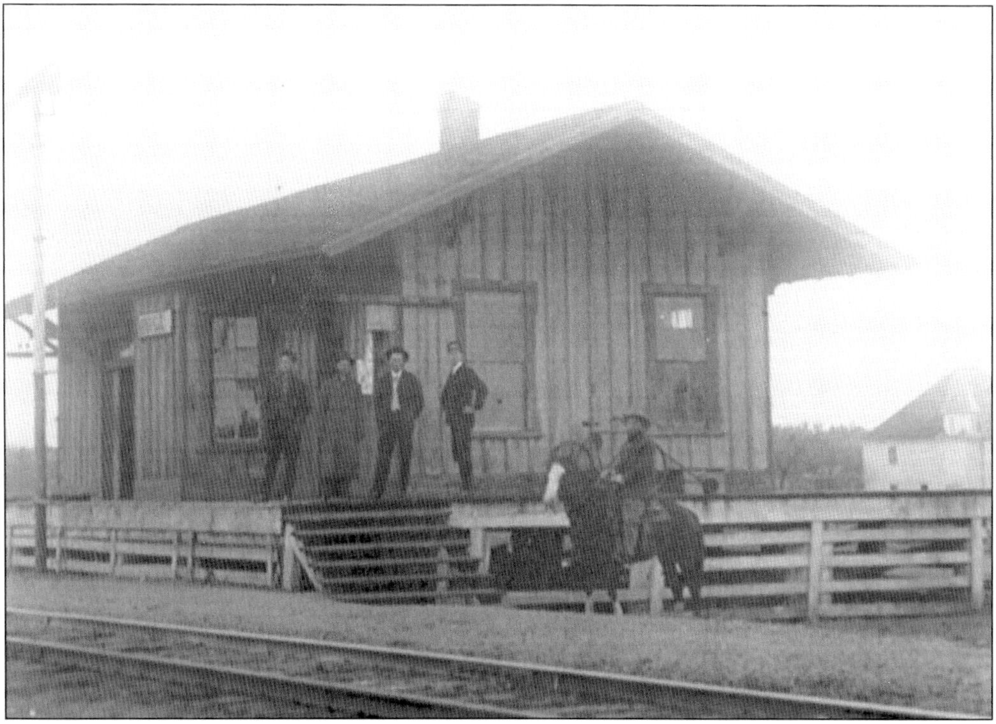

In 1881, when developer James Morrill drew up the plat of the town, the Argyle train depot was built on the west side of the railroad tracks. It had a loading dock and large cattle holding pens. Inside the passenger waiting room, the depot had a coal-burning, pot-bellied stove, and the railroad agent conducted business from behind a cage. (Courtesy of Kay Teer.)

Contents

ACKNOWLEDGMENTS

I want to thank the following for their help as I compiled and wrote this book: Crystal Wood of Tattersall Publishing for scanning photographs and sharing her advice and expertise, along with proofreading the manuscript; my husband, Dr. Larry Simmons, for assisting me in collecting research material and picking up and returning photographs; Katherine Boyer for proofing and correcting page numbers; Terry Lantrip editor/publisher of *The Argyle Sun* for proofreading this manuscript; and Pat Brown, Mary Anne Carroll, Jackie Carpenter, Mary Ann DeBerry, Kathy Emery, Greta Garrett, Jim Heath, Wallace Lynch, Martha Len Nelson, Karyl Smith, and Mary George Sullivan for sharing with me their knowledge of Argyle history.

Thank you to those who let me put their photographs in this book: Martha Beavers, Jody Bellinghausen, Pat Brown, Dr. Allen Buffington, Mary Anne Carroll, Jackie Carpenter, Joan Delashaw, Mary Ann DeBerry, Eagleton Photography, Kathy Emery, June Gentry, Greta Garrett, Jim Heath, Thom Horton, Arlene Kerr, Edwinna Kerr, Wallace Lynch, Martha Len Nelson, Denise Remfert, Dr. Larry Simmons, Kay Teer, Argyle United Methodist Church, Argyle Volunteer Fire District (AVFD), Argyle Police Department (APD), *Denton Record-Chronicle* (DRC), and *The Argyle Sun*.

I researched materials in the following books, articles, and personal interviews: *Argyle Community History* by Yvonne A. Jenkins; *The Place Is Argyle: Historical Facts and Recollections* by Lynn Sheffield Simmons, First Baptist Church of Argyle history written in 1980 and 1984 by Dixie Anderson; Argyle United Methodist Church directories and early history; *The Denton Record-Chronicle* (DRC) articles on Argyle; articles in *The Argyle Sun*; poems *The Place Is Argyle* and *The Sam Bass Poem* by Lynn Sheffield Simmons; and personal interviews with the people listed above who shared with me their knowledge of Argyle history and lent their photographs.

Introduction

As more people migrated west, members of the Peters Colony were the first to settle in Argyle. Fourteen families made Argyle their home between 1850 and 1867. It was an ideal place to live. The artesian wells provided plenty of water and the rich soil produced fine crops. Before the Texas and Pacific Railway built tracks through the southeastern part of Denton County in 1881, it was difficult to distinguish Argyle from the Pilot Knob community.

The tall hill with an elevation of 850 feet running beside Interstate 35W and three miles west of Argyle is known as Pilot Knob. The hilltop served as a reference point for wagon trains and a lookout for Indians. It was alleged that Denton County's famous outlaw Sam Bass hid some of the gold he robbed from the Union Pacific Railroad in a cave on the tall hill. Settlers living around the distinguished knoll called their community Pilot Knob. Besides being the highest hilltop in Denton County, Pilot Knob marks the beginning of the Grand Prairie and the end of the Eastern Cross Timbers. Nearby, the town of Argyle is part of the Eastern Cross Timbers, a narrow strip of land running from Waco, Texas, to the Red River Valley. This belt of rolling hills and tall trees is wedged between the Grand Prairie to the west and the Blackland Prairie to the east.

"Our farm was called the Long Point Farm because that was the last of the timber," 92-year-old Marcella Stewart Henderson of Denton said in a 1994 interview while telling about the 400-acre Stewart farm located on the south side of "the Knob."

The early settlers in the Pilot Knob–Argyle area were both black and white. Many of the landowners not only farmed their land but had other occupations, too. Dr. Daniel McIntyre Stewart, a white man, owned the Long Point Farm on the south side of Pilot Knob and he was the first physician. Nearby, Andy Walker, a member of a black family, owned a farm, and he was a famous horse wrangler well known for his successful horse liniment. John C. Heath's ranch is on what is now F.M. (Farm to Market) 407. He farmed his land and was also a cattleman.

In 1880, the Texas and Pacific Railway laid tracks through the Cross Timbers from Aubrey to Denton, through Roanoke, and down to Fort Worth. Developer James Morrill drew the plat of the town, calling the streets running parallel to the railroad track East Front Street (which is now US Highway 377) and West Front Street (which has kept its name). It is presumed that local physician Dr. Daniel McIntyre Stewart, whose family was from Argyll, Scotland, helped the railroad surveyor name the town Argyle on November 7, 1881, when it was established.

After the railroad was built, the mail site was moved from what is now C. Taylor Road to the railroad and mail was delivered four times a day. The cattle business began to grow and became the livelihood for many residents. Argyle farmers started growing wheat and oats as a commercial crop to be shipped elsewhere. In 1874, R.W. Fenton bought the land where the Meadows Building is today. In the late 1880s, a grocery store was built there. In 1888, Jeff Wimms operated a blacksmith shop to repair farm equipment and shoe horses. A dry goods store opened as well as the drugstore owned by "Doc" Fullingim, the town's doctor.

In 1895, a fire sweeping through downtown Argyle destroyed most of the businesses, but Argyle residents soon began rebuilding. The dry goods store reopened and also sold groceries as well as farm tools. The drugstore opened, as did blacksmith shops and other businesses. In 1888, the Argyle State Bank opened. The bank was in the front of the red brick building on what is now US Highway 377, and a drugstore was in the back. By the turn of the century, cotton had become the major cash crop and Argyle had a cotton gin that was built in 1908 by J.C. Smith. Wallace Lynch, a longtime resident born and raised in Argyle, said, "Nearly everyone grew cotton, and schoolchildren were dismissed from school early to help their families pick cotton."

In 1910, the automobile was instrumental in taking people to surrounding towns to do their shopping. Before long, the depletion of the soil made agriculture less profitable and people left the farm to work in the cities. In 1947, the population dropped to 147.

In 1960, the citizens of Argyle voted to become incorporated, but the election was challenged by the City of Denton and the courts ruled it illegal. In 1962, there was another election to incorporate and it passed, giving Argyle two square miles and a population of 200 people. In the mid-1960s there was a growth spurt of new people wanting to leave the city and move to the country. In 1962, the Argyle Water Supply Corporation was established. In 1963, the Argyle Volunteer Fire Department was organized, and in 1971, the Argyle Volunteer Fire Department Women's Auxiliary was formed to raise funds for firefighting equipment and a fire hall.

Through the years, as more people moved to Argyle, the local government grew, more services have been provided, new businesses have been established, and modern schools have been built. People in neighboring cities are envious of Argyle's rural atmosphere, its rolling hills, and lovely trees.

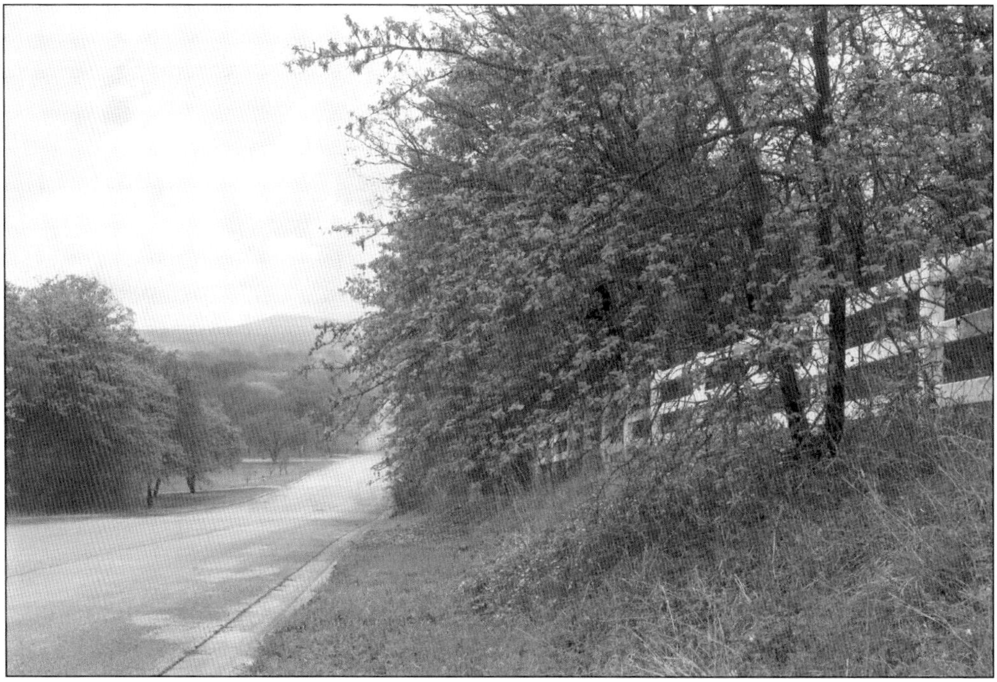

Argyle is situated among rolling hills and large trees east of Highway I-35W. With a population of 3,283, the small town is part of the Eastern Cross Timbers that runs from Waco, Texas, to the Red River Valley. Argyle is located six miles south of Denton and only minutes away from Fort Worth and Dallas. (Courtesy of Denise Remfert.)

One

Argyle Homes and Places

The Heart of the Town

The first homes in Argyle were located in the center of town, which is now called "Old Town Argyle."

After James Morrill laid out a map of the town in 1881, he named the street running parallel to the railroad track East Front Street (now US Highway 377) and West Front Street. On the east side of the railroad tracks, the streets running east and west are named for well-known counties: Rusk, Denton, Dallas, and Collin. Those crossing them, running north and south, are named for trees: Pecan, Ash, Cedar, Oak, Elm, Cypress, Mesquite, and Walnut.

Most of the early homes were modest, one- and two-story wood frame houses, except for Argyle's oldest home. The A.G. Schnably house had two stories that included a front gable, a turret, and a fancy wraparound porch. The house was built in the 1880s by Herman Fehleison and his sons on a high point east of Highway 377. Unfortunately, the house burned down in the 1950s.

Pilot Knob, the high hill with an elevation of 850 feet running alongside Highway I-35W, does not have a historical marker, nor is it inside Argyle's town limits, but it is included because "the Knob" and the Pilot Knob community played an important role in Argyle's history.

Argyle's historical markers are identified in this chapter. Each marker gives the details about why that particular location is part of Argyle's history.

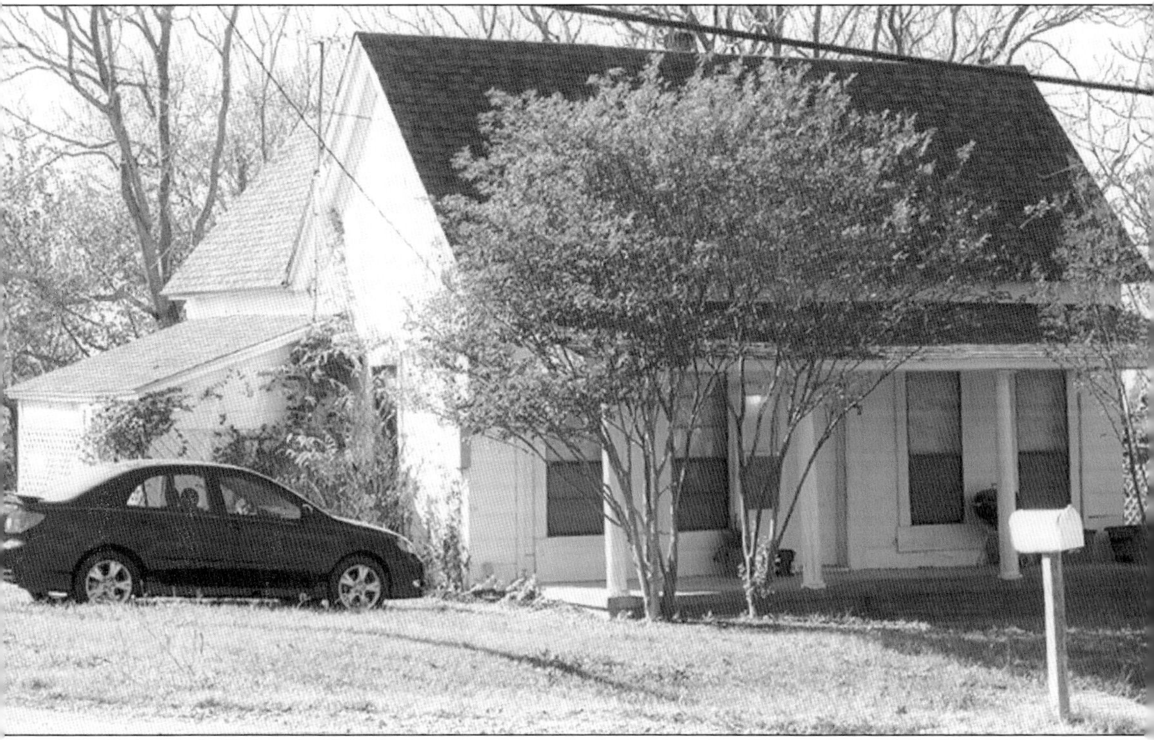

The Laura "Dinkin" Brown home on Denton Street is one of Argyle's older homes that is still standing. The home was built in the early 1900s. Many of the old homes in Old Town Argyle have been torn down and replaced with newer houses, unlike those built in the early days, which were generally built of unpainted wood, plain in style, and characteristic of a farming community. (Courtesy of Dr. Larry Simmons.)

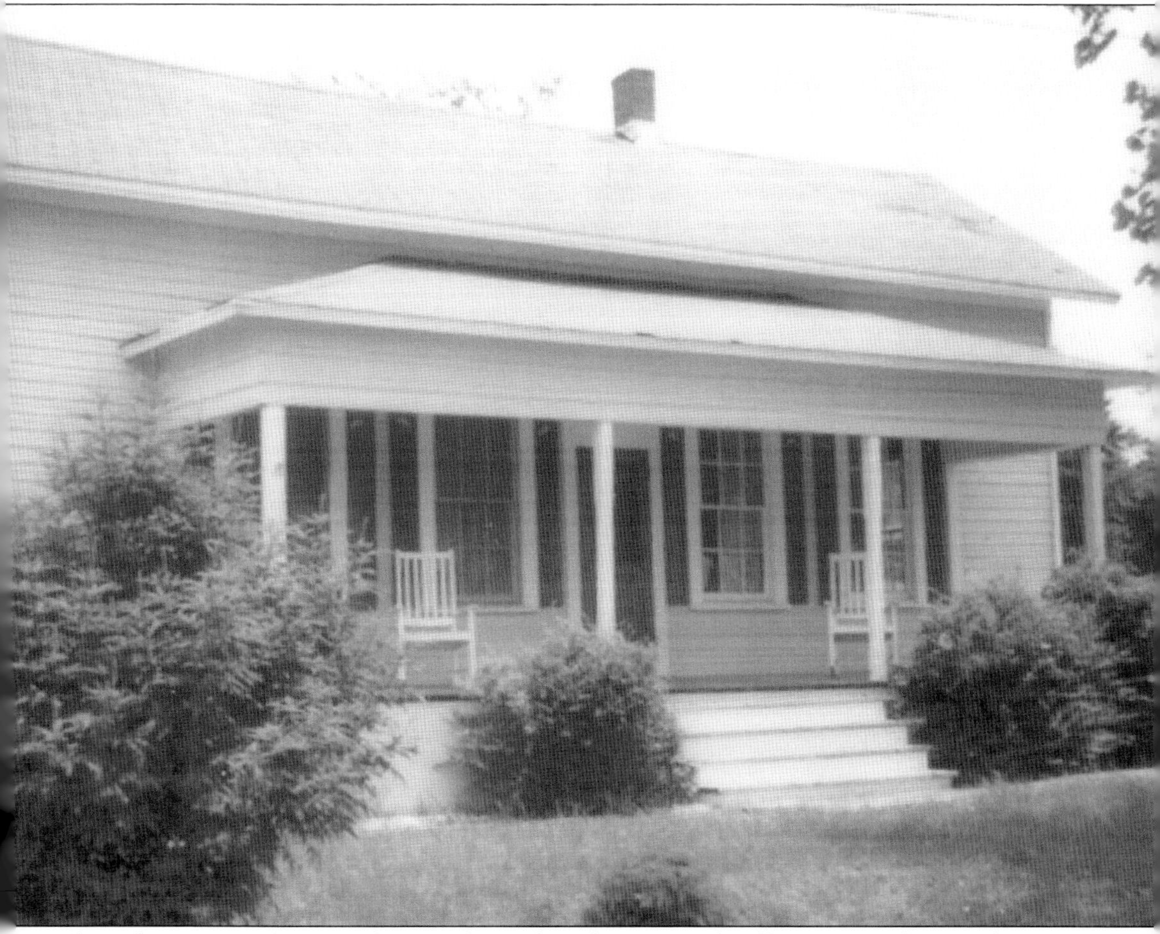

The railway section foreman's house is located on the corner of Dallas Street and US Highway 377. It was built after the Texas and Pacific Railway laid tracks through Argyle in 1881. The house was later bought by William and Oleta Carpenter. (Courtesy of Dr. Larry Simmons.)

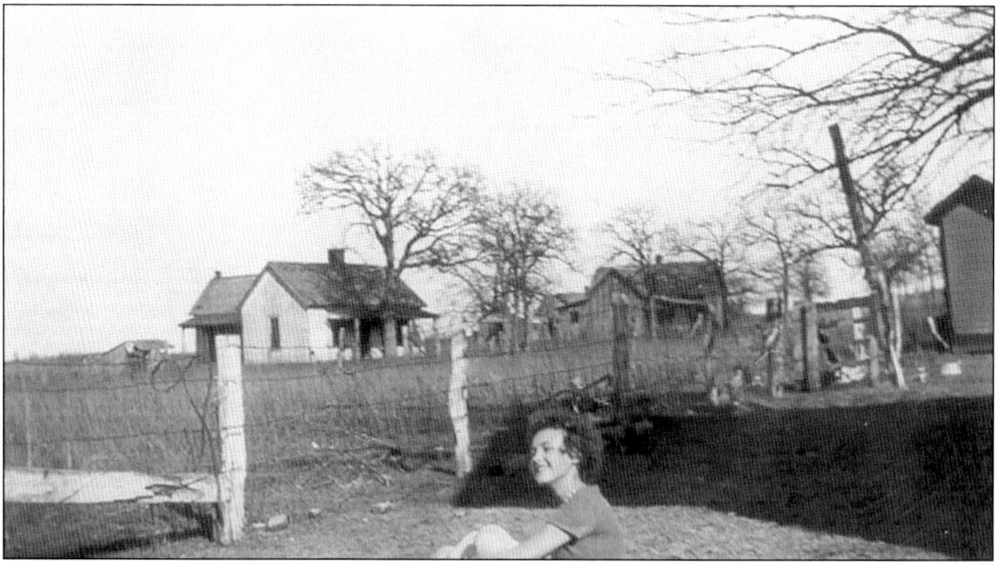

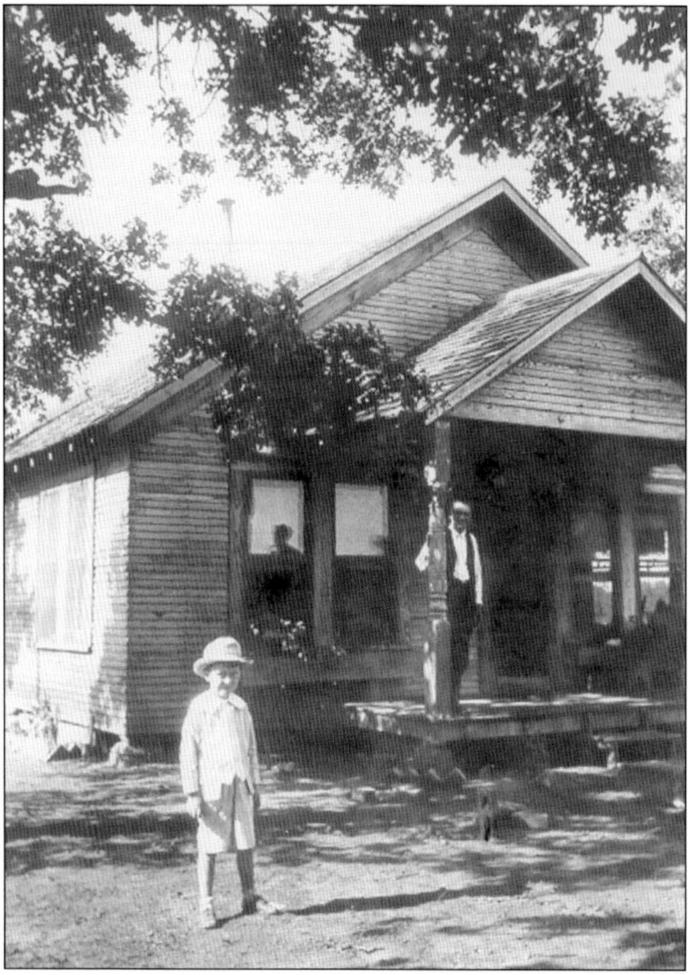

The two wood frame houses seen in this picture are viewed from the Texas and Pacific Railway (T&P) section foreman's yard on US Highway 377. They are typical of early Argyle homes. Vera Stubblefield, daughter of T&P railway foreman Pleasant "Plez" Stubblefield, is pictured in the foreground. (Courtesy of Mary Anne Carroll.)

The Perry and Clela Lynch Wood home was located at the top of the second hill on Denton Street. The first hill, where the Argyle Methodist Church was located, is now the site of the Argyle Town Hall. Although the new church has been relocated on Fort Worth Drive for a number of years, the hill is still referred to as "Methodist Hill." (Courtesy of Greta Garrett.)

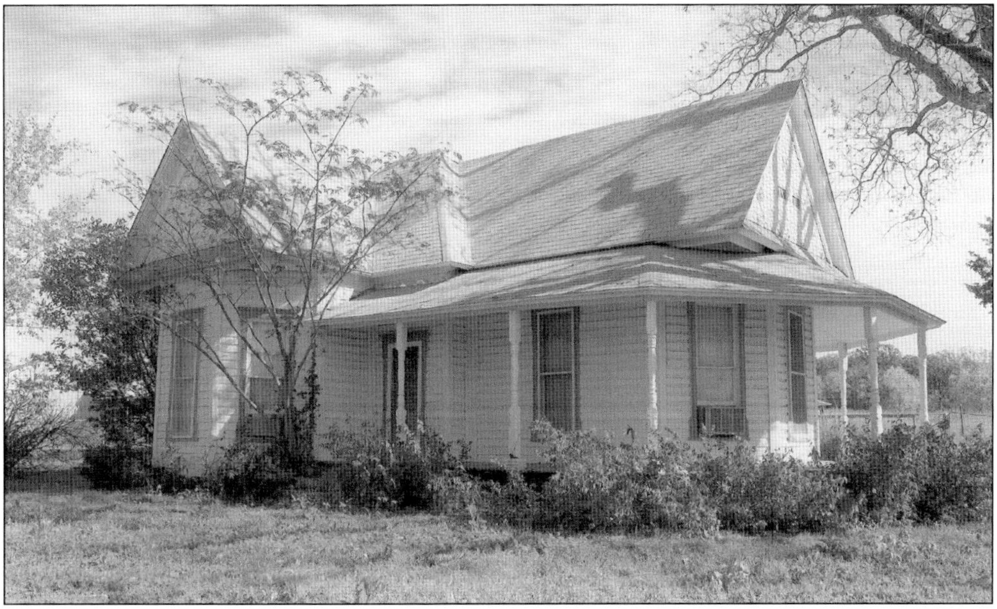

The home of "Uncle Bob" Keith, who was a Baptist preacher, was located on US Highway 377. In the early 1900s, it was customary for an Argyle bride and her husband-to-be to drive in a horse-drawn carriage to Uncle Bob's house and wait for him to come outside to perform the wedding ceremony. Afterward, the couple drove off properly married, Argyle-style. (Courtesy of Denise Remfert.)

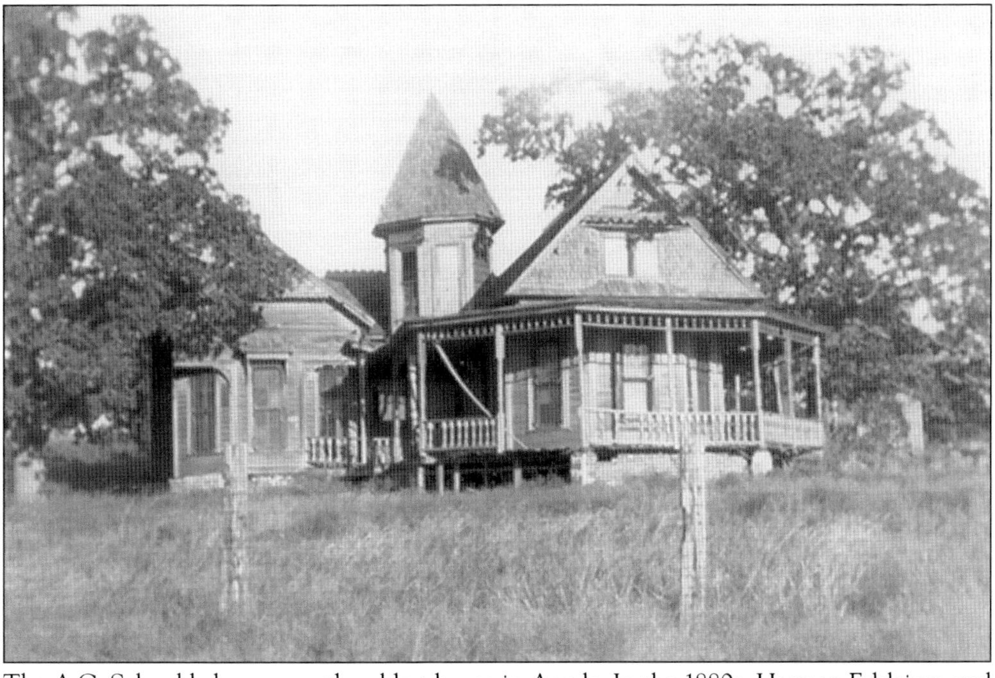

The A.G. Schnably house was the oldest house in Argyle. In the 1880s, Herman Fehleison and his sons built the house for Schnably, who was a ticket agent for the Texas and Pacific Railway. It took two days to haul the lumber by oxen and wagon from Fort Worth. The house was on a high point east of US Highway 377 and burned down in the 1950s. (Courtesy of Pat Brown.)

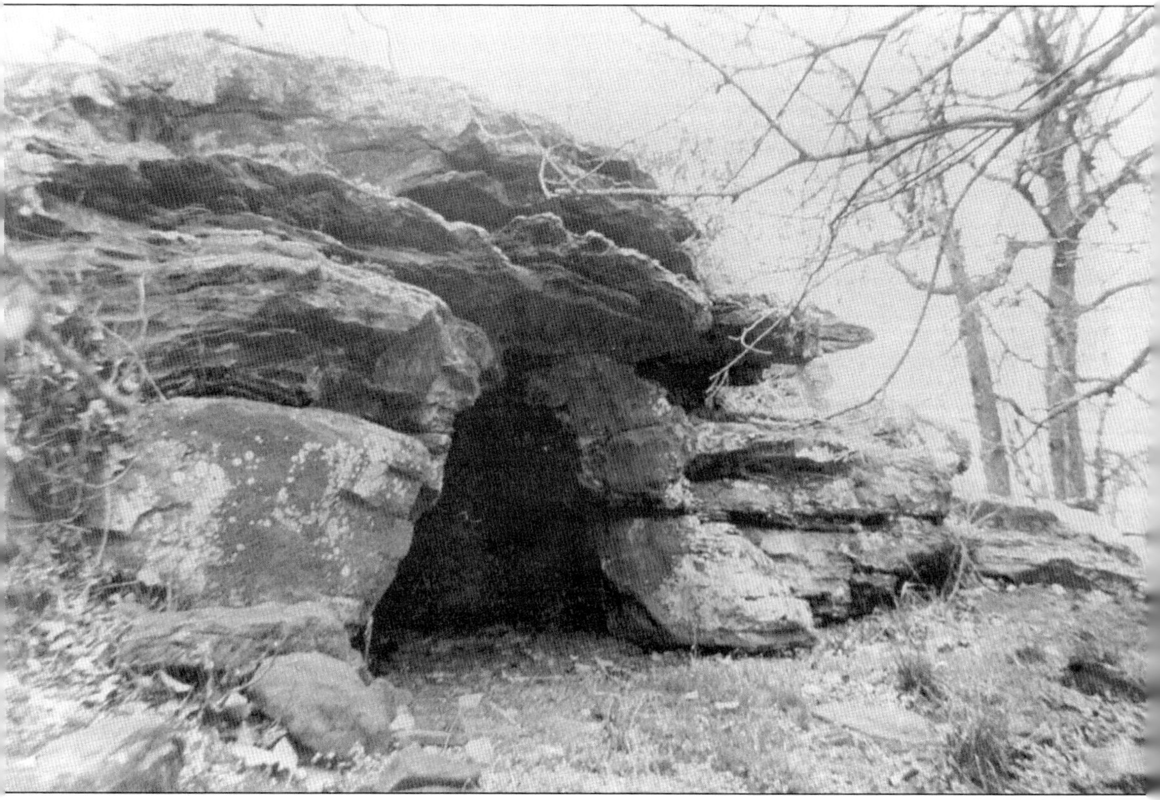

This cave on Pilot Knob was thought to have been a hideaway for the outlaw and train robber, Sam Bass. After Bass's gang robbed the Union Pacific Railroad before returning to Denton from Nebraska, some people thought Sam hid his share of the $60,000 in newly minted $20 Double Eagle gold pieces in or around the cave. For years, visitors combed "the Knob" unsuccessfully looking for Bass's gold. (Courtesy of Kay Teer.)

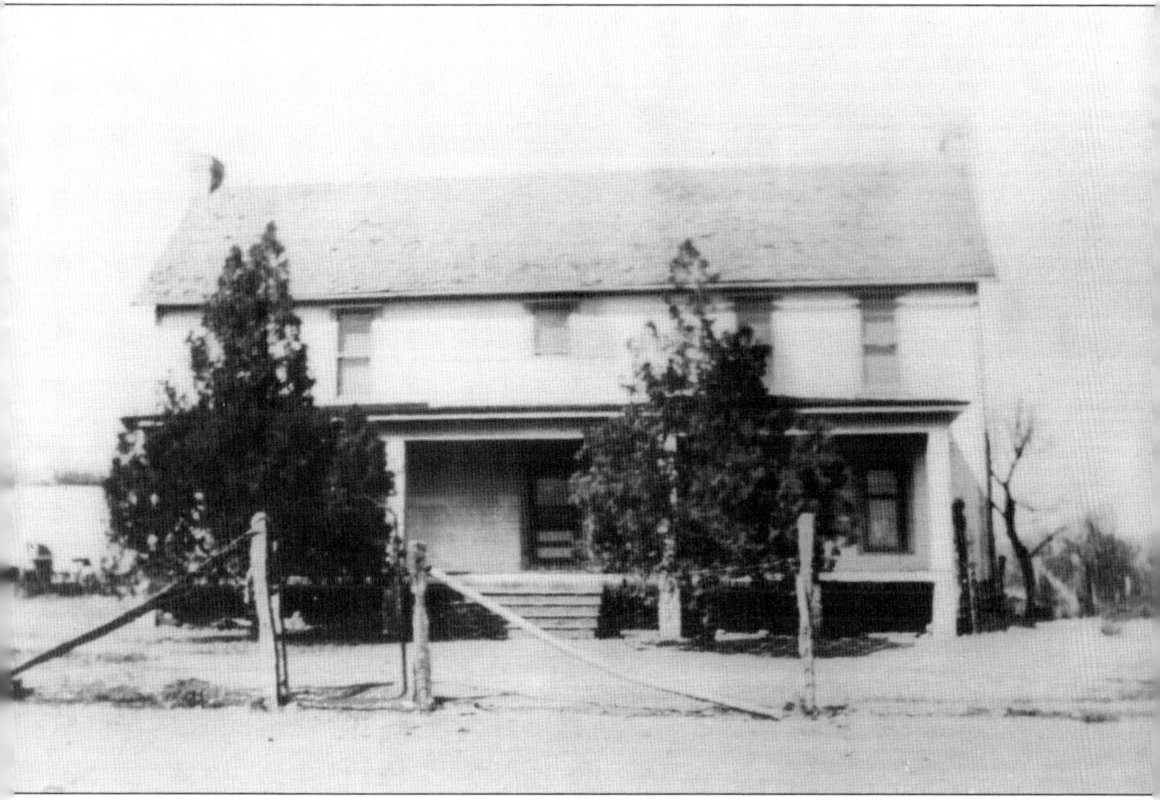

Long Point Farm was located on the south side of Pilot Knob. It was the home of Dr. Daniel McIntire Stewart. The house was built after Doctor Stewart came to the Argyle–Pilot Knob area in 1877. Lumber for the house was brought by oxen from Fort Worth, Texas. (Courtesy of Martha Len Nelson.)

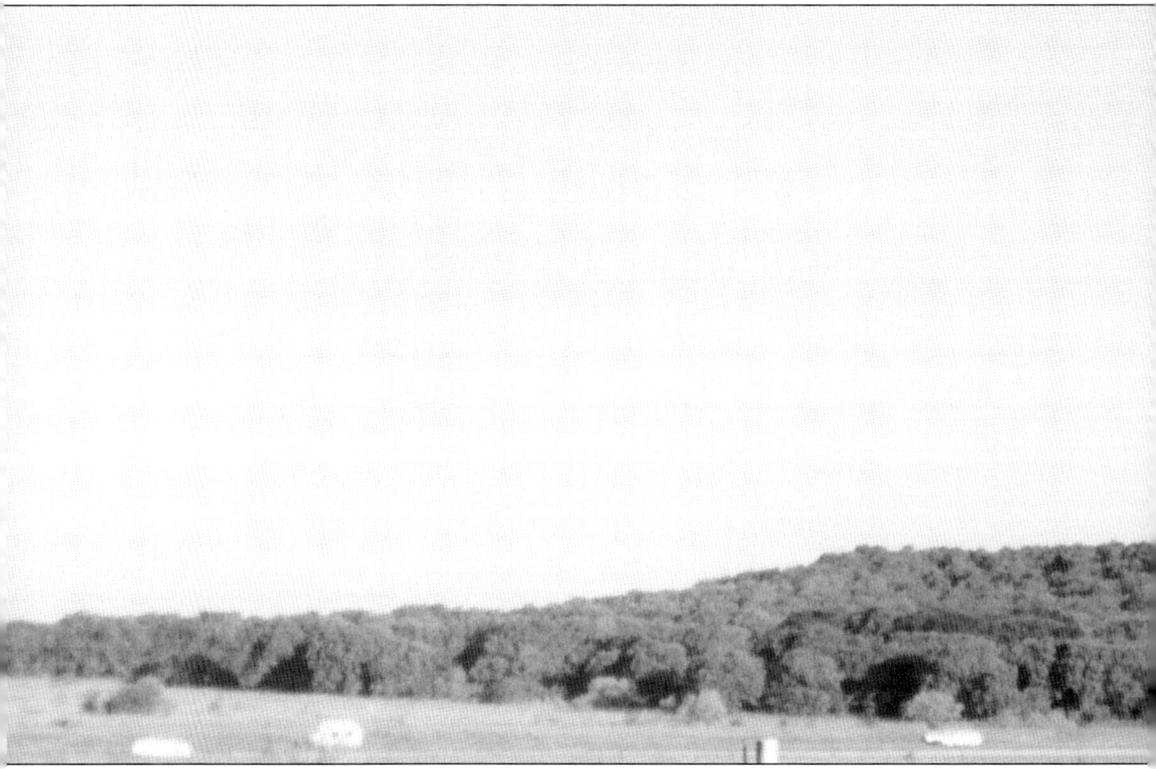

Pilot Knob, a tall hill with an elevation of 850 feet that runs alongside Interstate 35W, was owned by Laura J. Evans McReynolds (born 1863). She grew up at Pilot Knob, and after she married, the couple made their home there. The Evans heirs sold the land to John Paine, who bought

more land around the Knob, and his property became known as Pilot Knob Ranch. (Courtesy of Pat Brown.)

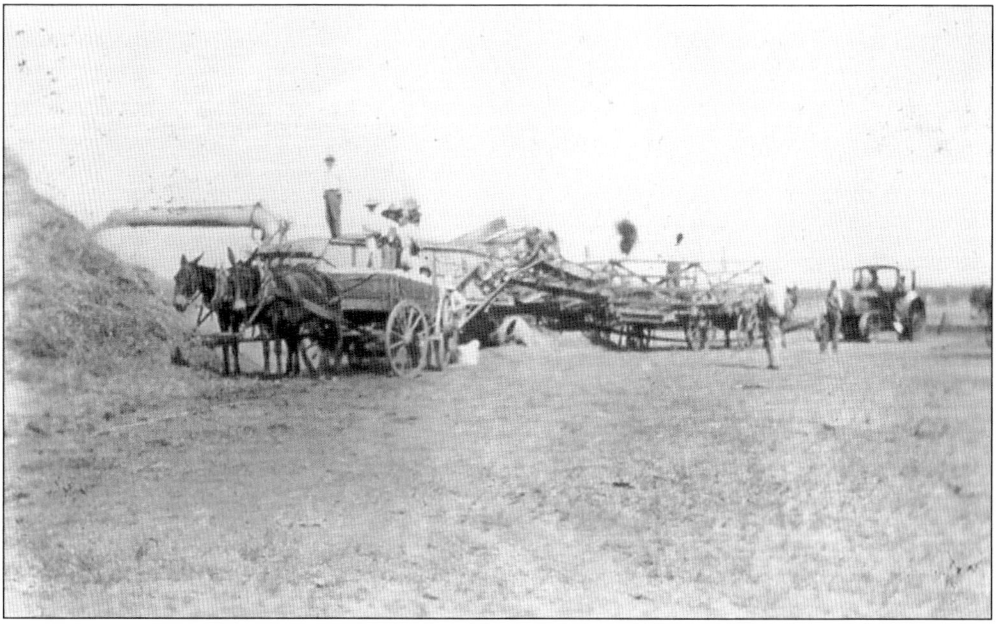

On Long Point Farm, as on the other farms in the Argyle area, winter wheat was planted from August to October and harvested from May to mid-July. This picture was taken in June 1918 of the threshing machine belonging to Henry Stewart and used on Long Point Farm during harvest time. Argyle farmers used similar equipment to separate the wheat from the straw. (Courtesy of Martha Len Nelson.)

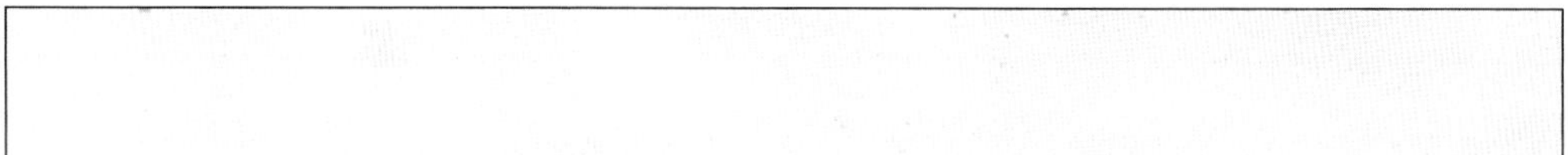

Shown in this photograph is the wheat binder that belonged to Henry Stewart and was used on Long Point Farm at harvest time. Wheat was, and still is, an important cereal for many people who use it as a food staple. This wheat binder is an example of the machinery used and operated by farmers in Argyle and the surrounding area in the early 1900s. (Courtesy of Martha Len Nelson.)

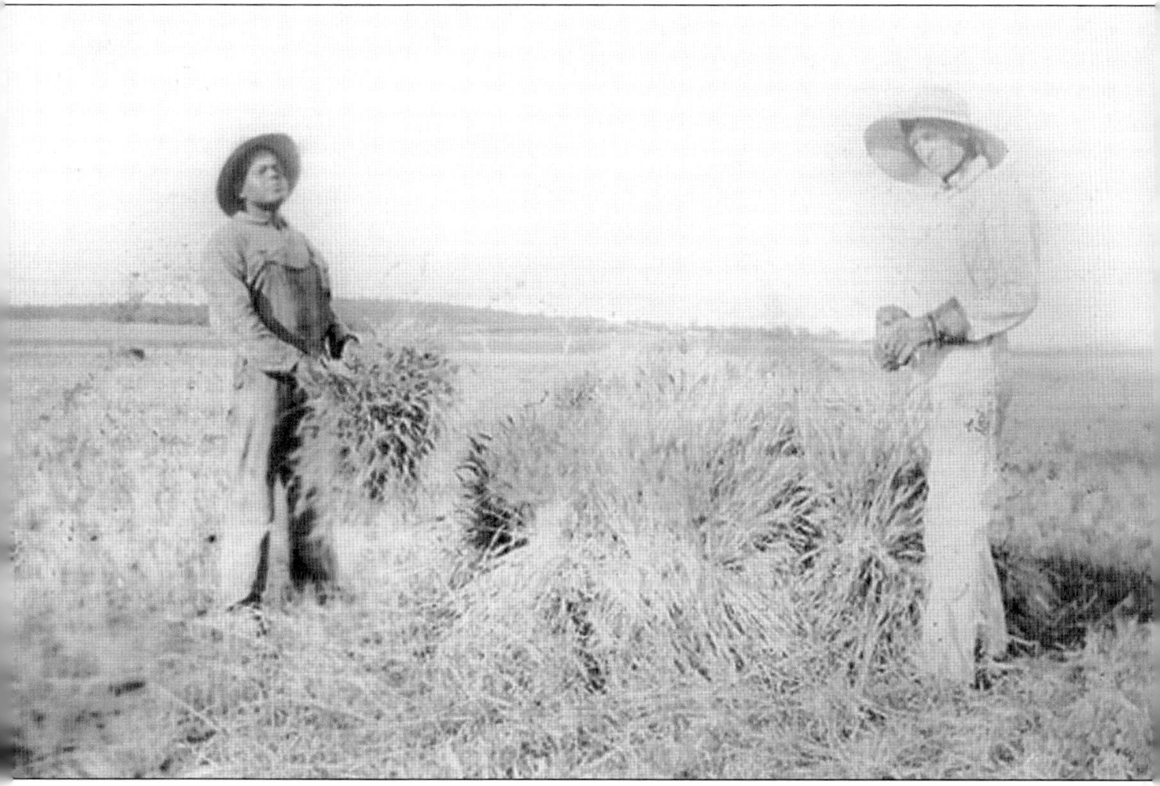

Farmworker Leon Hemby and Bill Cook, a Long Point Farm neighbor, are shown baling wheat at Long Point Farm on June 11, 1918. Farm hands and neighbors worked together to prepare the wheat for market. Between 1890 and 1920, Denton County ranked at the top of wheat production in Texas. (Courtesy of Martha Len Nelson.)

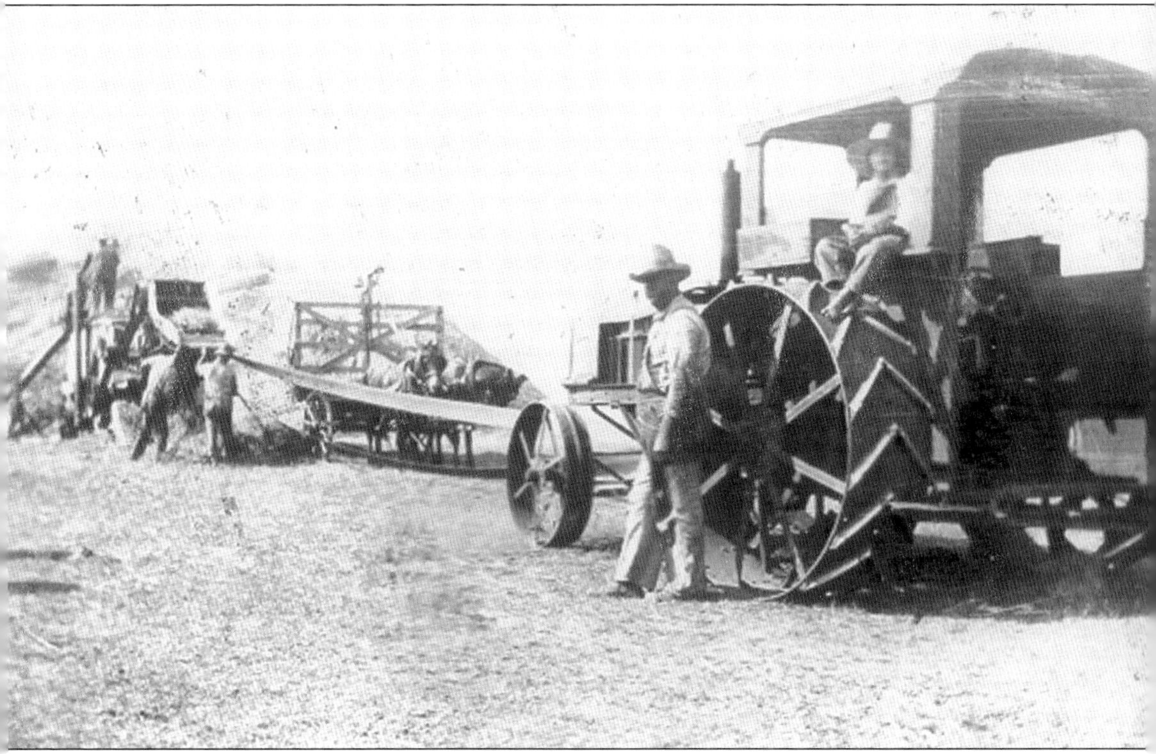

The tractor used on Long Point Farm was like other tractors used by farmers in the Argyle area in 1918. Cotton and wheat were the major cash crops, and in 1908, J.C. Smith built a cotton gin east of the Argyle train station. "Children were dismissed from school to help their families pick cotton," said 88-year-old, longtime Argyle resident Wallace Lynch. (Courtesy of Martha Len Nelson.)

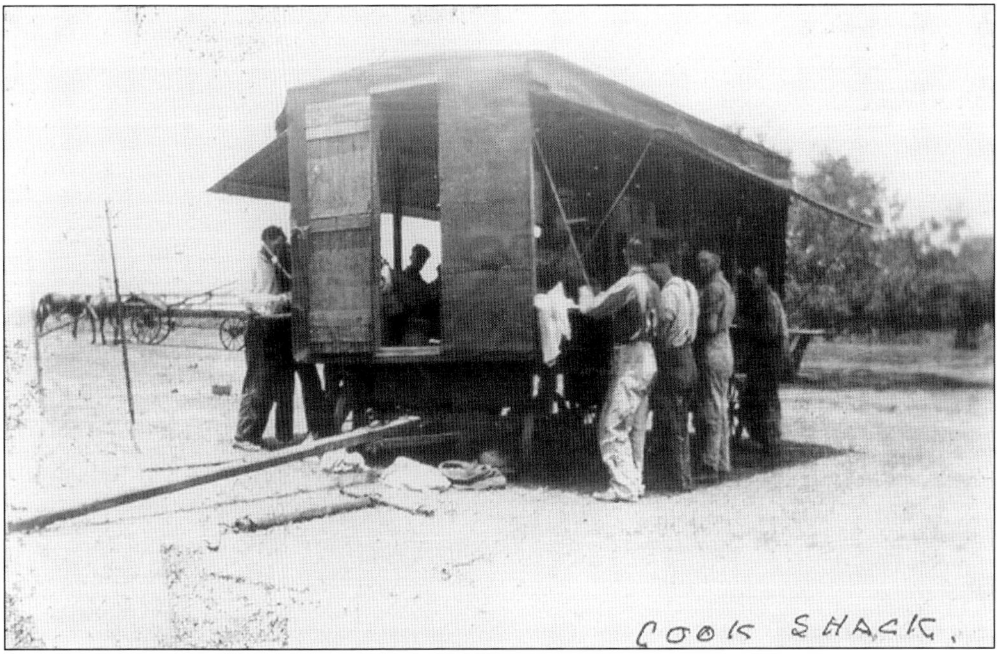

Men working at Long Point Farm during harvest time gathered around the cook shack for a hot meal. Since the men stayed outside all day, Marcella Stewart Henderson, who grew up on Long Point Farm, said in a 1994 interview, "The only time we got to really be with our father was on a rainy day." (Courtesy of Martha Len Nelson.)

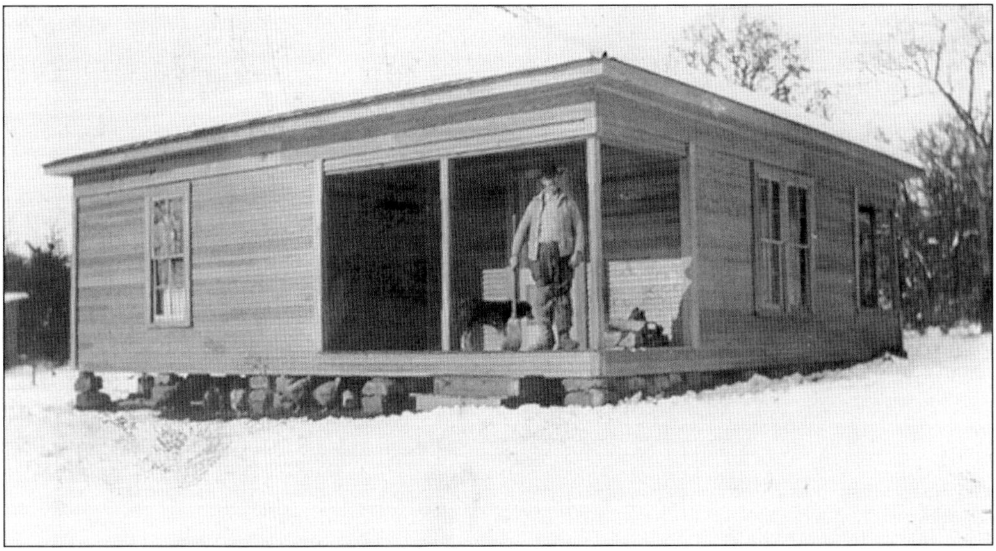

Henry Stewart is seen here standing on the porch of the rent house on Long Point Farm. Renters staying at the house worked on the farm instead of paying rent. Farmworkers often lived on the premises as they moved from farm to farm during the harvest season of major crops. (Courtesy of Martha Len Nelson.)

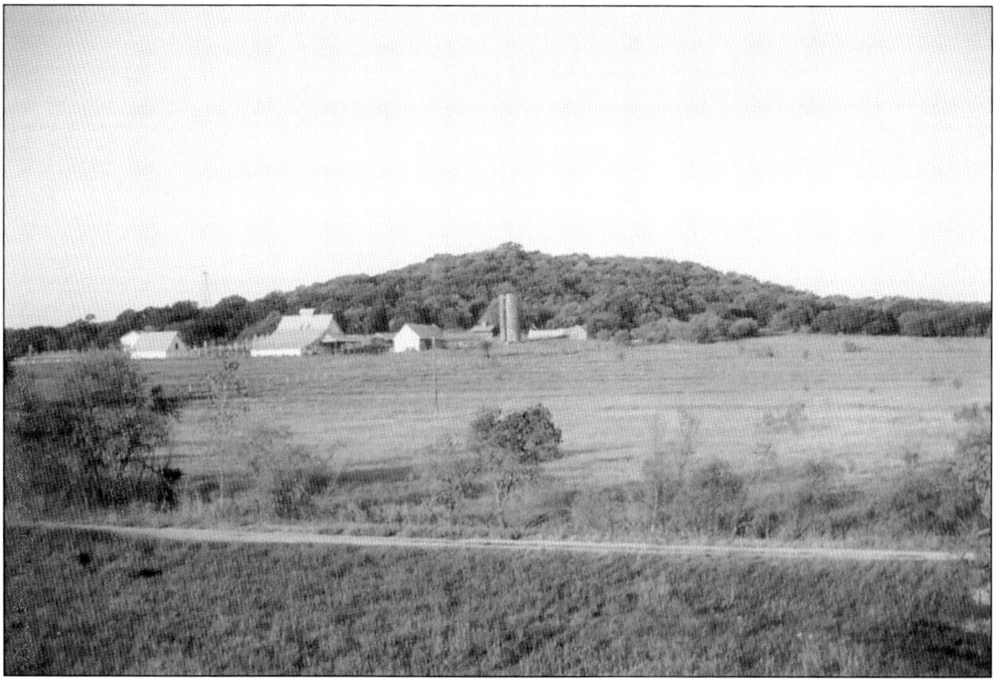

This 1986 photograph shows Pilot Knob Ranch along with its buildings before it was bought from the Alex McCutchin family by H. Ross Perot. Prior to the sale, Pilot Knob was a working ranch with a house, silo, barn with a sweeping roof, outbuildings, and all that was needed to have a cattle operation. (Courtesy of Dr. Larry Simmons.)

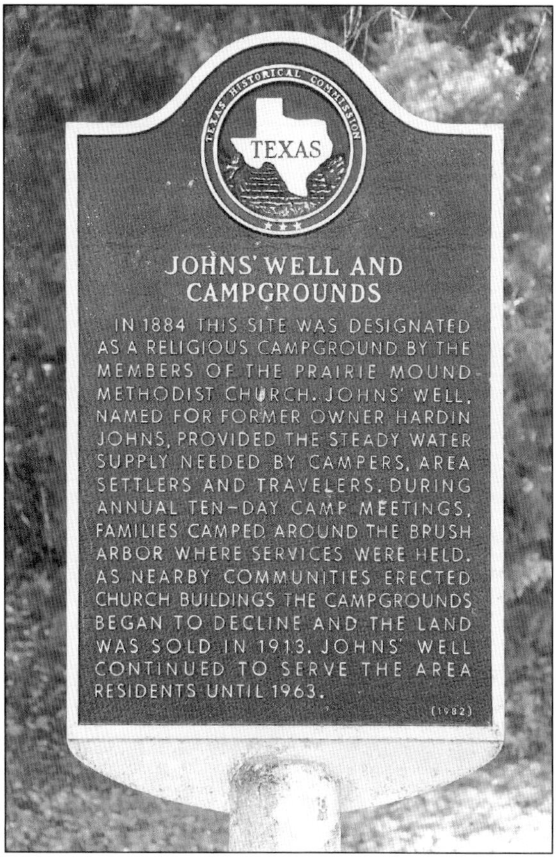

Johns' Well and Campgrounds is an important Argyle landmark. The well was named for the Johns family, who bought the land in 1875. The first Johns' Well was located on the north side of Old Justin Road and the second well was across the road where the camp meetings were held. Both wells provided water for neighboring families, the campground meetings, and cattle drives passing through. (Courtesy of Denise Remfert.)

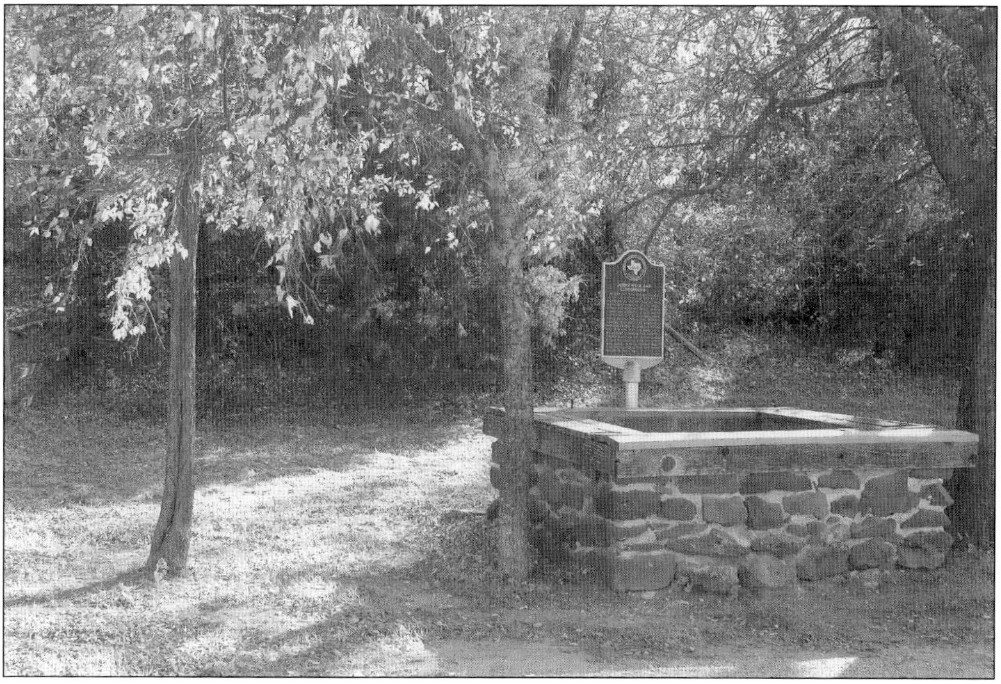

The Methodist Episcopal Church owned the land where the nondenominational campground meetings were held at Johns' Well during the second week in July. People from Argyle and the Pilot Knob communities attended the meetings, including families from as far away as 25 miles. They traveled in horse-drawn wagons, bringing with them stoves, bedding, and enough food for two weeks. (Courtesy of Denise Remfert.)

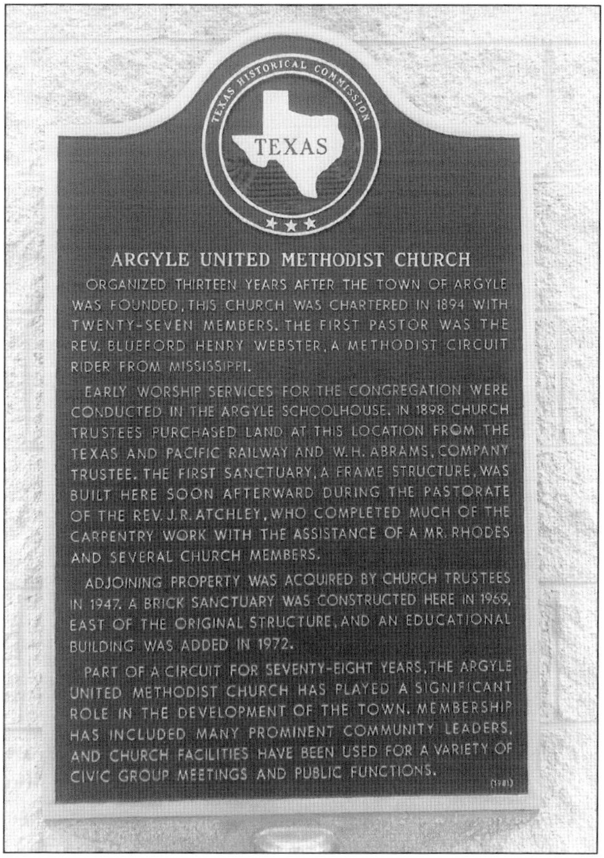

The Argyle United Methodist Church historical marker is located at the new church on Fort Worth Drive (US Highway 377). In 1981, the marker was placed at the church's original location on Denton Street. The church was chartered in 1894 with 27 members attending; early church services were held at the Argyle schoolhouse. In 1898, the trustees purchased land on Denton Street and a frame structure was built. (Courtesy of Dr. Larry Simmons.)

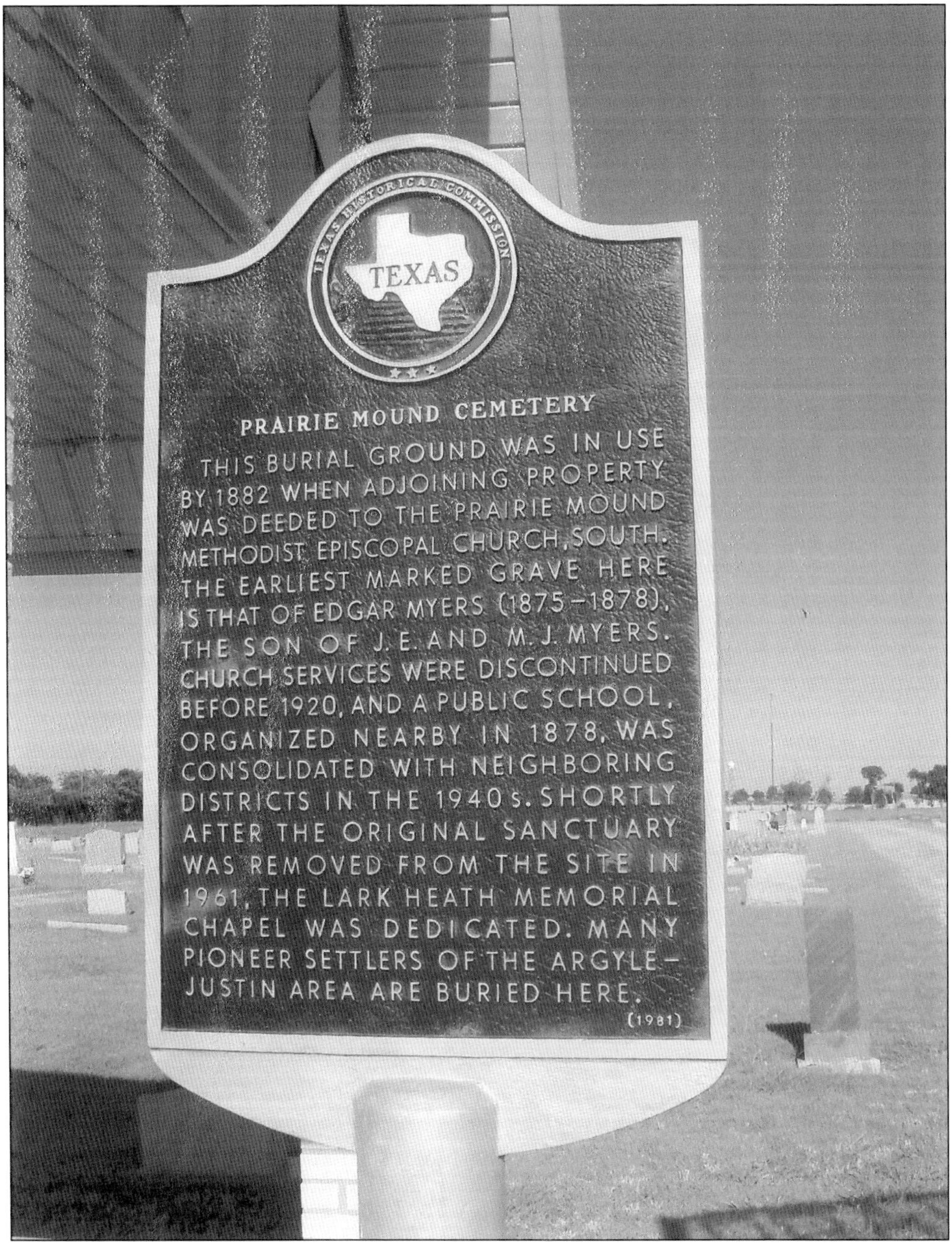

The Prairie Mound Cemetery historical marker tells how the burial ground was in use by 1882 when the adjoining property was deeded to the Prairie Mound Methodist Episcopal Church, South, to build a church. Soon after the church's original sanctuary was removed in 1961, the Lark Heath Memorial Chapel was built in its place. (Courtesy of Jody Bellinghausen.)

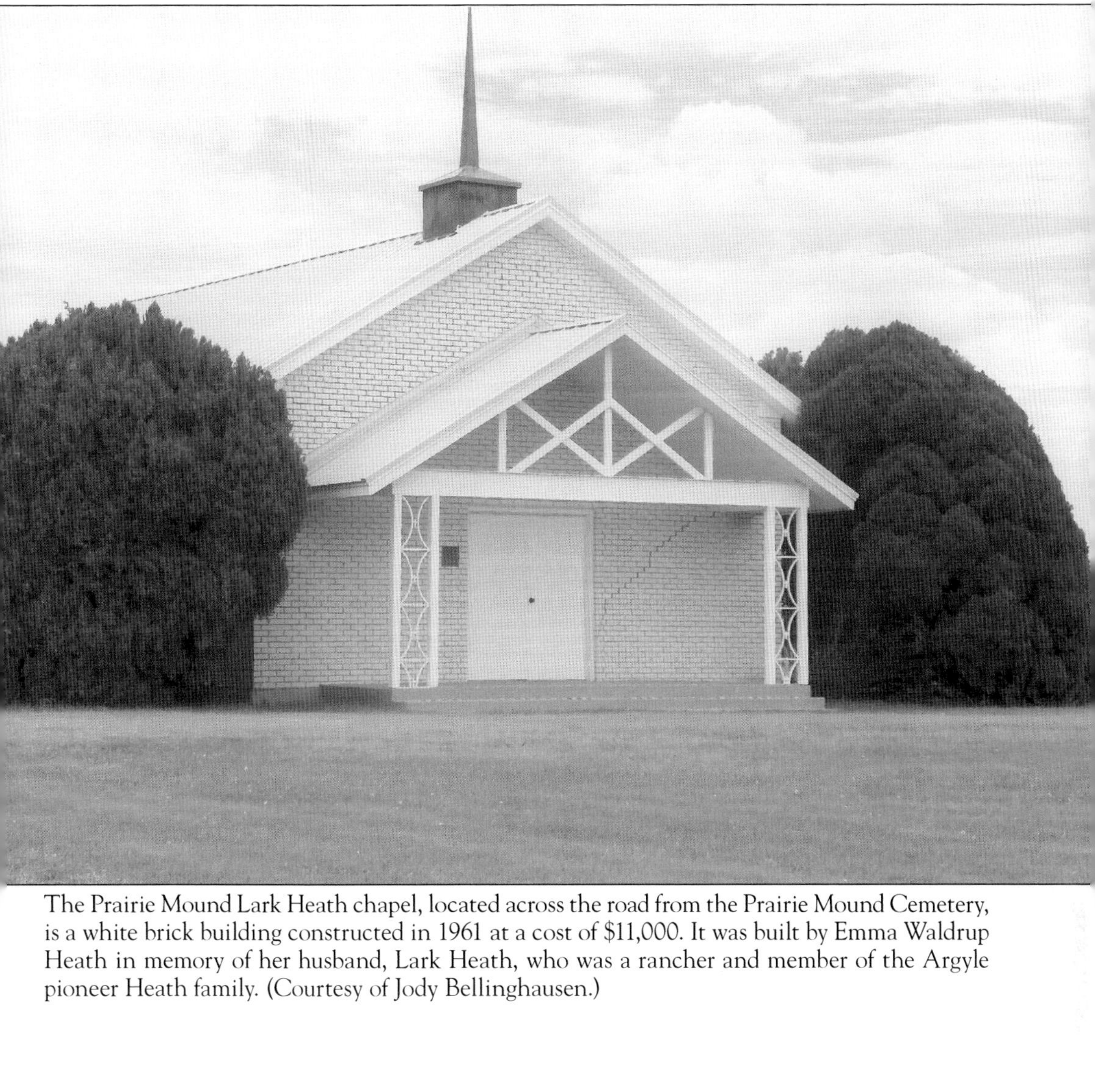

The Prairie Mound Lark Heath chapel, located across the road from the Prairie Mound Cemetery, is a white brick building constructed in 1961 at a cost of $11,000. It was built by Emma Waldrup Heath in memory of her husband, Lark Heath, who was a rancher and member of the Argyle pioneer Heath family. (Courtesy of Jody Bellinghausen.)

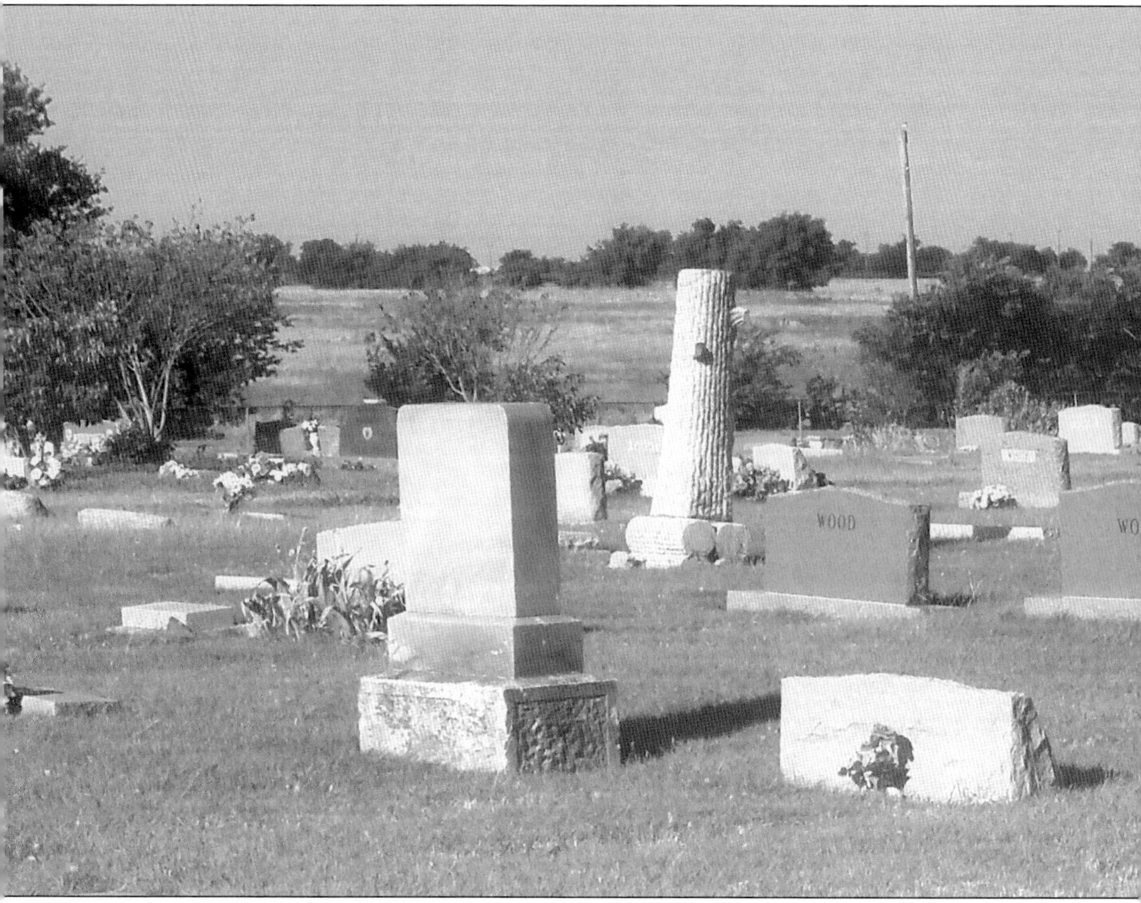

The Prairie Mound Cemetery is located on flat prairie land that marks the beginning of the Grand Prairie and the ending of the Eastern Cross Timbers. The earliest marked grave was Edgar Myers (1875–1878). He was the son of J.E. and M.J. Myers. The first Sunday in May is the Prairie Mound Cemetery Decoration Day. The event begins with a church service followed by lunch and

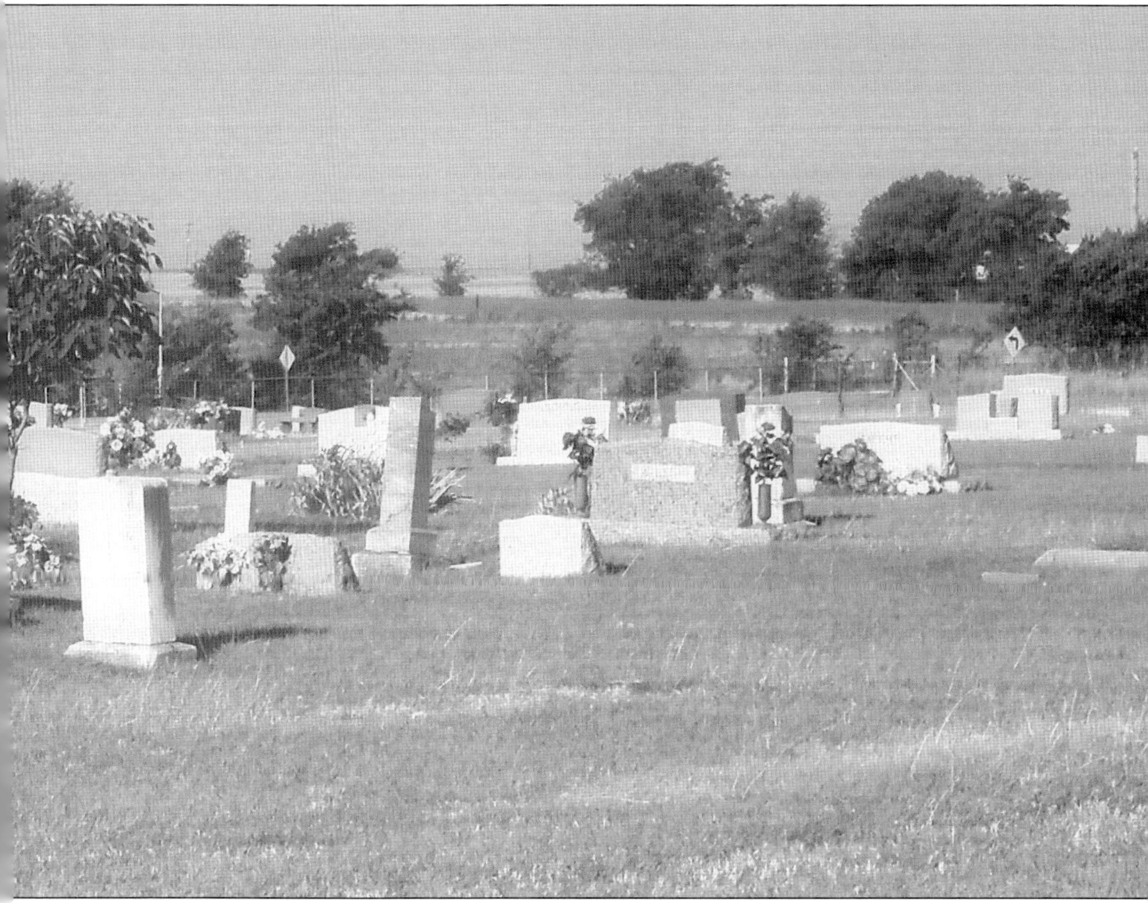

a business meeting. The Saturday before, members of the Prairie Mound Association meet for a cleanup day to prepare the grounds and chapel for the annual affair. The upkeep of the cemetery is made possible through private donations. (Courtesy of Jody Bellinghausen.)

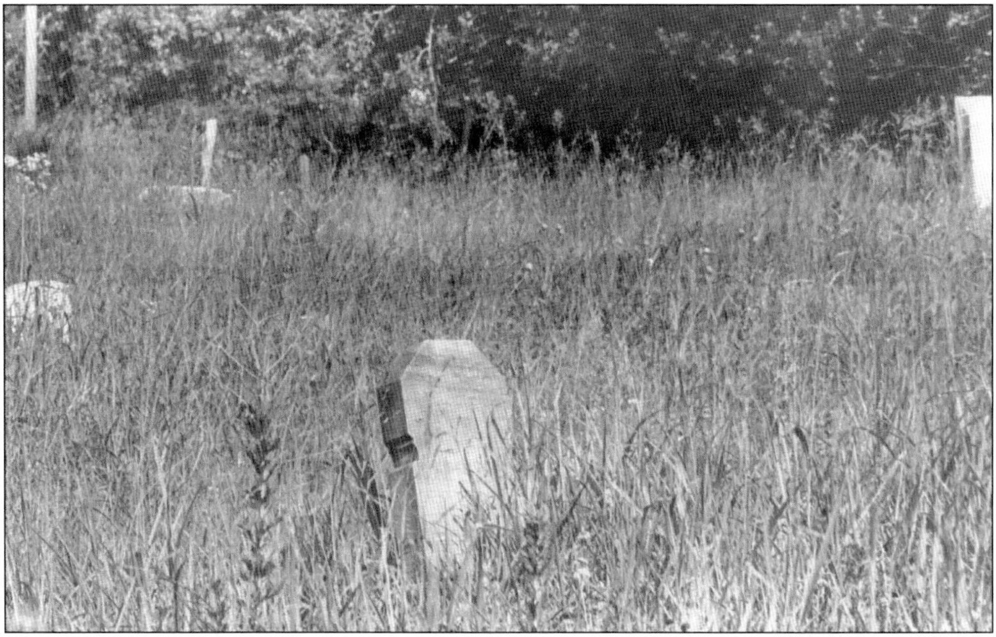

Neglect, along with overgrown grass hiding headstones, made the Graham-Argyle Cemetery unknown to most people. In 1974, Yvonne A. Jenkins of Argyle and Mrs. W.H. Matthews of Denton organized a Graham-Argyle restoration and financial campaign. Volunteers were W.T. "Bill" Meadows, John Thompson, Gus Cogdell, Wilton Newborn, Ralph Ayers, C.R. "Happy" Salmon, and members of the Argyle Volunteer Fire Department and Boy Scouts of America. (Courtesy of DRC.)

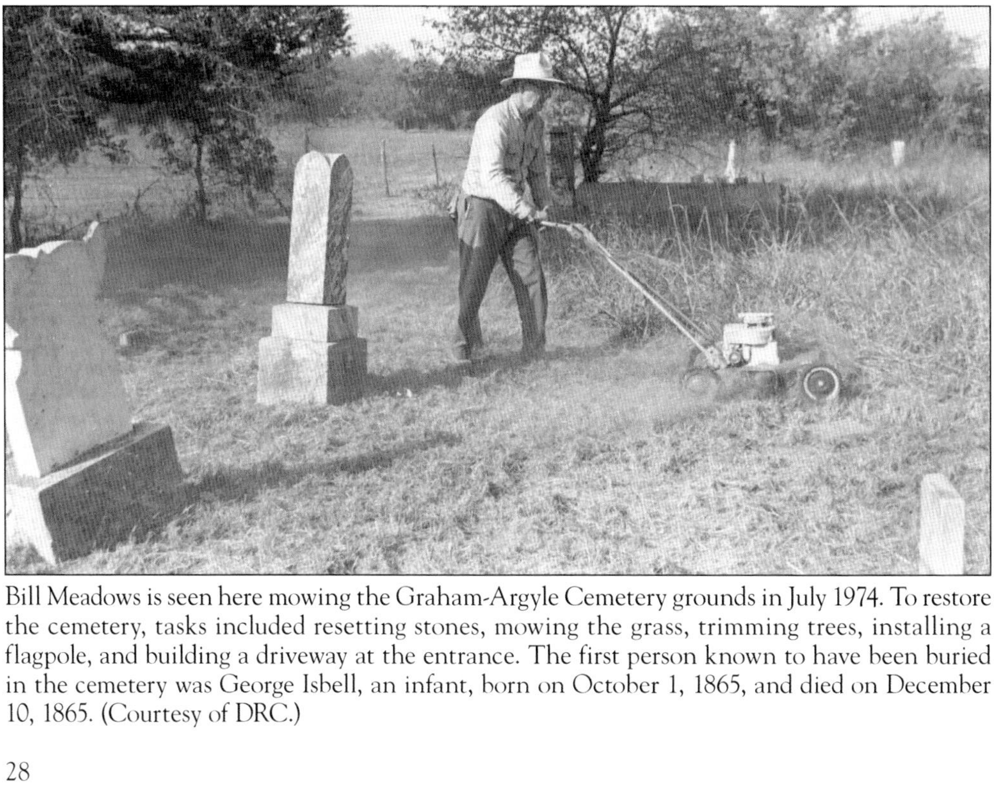

Bill Meadows is seen here mowing the Graham-Argyle Cemetery grounds in July 1974. To restore the cemetery, tasks included resetting stones, mowing the grass, trimming trees, installing a flagpole, and building a driveway at the entrance. The first person known to have been buried in the cemetery was George Isbell, an infant, born on October 1, 1865, and died on December 10, 1865. (Courtesy of DRC.)

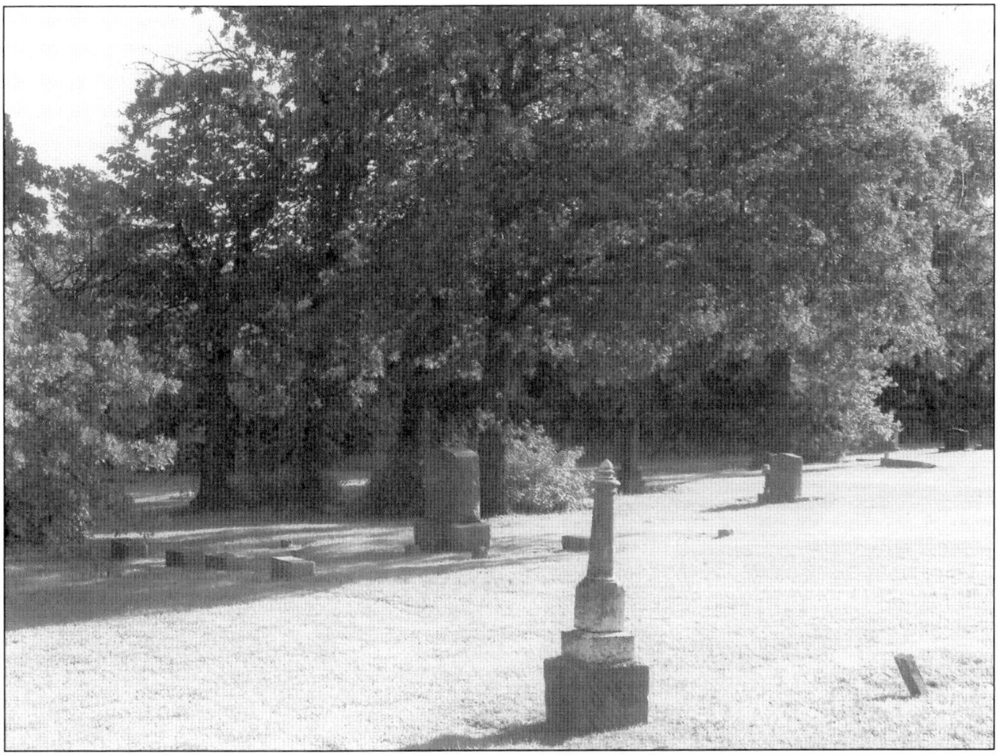

The Graham-Argyle Cemetery on Country Club Road is located in the Eastern Cross Timbers, well known for its tall trees and gently sloping hills. The Graham-Argyle Cemetery Association has a decoration day each May when the board of directors and members meet to cut the grass, trim trees, and clean up the grounds, followed by lunch and a business meeting. (Courtesy of Jody Bellinghausen.)

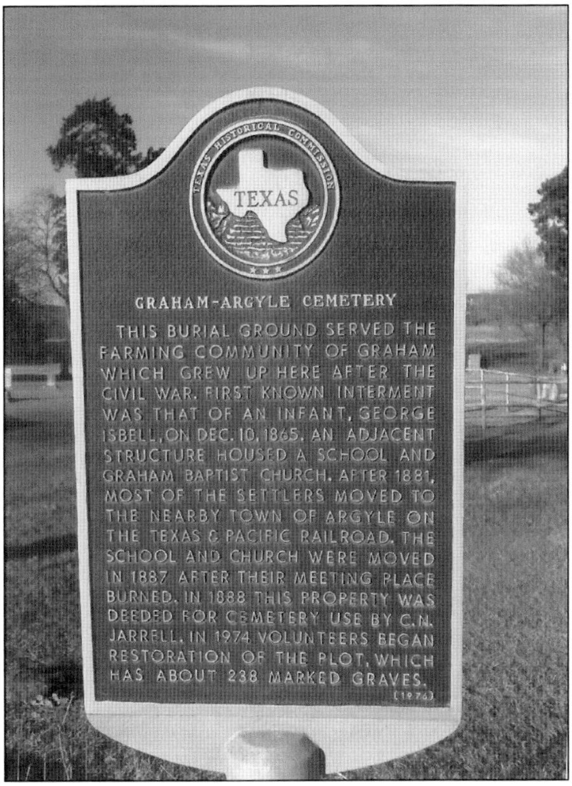

The Graham-Argyle Cemetery, located inside the cemetery, states that the burial grounds served the farming community of Graham that emerged shortly after the Civil War. Adjacent to the cemetery was a structure housing both a school and the Graham Baptist Church. In 1887, the building burned down and the school and church were moved to the town of Argyle. (Courtesy of Jody Bellinghausen.)

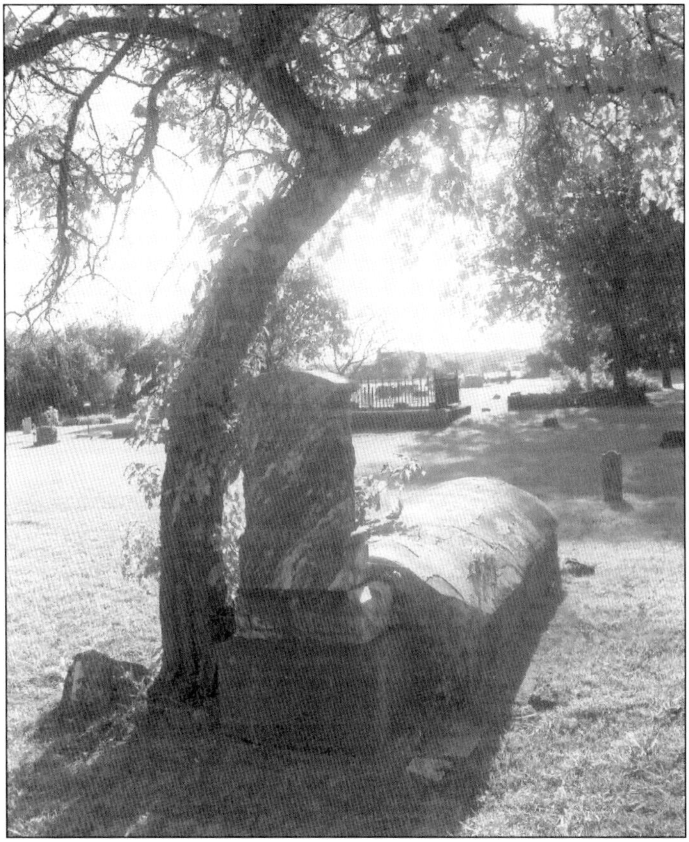

This is the only aboveground grave in the Graham-Argyle Cemetery. The concrete crypt is the gravesite of local shopkeeper H.R. Fehleison (born on August 12, 1857, and died on April 20, 1902). Beside him is Randolf, his infant son (born on January 13, 1885, and died on January 24, 1885). (Courtesy of Jody Bellinghausen.)

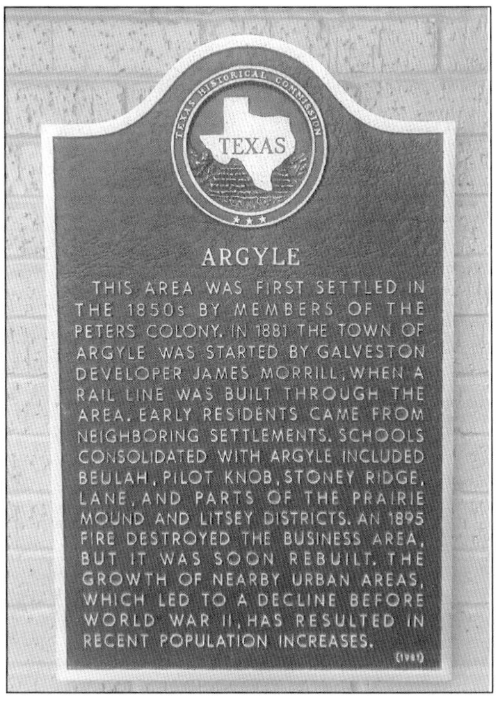

The Argyle historical marker is now located at the Argyle Town Hall on Denton Street. It was originally placed on the Argyle City Hall building located on US Highway 377. The marker's dedication was made in 1981 as part of the Argyle Centennial Celebration. Argyle became a town in 1881 after the Texas and Pacific Railway laid tracks through Denton County. (Courtesy of Dr. Larry Simmons.)

Two

Schools and Churches
The Strength of the Town

In the 1870s, it was easy to start a school in Texas. Interested parents could file an application with the county judge, and the amount of money the school received was determined by the number of students enrolled. Since the students had to walk or ride their ponies to school, there were numerous schools in the area that included the Graham, Lane, Pilot Knob, Litsey, Stony Ridge, Prairie Mound, Beulah, and Argyle Schools. In the 1930s, with the introduction of school buses, the smaller districts consolidated with the Argyle Rural School District. The Argyle School was built at the corner of Old Justin Road and West Front Street in 1885.

In 1898, the Methodist church purchased land on Denton Street and a wood structure was built. In 1909, after a Baptist church revival at the Methodist church building, Dr. M. D. Fullingim donated two lots on Dallas Street to build the Argyle Baptist Church.

The Argyle Church of Christ held its first church meeting in 1971 in the Argyle Community Center and later built a church on F.M. 407. The Oak Hills Community Evangelical Free Church met in the Argyle School cafeteria until its new church was built in 1986.

Through the years, school board trustees and Argyle church members have worked together to sponsor special events to benefit the community. In their facilities they have held Thanksgiving dinners, Easter Sunrise services, the Argyle Seniors' Activities Center, barbecue dinners, talent shows, church services, Fourth of July celebrations, political forums, and many more.

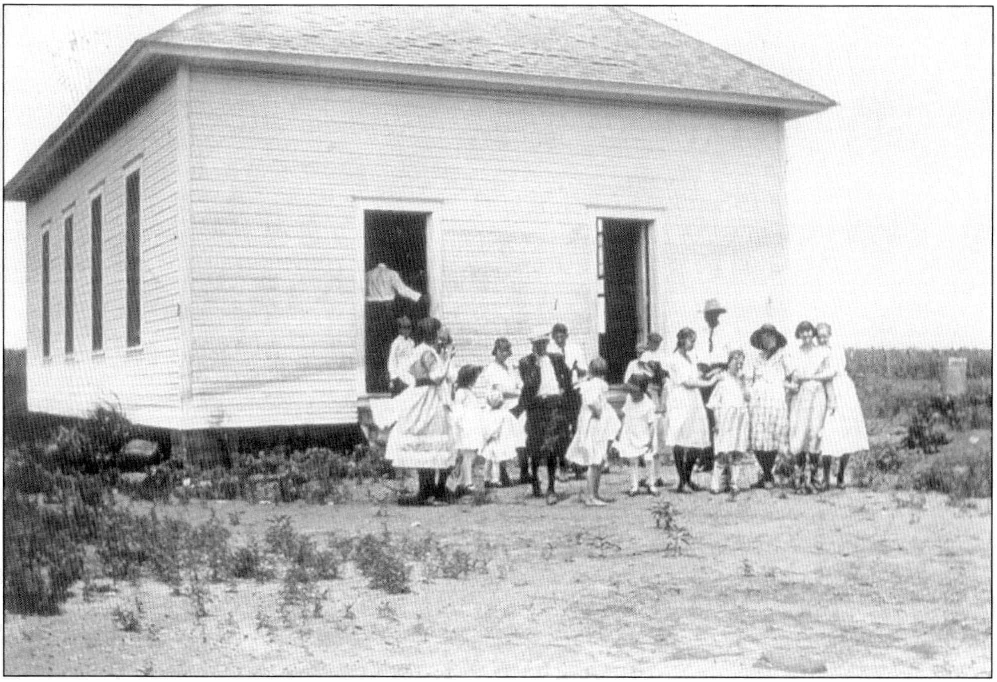

The Pilot Knob School in the early 1900s was a big square room with two doors. The girls went in one door and the boys went in the other. The grades were from first grade through sixth, and then the students were transferred to the Argyle School. (Courtesy of Martha Len Nelson.)

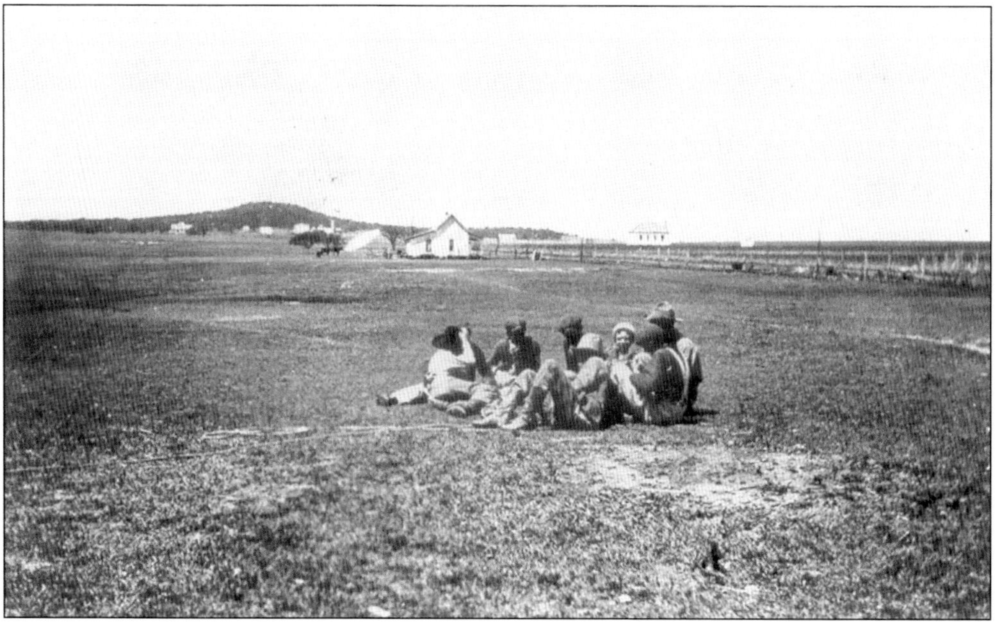

Schoolchildren are seen in the foreground with Pilot Knob and the Pilot Knob School in the background. When Marcella Stewart Henderson and her brother attended the Pilot Knob School, they traveled in a horse-drawn cart. "The cart had two wheels and only one seat with a 'little lattice thing' to put your feet on," said 92-year-old Henderson in a 1994 interview. (Courtesy of Martha Len Nelson.)

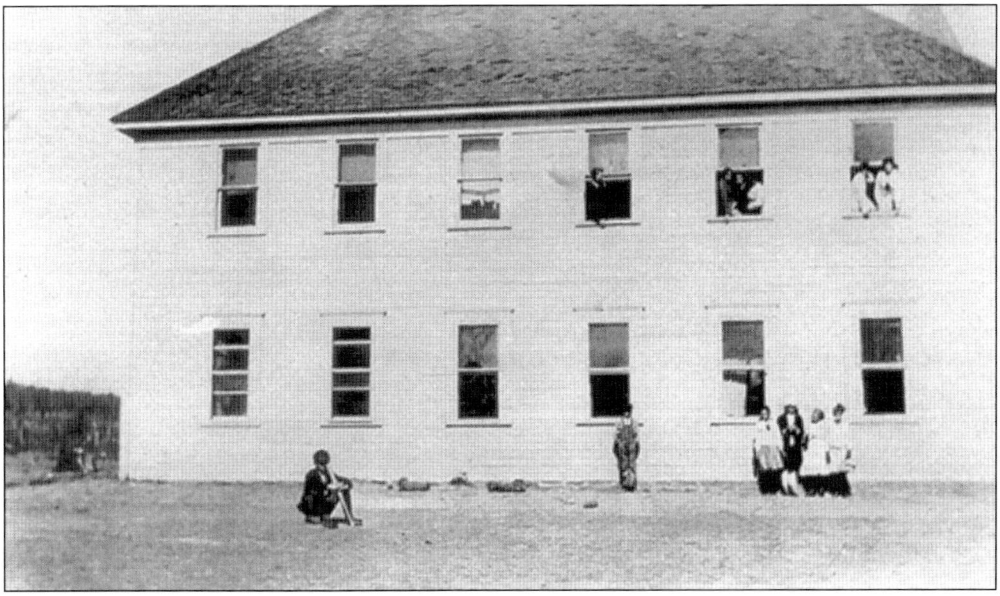

The Argyle School opened on November 2, 1885. The "downtown," white, two-story, wooden building, heated with a wood-burning stove, was located at the corner of West Front Street and Old Justin Road. When students wanted a drink of water, they pumped it from a well behind the school, which was close to the branch (creek), and while there, they frequently caught crawfish. (Courtesy of Martha Len Nelson.)

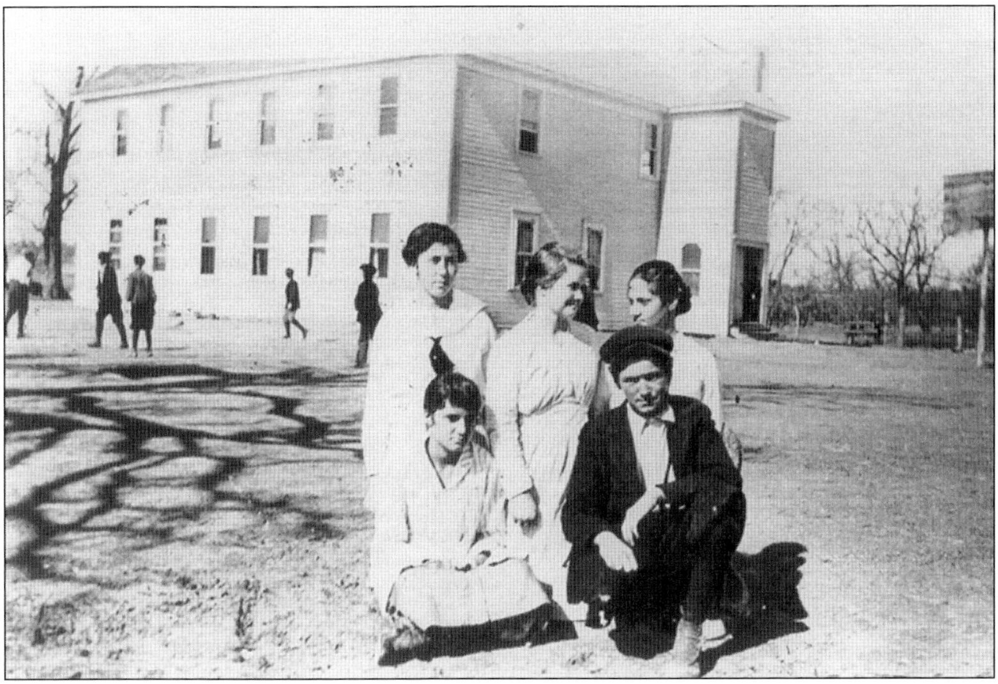

Classes were held on both the first and second floor of the wooden, two-story Argyle schoolhouse. It had only one door and there were no screens on the windows. In this photograph, the students in front of the building are (standing) Clela Lynch, Grace McMakin, and Maud McMakin; and (seated) Sallie McMakin and her brother Dick McMakin. (Courtesy of Martha Len Nelson.)

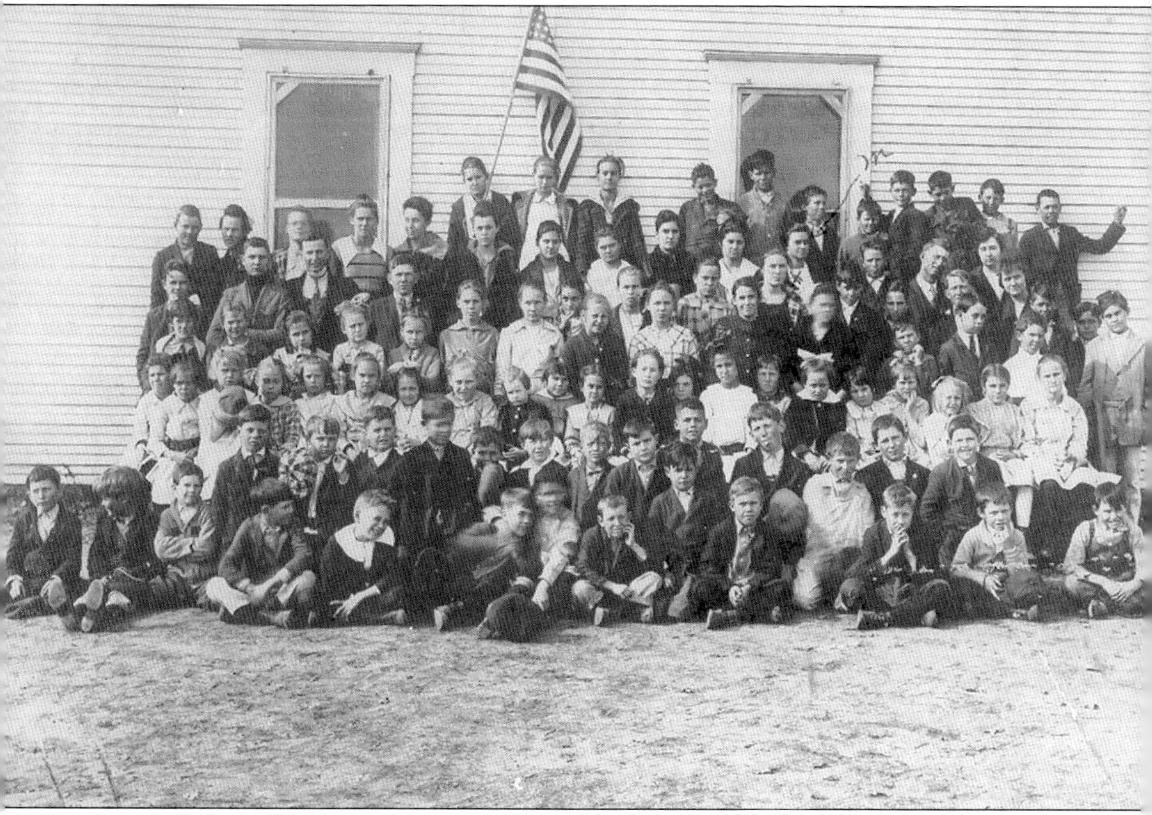

Mary George Billingsley Sullivan, Argyle's oldest citizen, who lived to be 102 years of age, identified some of the students in this 1918 Argyle School photograph. Pictured in the first row, the fifth boy from the left is Herman Cook and the 10th boy from the left is Edgar Horton. In the third row, the sixth girl from the left is Lessie Coggell, and next to her is Eugenia Stewart. In the fourth row, from left to right starting with the third girl, are Ola Jeter, Winifred Carpenter, Mary George Billingsley (Sullivan), Georgia Belle Meadows (Allen), and the eighth student from the left is Doyle Chambers. In the sixth row, the seventh student from the left is Lala Crawford, the 11th student is Marcella Stewart (Henderson), the second man to her left is principal Luther Johnson, next to him is teacher Mrs. Hodges, and below her is teacher Mackie Cook. In the back row, the third student from the left is Nell Horton. (Courtesy of Martha Len Nelson.)

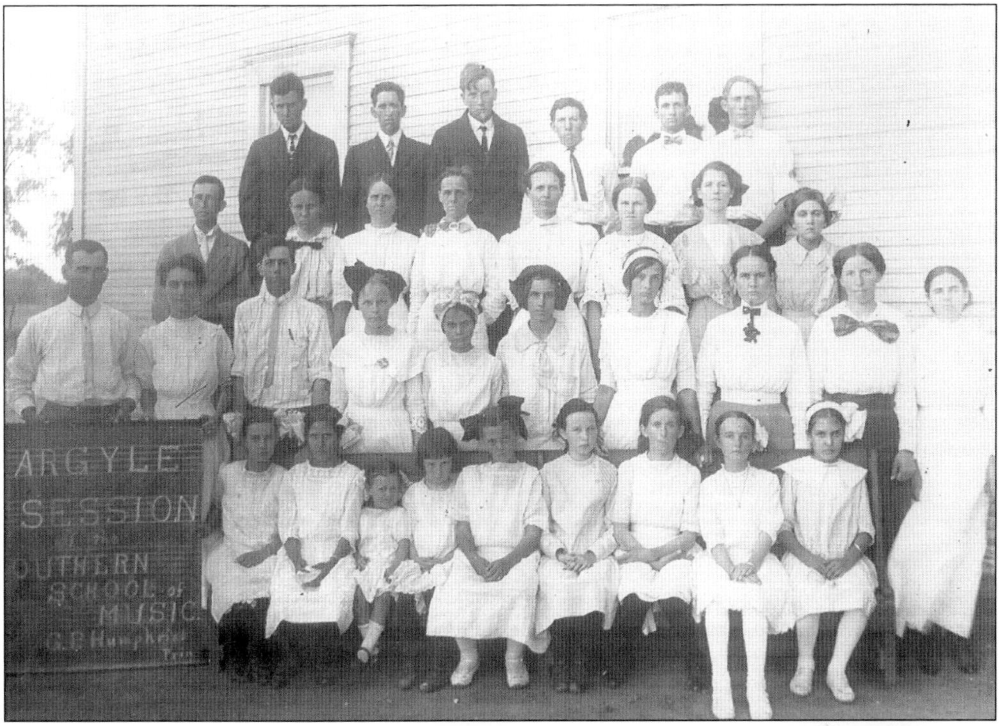

This photograph is of the Argyle Session of the Southern Music Singing School that was taken about 1910. Pictured in the first row, from left to right, are Marcella Stewart (Henderson), her best friend Lala Crawford, and her little sister Eugenia Stewart. In the third row, the fifth woman from the left is Marcella's mother, Ina Lively Stewart, and her Aunt Daisy Lively is left of the director. (Courtesy of Martha Len Nelson.)

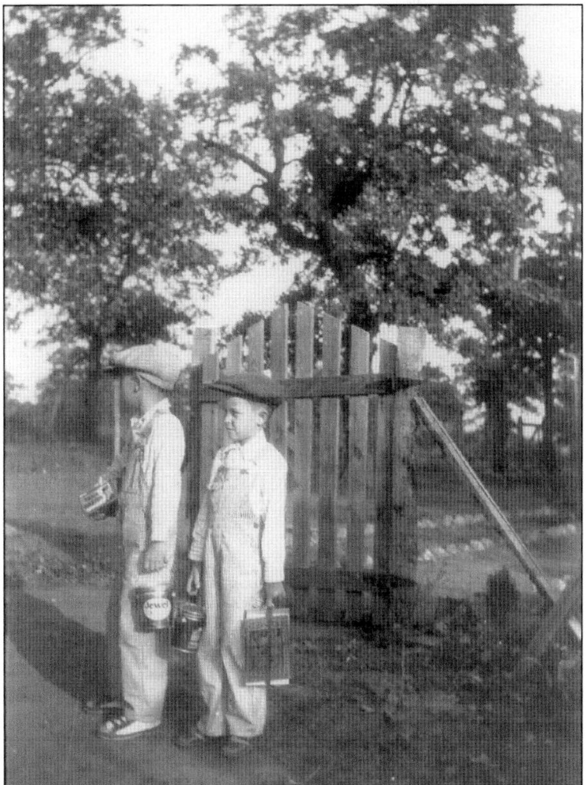

Dressed in new overalls and carrying shiny new lunch pails (syrup buckets), first-graders Wallace Lynch and his nephew Perry Wood (who was five months younger) are seen leaving home to attend the first day of school at the new 1929 red brick Argyle School. "We thought we were in tall cotton moving into that new brick building," remembers Wallace Lynch, who was born and raised in Argyle. (Courtesy of Wallace Lynch.)

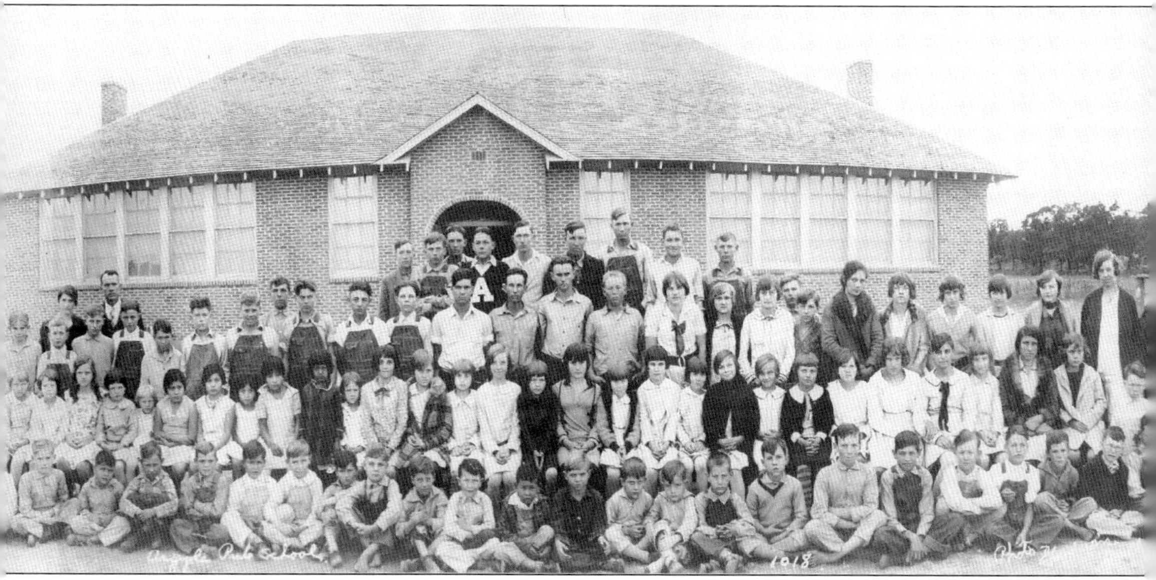

This photograph was taken in 1929 when Argyle students moved into the new, red brick Argyle schoolhouse. Seated on the first row, fourth from the left, is Crawford Morris; sixth and seventh from the left are Tommie Horton and Wallace Lynch; 11th and 12th are Perry Wood and J.D. Massey. Those with perfect attendance received certificates, and most students attended class regularly to receive one. (Courtesy of Wallace Lynch.)

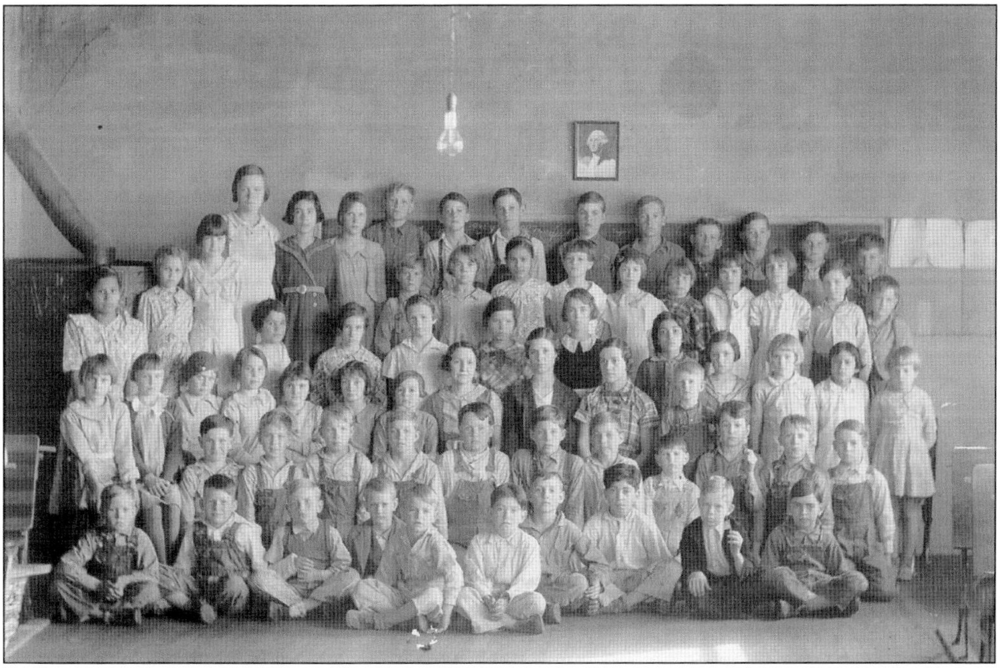

Wallace Lynch is the fourth boy from the left in the second row, and his nephew Perry Wood is next to him in this 1930 Argyle School photograph. Both boys were in third grade. They skipped second grade, as did most of students who successfully passed a written test after first grade. (Courtesy of Wallace Lynch.)

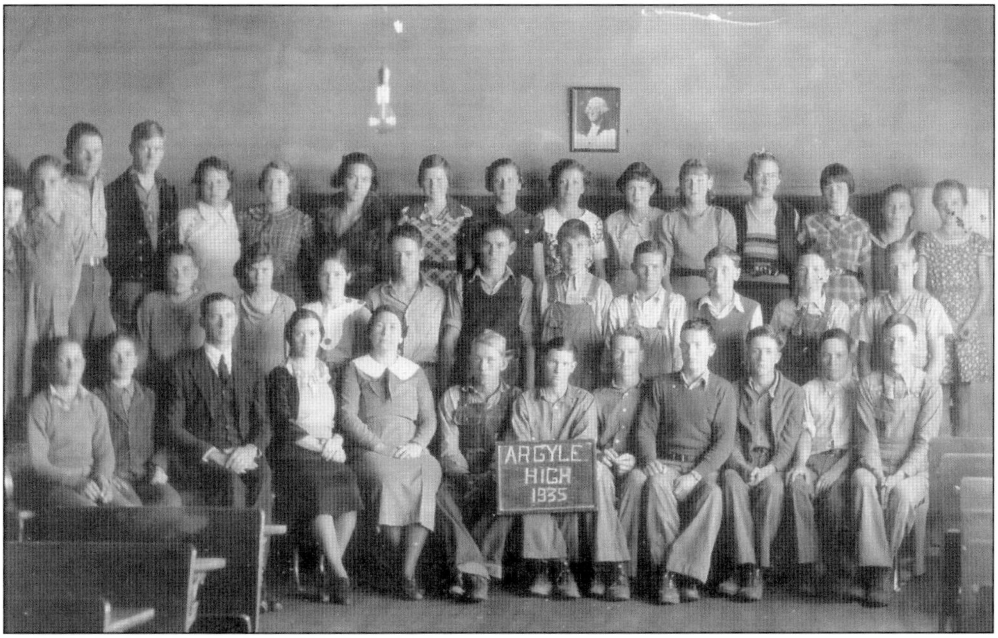

In this 1935 Argyle School photograph, the first boy standing is Perry Wood, and in the second row, the third boy from the end is Wallace Lynch. The Argyle School had classes from first through ninth grade, then students transferred to Denton for 10th and 11th grades to graduate from high school. (Courtesy of Wallace Lynch.)

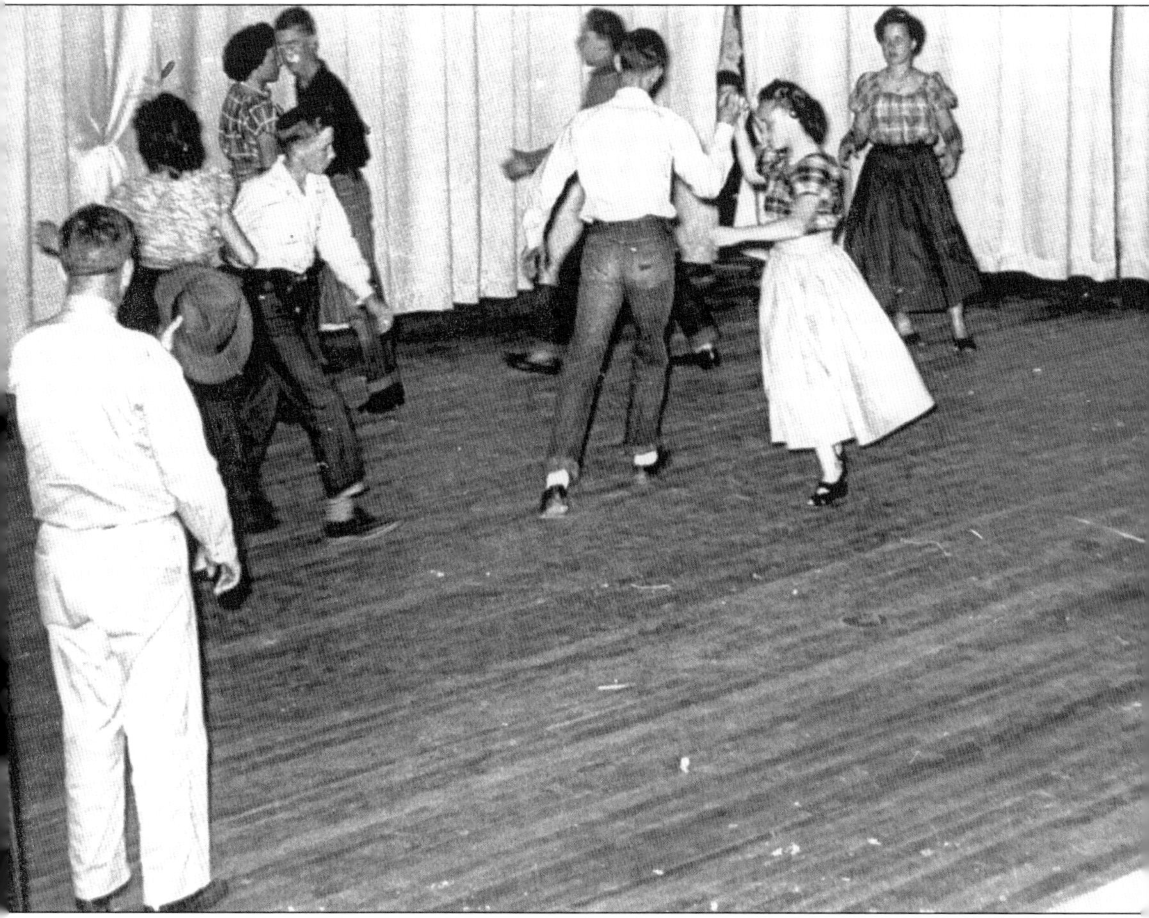

In the mid-1940s, members of the Argyle 4-H Club learned to square dance. One night a week the students rode a school bus to the Denton World War II United Service Organization (USO) to practice. After it closed, they practiced at the Argyle School auditorium. The students became so proficient at square-dancing that they traveled Texas performing and giving demonstrations to different organizations. (Courtesy of Kay Teer.)

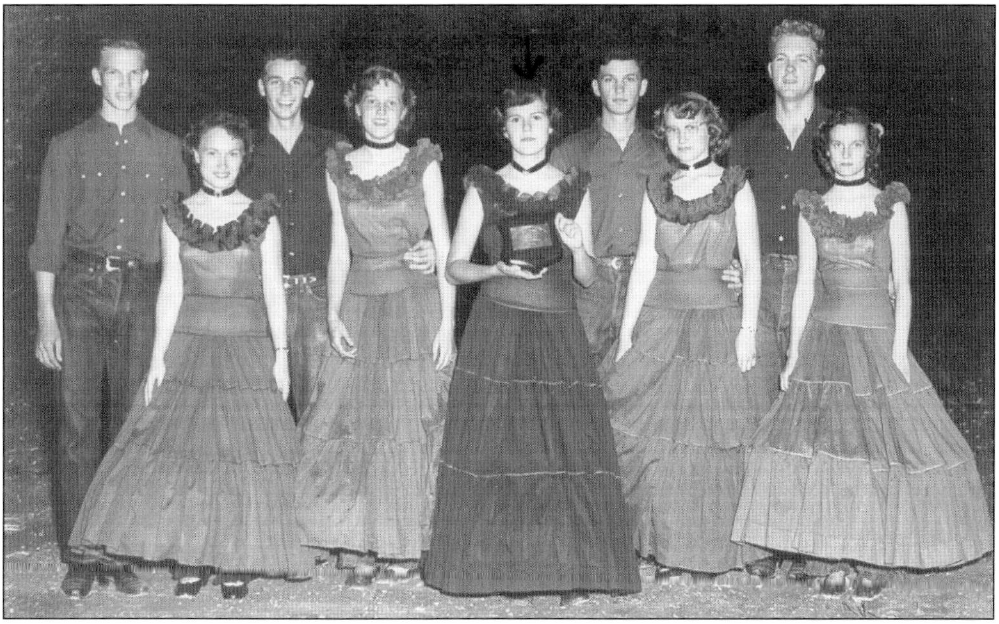

"All of us had dresses alike and I was the caller," said longtime resident and former mayor Yvonne A. Jenkins, who was born and raised in Argyle. The Argyle 4-H Club square-dancing members pictured above are, from left to right, John Burl Price, Margie Crawford Austin, Beverly Wilson, Jo Ann Matthews Brown, Yvonne Allen Jenkins, Bill Oxford, Shirley Taylor, Bobby Allman, and Mary Anne Boyles Carroll. (Courtesy of Kay Teer.)

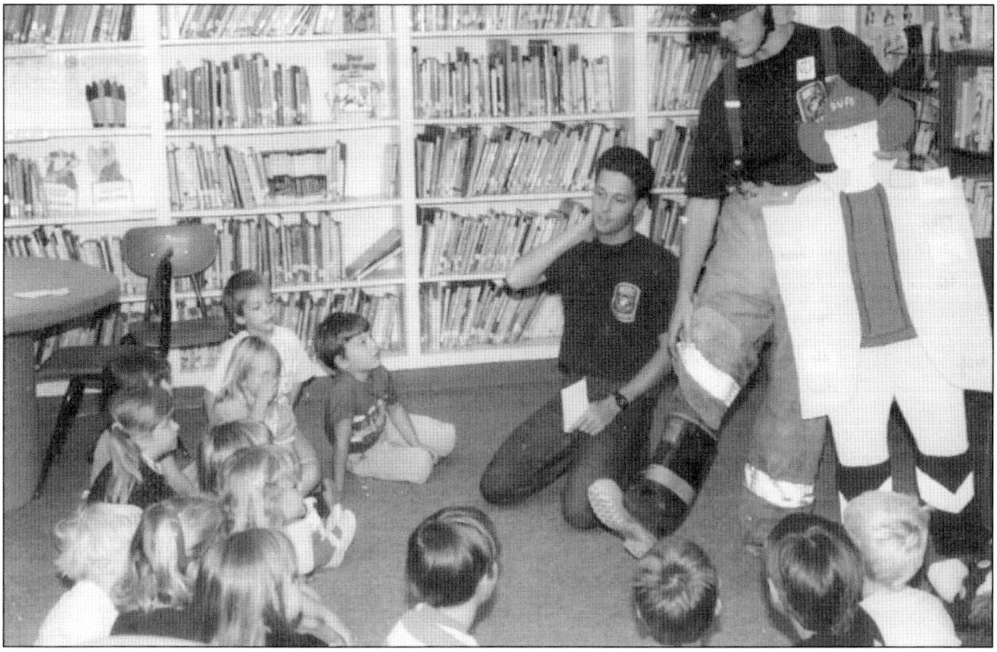

In the late 1970s and early 1980s, the Argyle Volunteer Fire Department (AVFD) gave presentations on fire safety to the Argyle Elementary and Middle School students. In this photograph, AVFD Fire Prevention Officer Loren Tracy shows students the standard firefighting gear firemen wear and the equipment they use. (Courtesy of AVFD.)

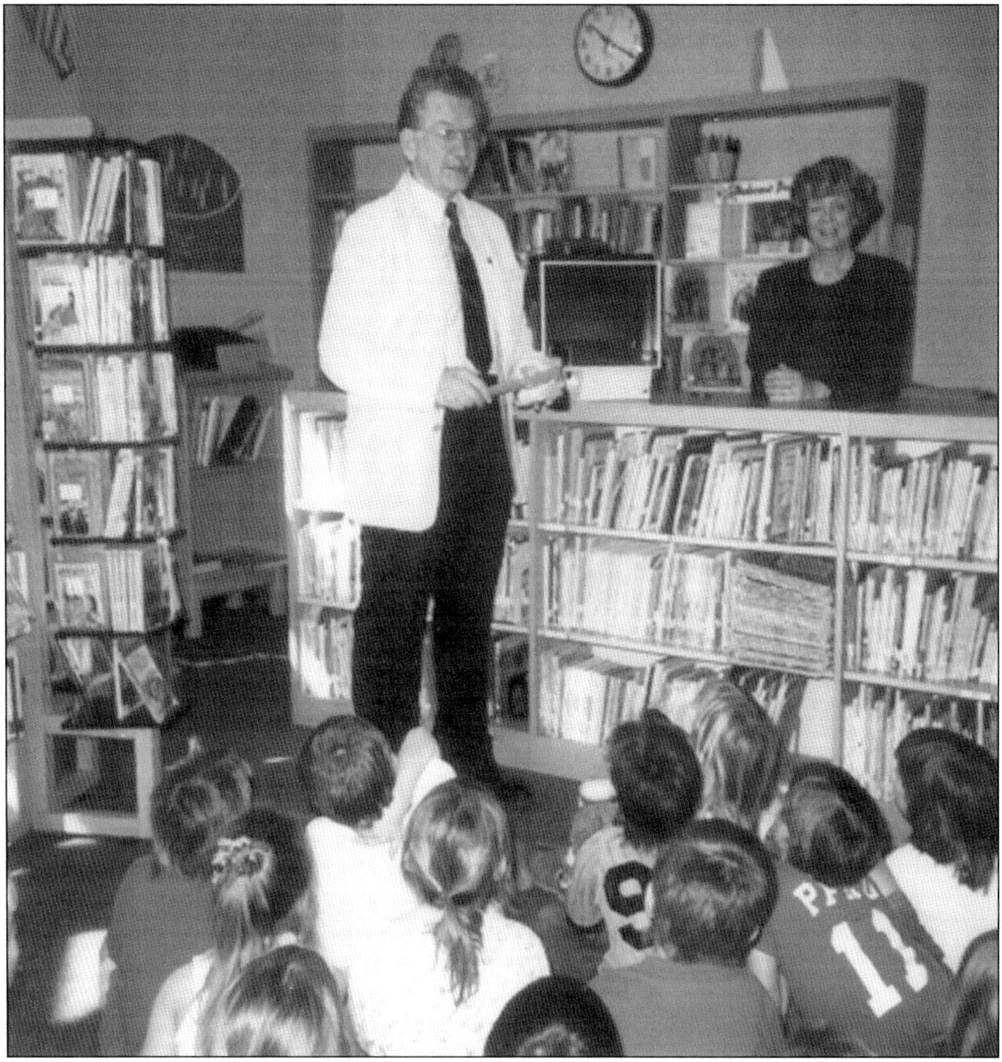

During Dental Health Month in the 1990s, Dr. Larry Simmons gave presentations to Argyle Elementary School students on taking care of their teeth. The students were given toothbrushes, toothpaste, and a *Happy Tooth* coloring book. Doctor Simmons was chairman of the Argyle Planning and Zoning Commission when the first zoning ordinance, 7-7-77, was passed. He practiced dentistry in Denton for 35 years before retiring. (Courtesy of *The Argyle Sun*.)

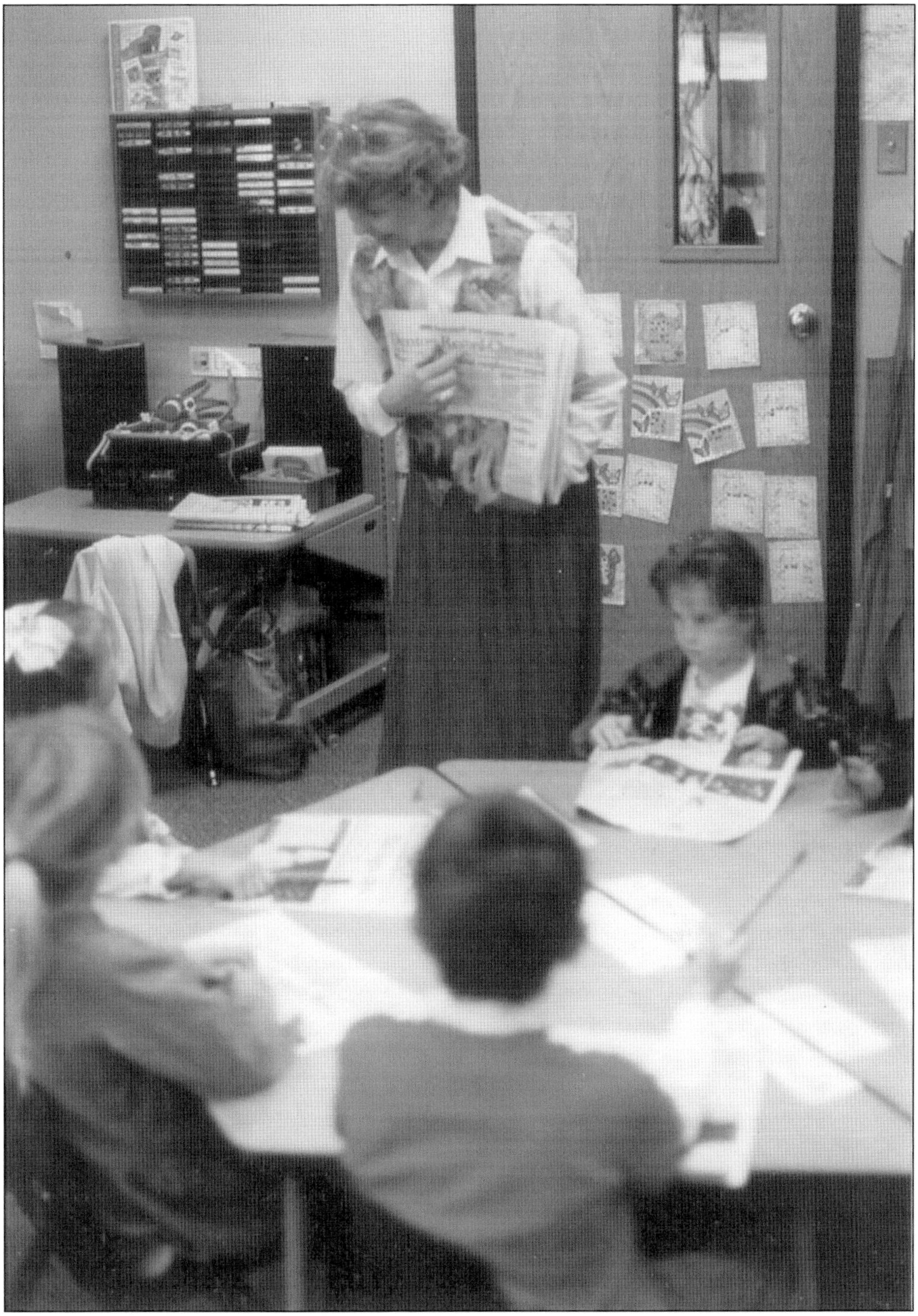

The Argyle Sun Newspaper-in-Education coordinator and former public school teacher Lynn Sheffield Simmons is seen in this 1995 photograph showing Argyle Elementary School kindergarteners how to use the newspaper as an educational tool to help them with their classroom assignments. Copies of *The Argyle Sun* were given to the students every week. (Courtesy of *The Argyle Sun*.)

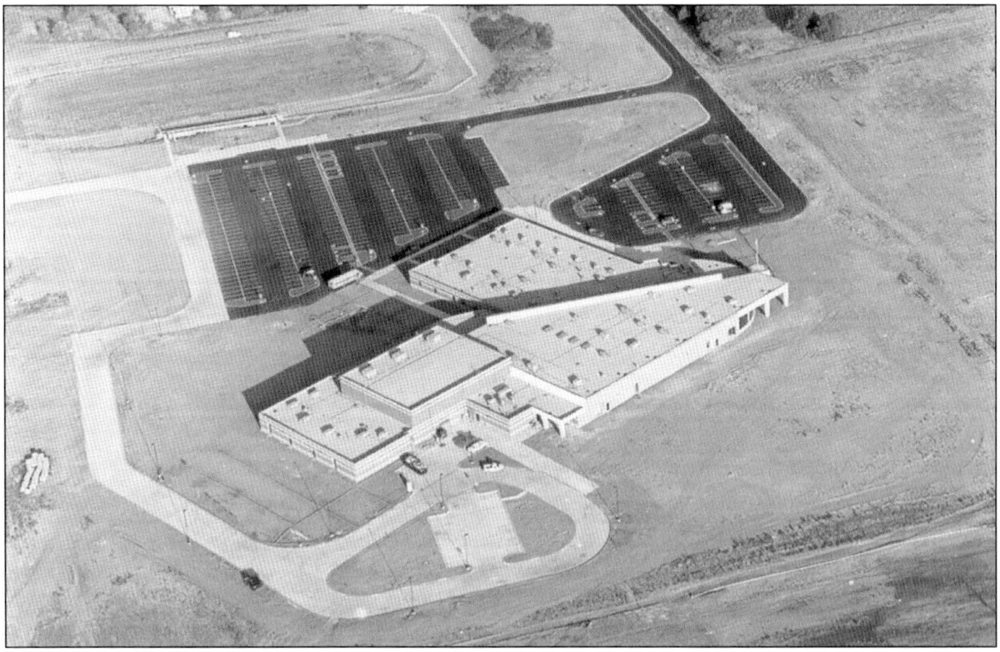

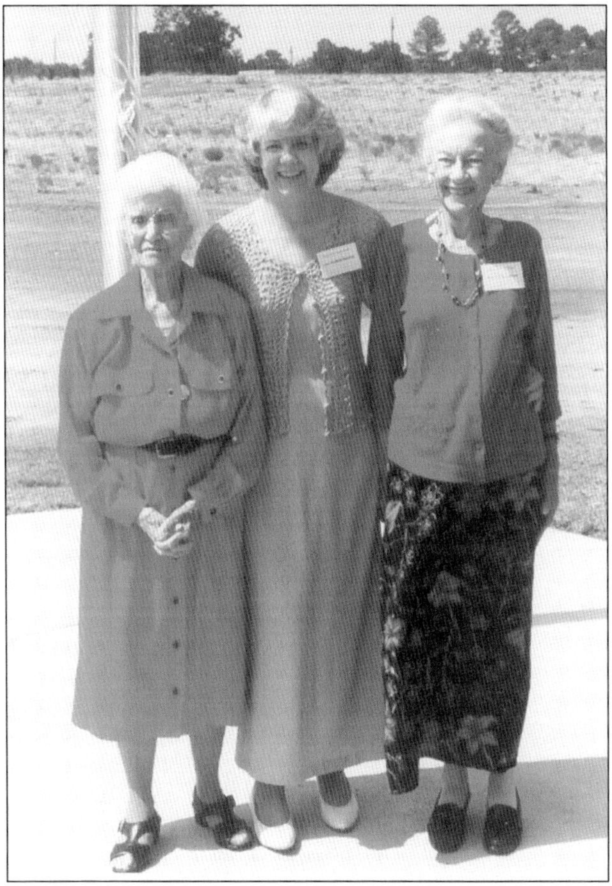

This is a 1999 aerial view of the new Argyle High School and Middle School on US Highway 377. The campus encompasses more than 100 acres. The old Argyle School closed because of the creek flooding. In 1929, B.W. Meadows bought the land for $50 and donated 6.074 acres of his farm to the Argyle School District, where the Argyle Elementary School is located. (Courtesy of Joan Delashaw.)

Ninety-eight-year-old Marcella Stewart Henderson (left), and 91-year-old Mary George Sullivan (far right) are seen with Lynn Sheffield Simmons at the 1999 opening of the Argyle High School. Henderson and Sullivan went to the old Argyle School on the corner of West Front Street and Old Justin Road. When they attended school, students graduated from high school after completing 11 grades. (Courtesy of *The Argyle Sun*.)

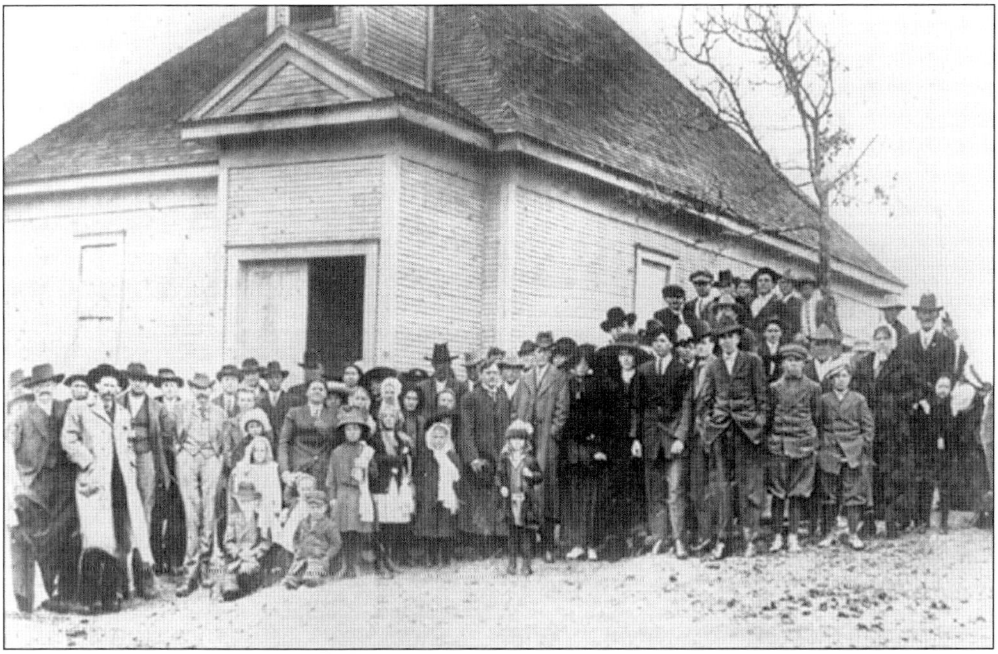

Shown here are the Argyle Baptist Church and members of its congregation in 1909. Originally, the church was Graham Baptist Church, organized in 1876 at the Graham schoolhouse. After the schoolhouse burned in 1887, church services were held at various locations in Argyle. Following a 1909 revival, Dr. M.D. Fullingim gave the Argyle Baptist Church two lots at Mesquite and Dallas Streets for a new church. (Courtesy of Wallace Lynch.)

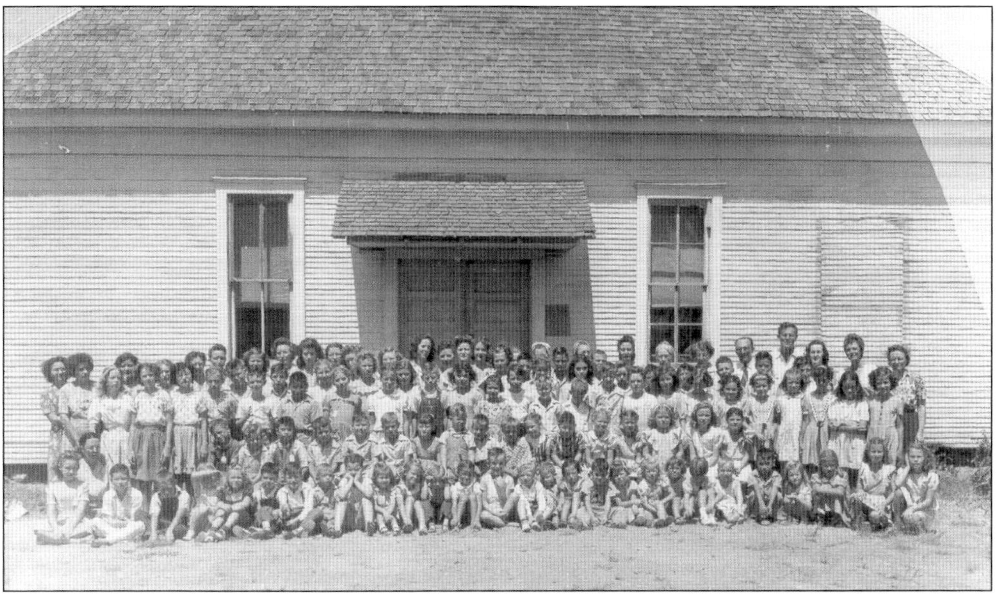

This 1946 photograph is of the Argyle Baptist Church Vacation Bible School held at the old Baptist Church. The previous year, a basement was dug under the main part of the building for Sunday school classrooms. On January 28, 1909, the Argyle Baptist Church held its "Fifth Sunday" meeting that continued for three days and nights. Dinner was held on the grounds on Friday and Saturday. (Courtesy of Wallace Lynch.)

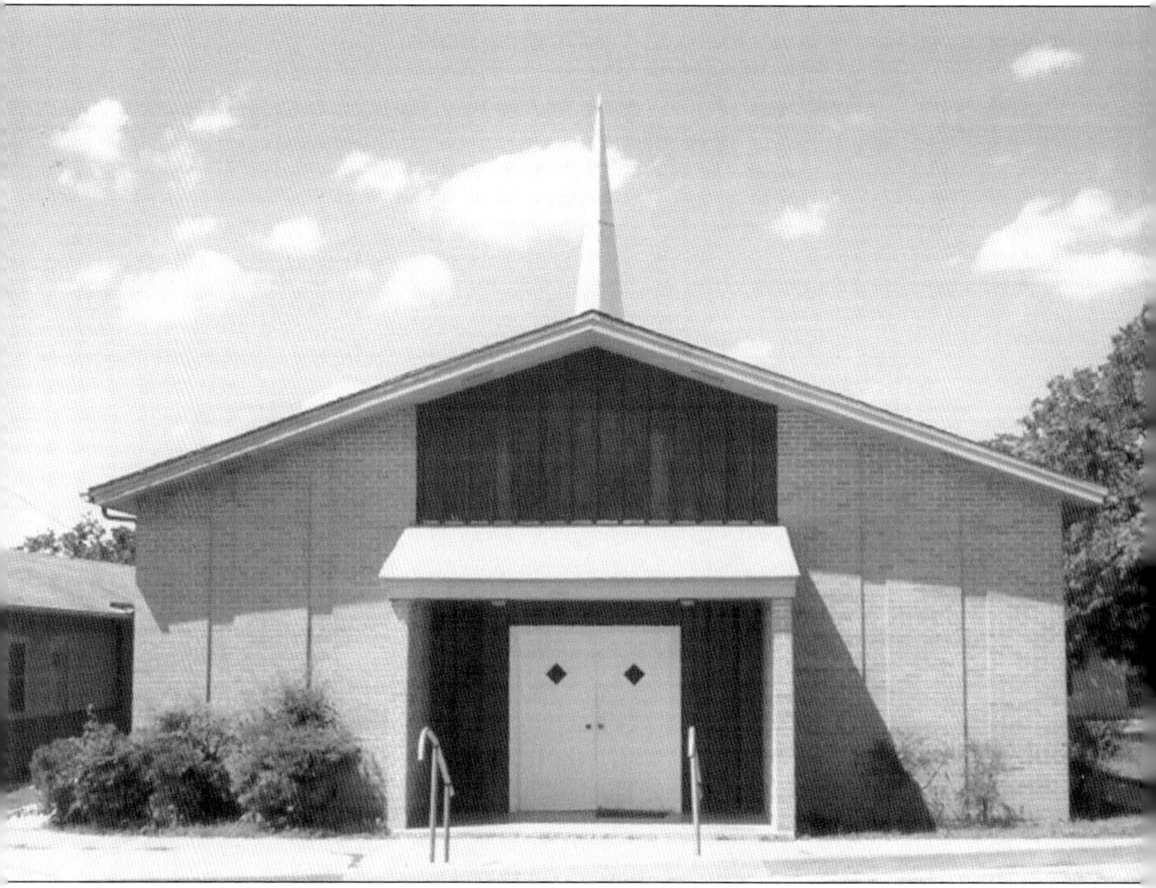

In 1962, the Sam Haynes family gave one lot and the church bought two more lots to build a new Argyle Baptist Church at the corner of Dallas and Cypress Streets. The classroom building, partly seen on the left, was the old railroad section gang house where the railroad workers' families lived. The house was moved from West Front Street and attached to the new church building. (Courtesy of Joan Delashaw.)

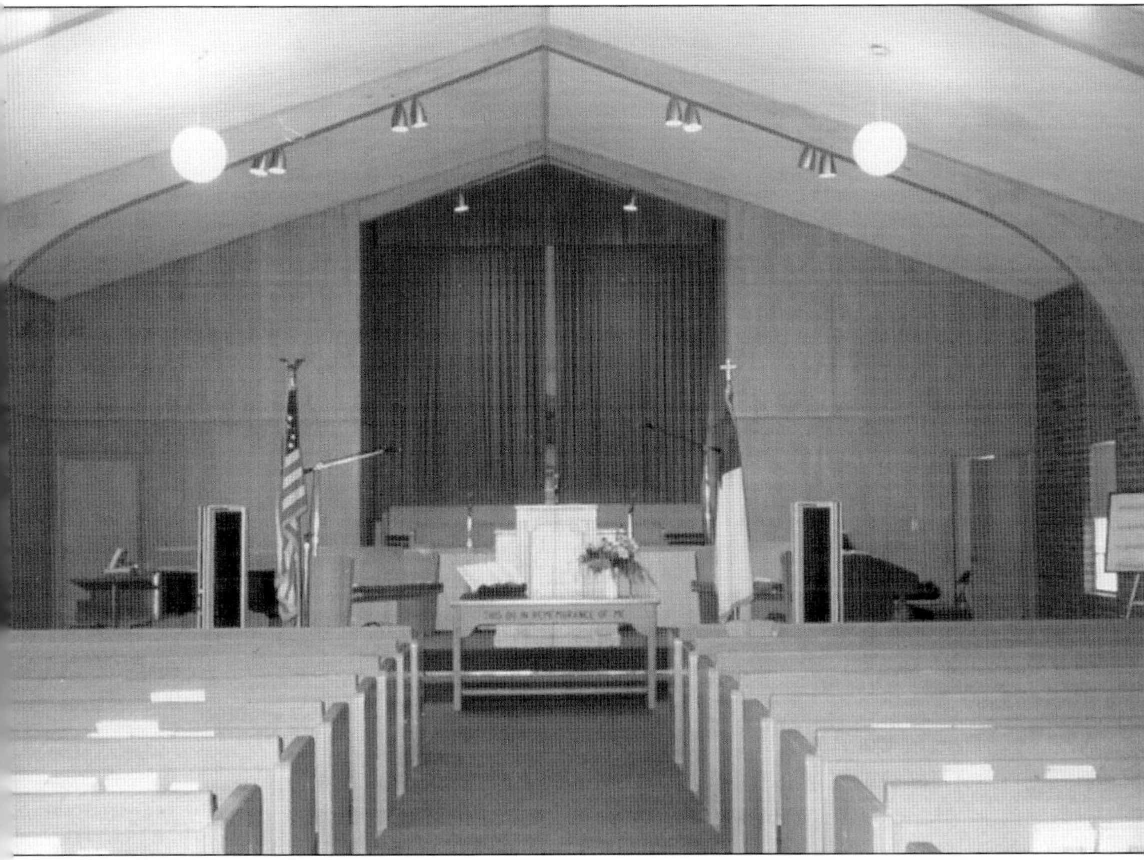

This is the sanctuary of the Argyle Baptist Church on Dallas and Cypress Streets. Church services in the new church began in 1963. The first church was the Graham Baptist Church, organized in the Graham schoolhouse in 1876 with three charter members: Dick Lane, Tell Lane, and Doctor Jarrell. The Jarrell girls later became Mrs. Turner Faught, Mrs. John Faught, and Mrs. Will Fincher. (Courtesy of Joan Delashaw.)

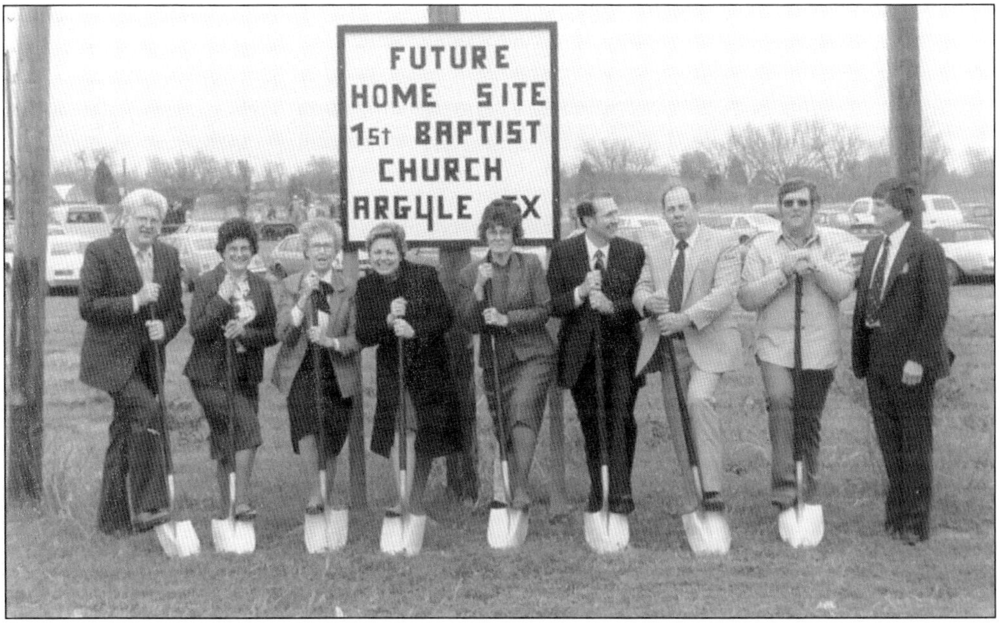

New shovels were used in the April 1984 ground-breaking for the new First Baptist Church of Argyle at 414 North US Highway 377. When the church was incorporated in 1977, the name was changed to the First Baptist Church of Argyle. Pictured from left to right are George Morgan, Dixie Anderson, Pat Ayres, Ruth Anderton, Myrtle Lee Lynch, Pastor Harold Henderson, Kieth Sheets, Kim Taylor, and Warren Oats. (Courtesy of Joan Delashaw.)

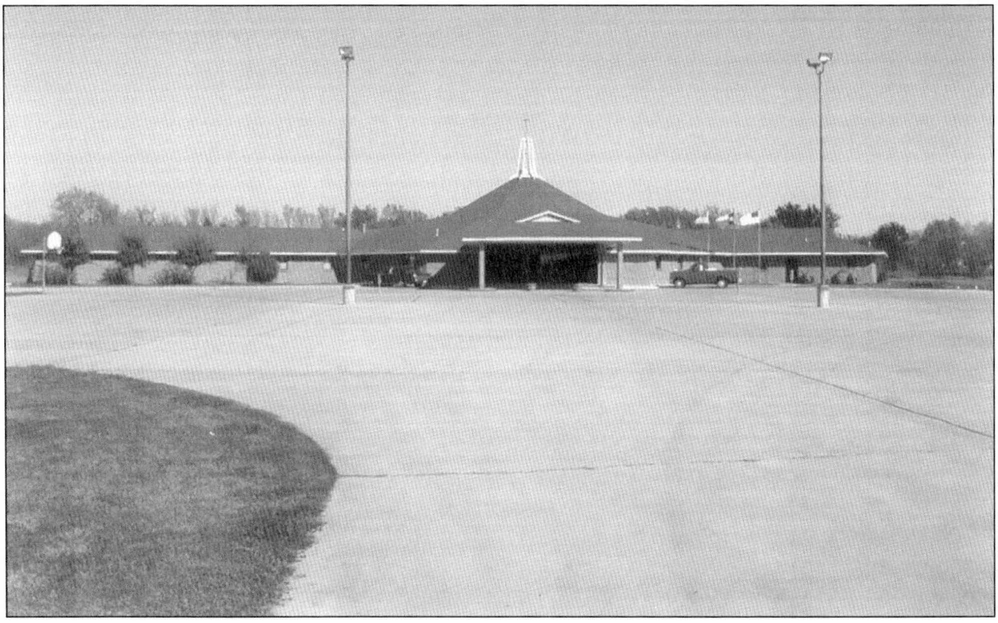

Seen here is the new First Baptist Church of Argyle, built in 1984. The building includes Fellowship Hall, which has a meeting room and a large kitchen. Many church and community activities have been held there, including Mothers' Day Out, Argyle Seniors' Activities Center, lunches in combination with community garage sales held in the parking lot, Fourth of July celebrations, and more. (Courtesy of Joan Delashaw.)

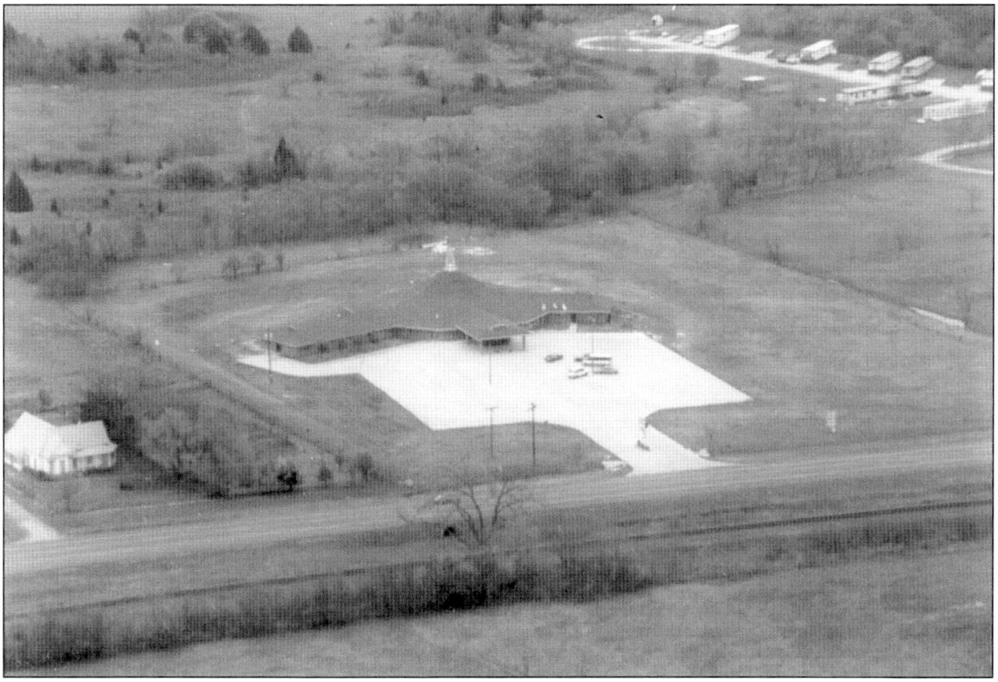

This aerial view of the new First Baptist Church of Argyle also shows the mobile home park before the Settlers Point subdivision was built. To the left, on US Highway 377, is the home of "Uncle Bob" Keith, a Baptist preacher in the early 1900s, who performed wedding ceremonies after couples drove their buggy to his house and waited for him to come out to perform the ceremony. (Courtesy of Joan Delashaw.)

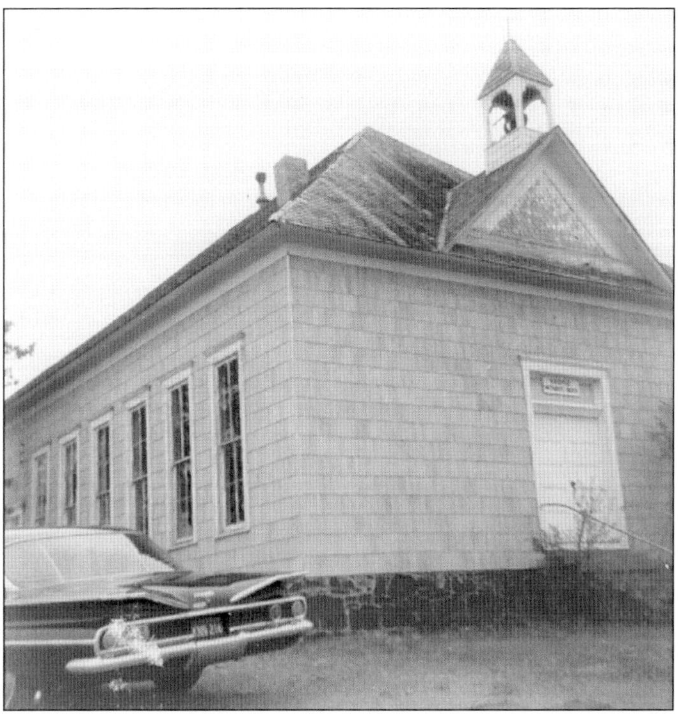

The wood frame Argyle Methodist Church building was located on Denton Street, which is often referred to as "Methodist hill." When the church was constructed, it did not have a belfry; the bell tower was added later. After the church was built, the Argyle Baptist Church congregation met there when the building was not in use, before the Argyle Baptist Church was built in 1909. (Courtesy of Mary Anne Carroll.)

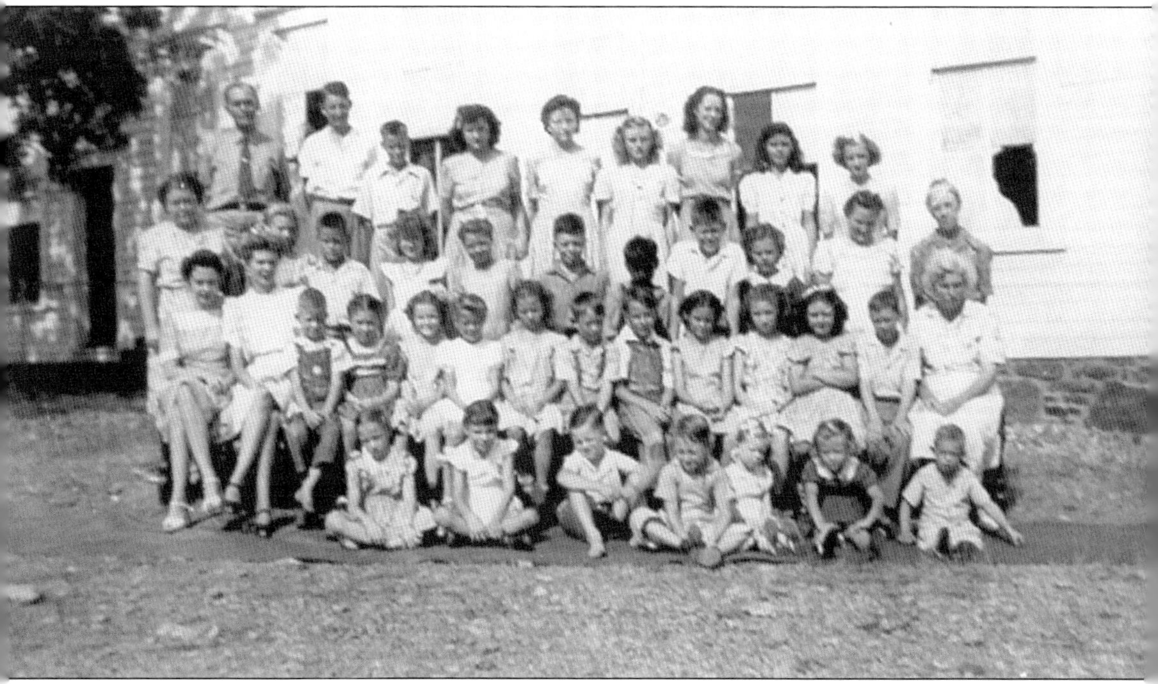

This mid-1940s photograph is of the Argyle Methodist Church Vacation Bible School that was directed by Brother Pollard. The Vacation Bible School was usually held the first week in June. Children in the first row are unidentified. The children in the first row are unidentified. Pictured from left to right, are (second row) Greta Wood (Garrett), Barbara Pruitt, unidentified, Sue Wallace, Susie Boyles, Barbara Horton, unidentified, Guy Fincher, Bobby Starnes, Mary Anne Boyles (Carroll), Margie Crawford, unidentified, John Wesley Taylor, and Mrs. Pollard; (third row) church helper Artie May Jones, unidentified, Lewis Boyles, unidentified, Wynema Harper, Sam Brown, unidentified, Bill Jones, Yvonne Allen (Jenkins), Willie Jo Cottle, and Mattie Brown; (fourth row) Brother Pollard, unidentified, Jimmy Boyles, Edrina Faught, Merle Faught, Mary Taylor, Betty Mae McGee, Elaine Harper, and Vera Shockey. (Courtesy of Mary Anne Carroll.)

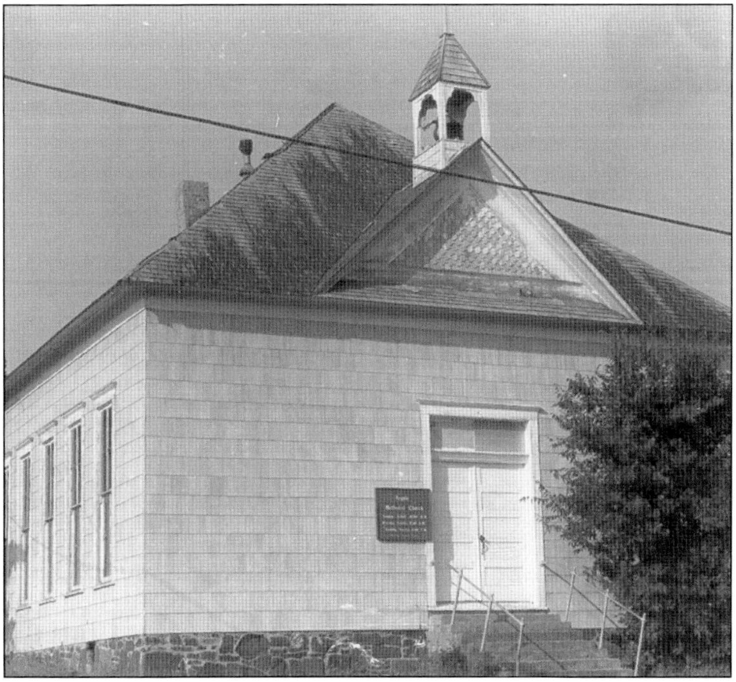

The Argyle Methodist Church was chartered in 1894 with 27 members. Its first pastor was Rev. Blueford Henry Webster, a Methodist circuit rider from Mississippi. This first church building was built by Rev. J.R. Atchley, who was also a carpenter. Church members helped to complete the construction. Land adjoining the church property was bought in 1947 and additional land was purchased in 1973. (Courtesy of Argyle United Methodist Church.)

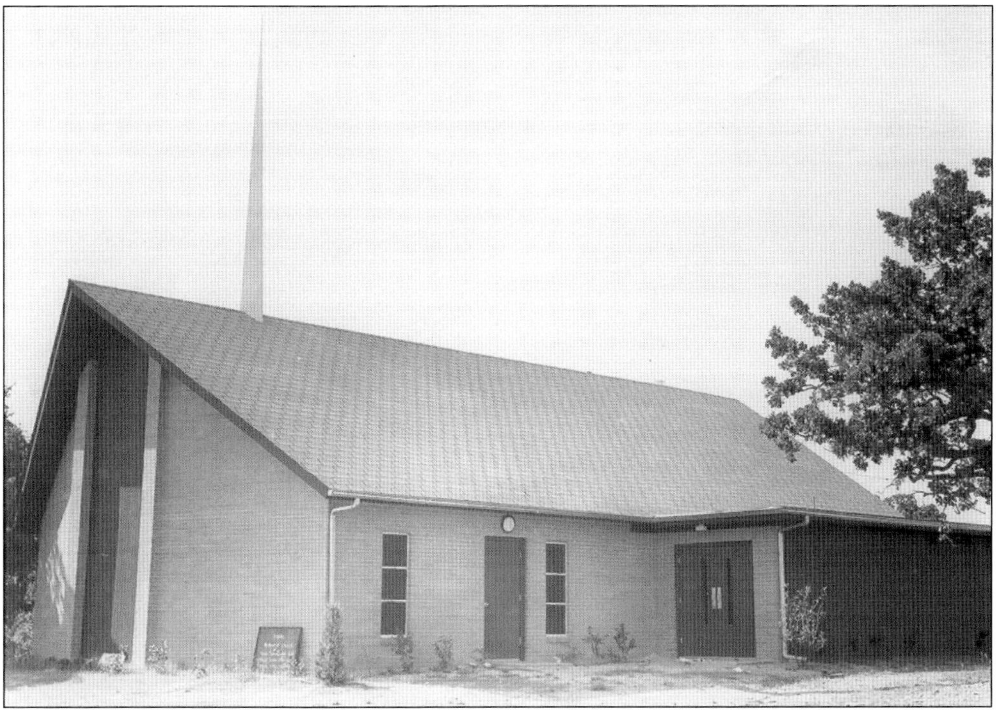

In 1969, the Argyle United Methodist Church built a brick sanctuary and, in 1972, an educational building. When the sanctuary was renovated in 1986, George Lewis was pastor, and Grover and Clara Faye Wallace were longtime members. Grover worked for the telephone company and helped organize the Argyle Volunteer Fire Department in 1963. He installed fire emergency telephone lines in the firefighters' homes. (Courtesy by Argyle United Methodist Church.)

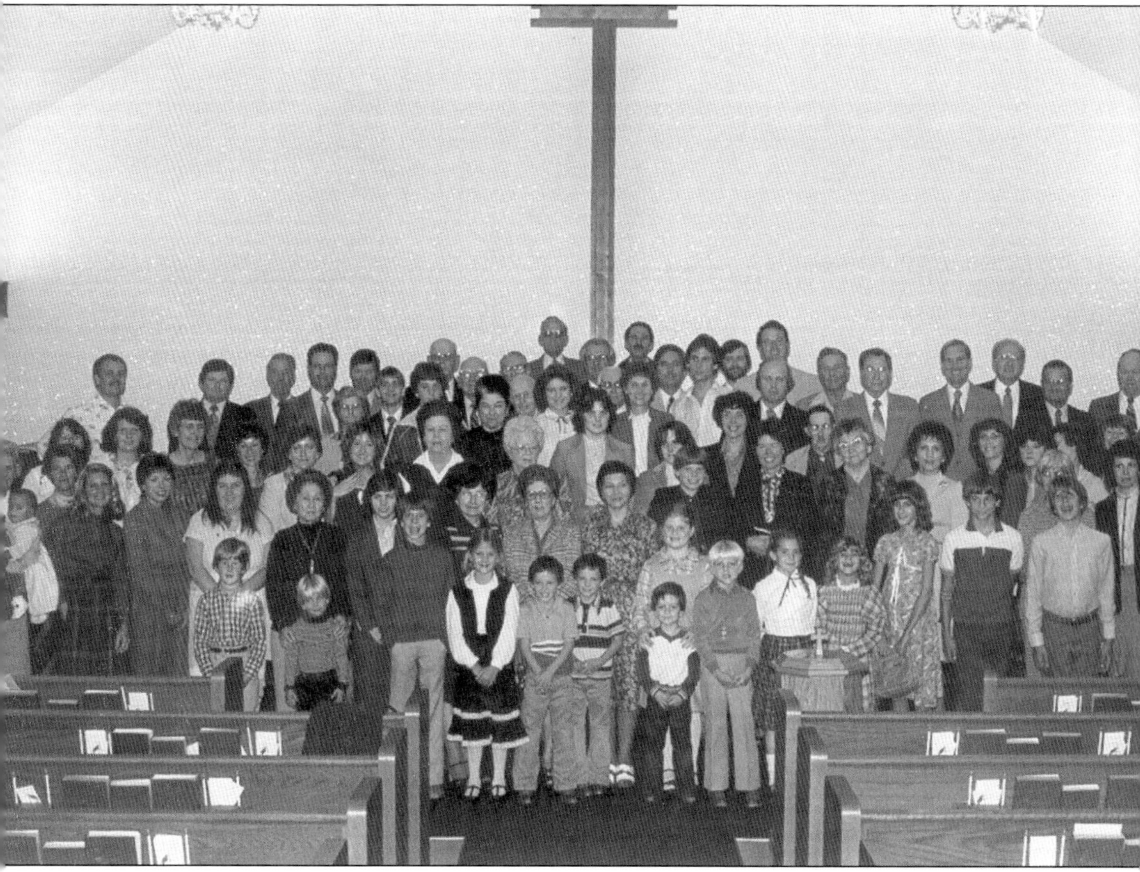

This photograph of church members in the sanctuary of the Argyle United Methodist Church was taken by Royce Gossett on November 2, 1981. The church had always been called the Argyle Methodist Church until 1968 when the General Conference took action to create the United Methodist Church. (Courtesy by Argyle United Methodist Church.)

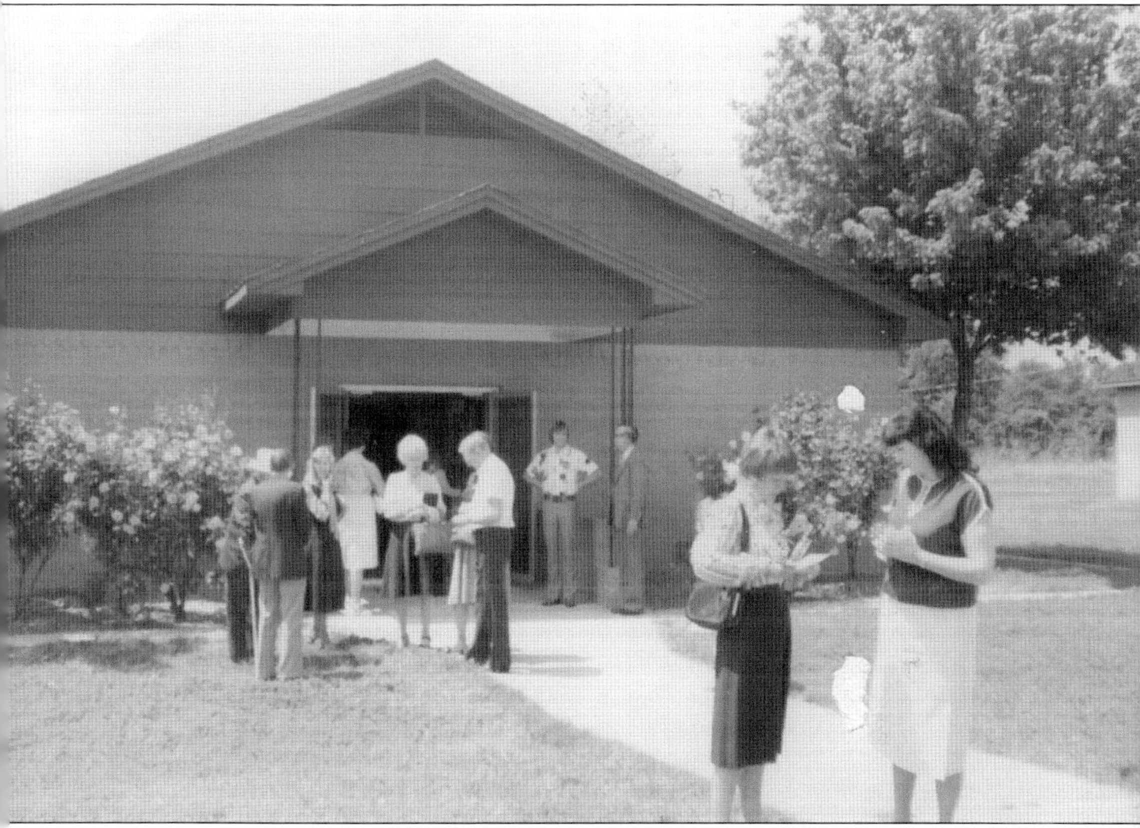

On March 7, 1971, the Argyle Church of Christ met at the Argyle Community Center with Dick Kerr, minister of the Justin Church of Christ, serving as the preacher and Jim McMahan as the song leader. The congregation bought more than six acres at F.M. 407 and US Highway 377, where an old house was remodeled into a sanctuary, and later, this new brick building was constructed. (Courtesy of June Gentry.)

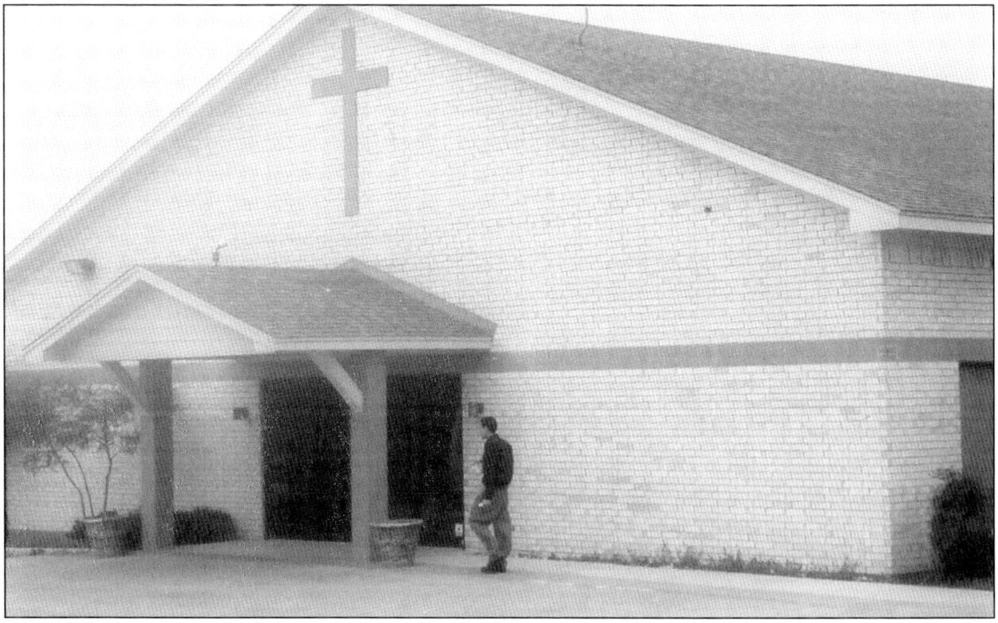

This is a photograph of the new Argyle Church of Christ building with the previous sanctuary remodeled into a classroom building. Early Argyle families who started the church were those of Dan Owens, Clyde Gentry, Jim McMahan, Jim Coffey, Sam Rountree, Tim Wagner, and James Mason. (Courtesy of Arlene Kerr.)

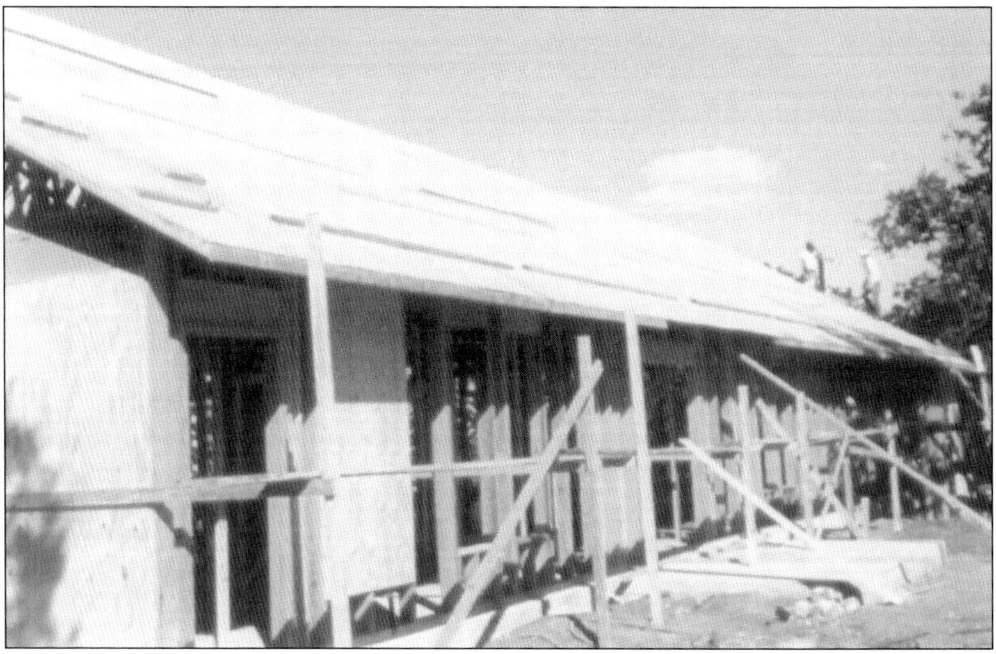

Oak Hills Community Evangelical Free Church was established in 1980. The founders were Dick and Kathy Emery and Doug and Jan Emery, who all grew up in Nebraska and were longtime members of the Evangelical Free Church. Tom Bulick became pastor of the new church. On the first Sunday, a congregation of about 25 people met at the Argyle school cafeteria. (Courtesy of Kathy Emery.)

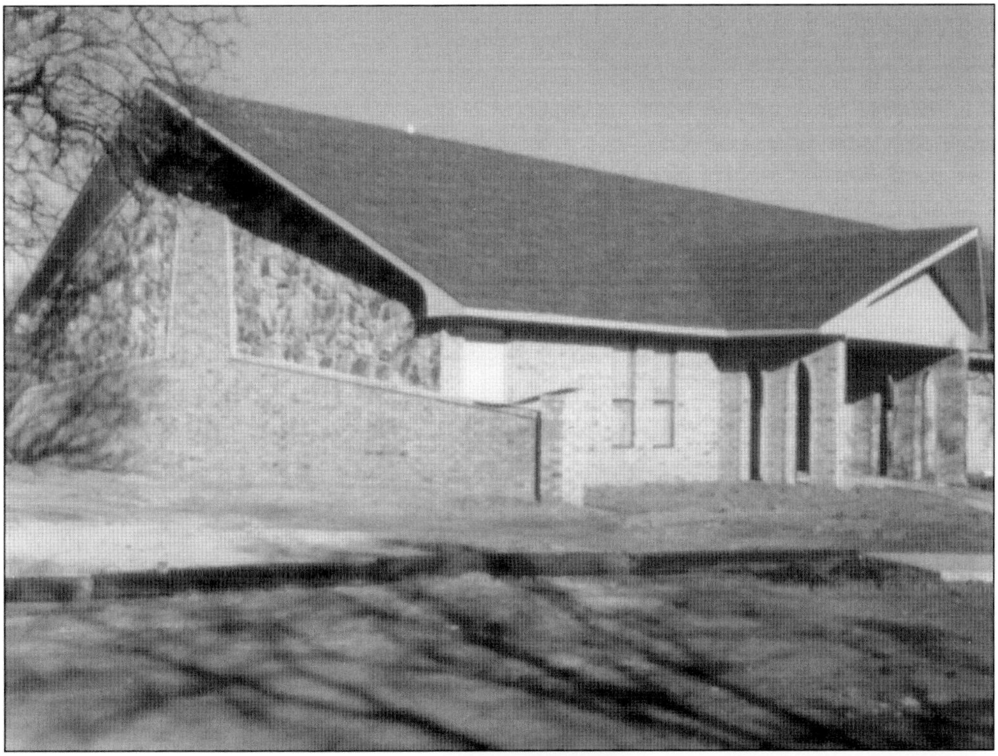

The Oak Hills Community Church continued to meet at the school cafeteria for the next five years. As the membership grew, the church purchased three acres on US Highway 377. In 1985, with a membership of more than 100 people, construction on the Oak Hills Community Church began at 601 South US Highway 377. John Eppler was the pastor when the church was completed in 1986. (Courtesy of Kathy Emery.)

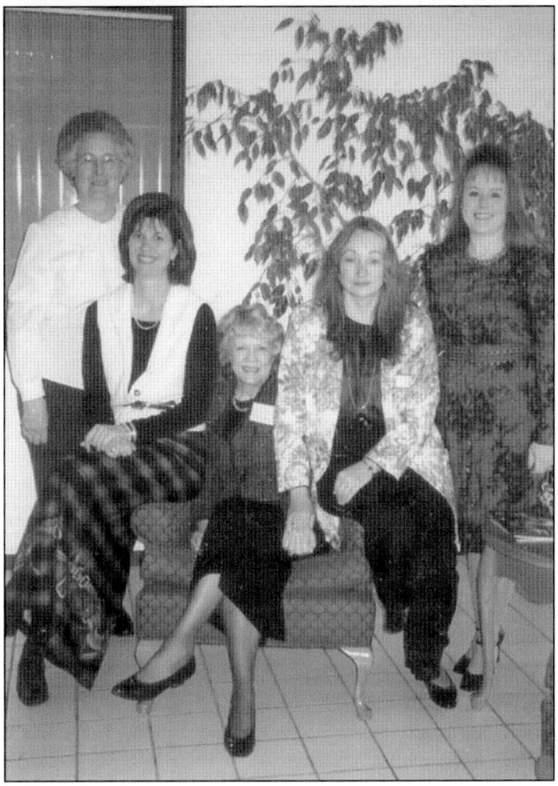

In 2000, the Argyle Christian Women's Fellowship began a Bible study group, with those attending and holding office representing different Argyle church denominations. Committee members were, from left to right, secretary June Gentry; coordinator Melissa Vinton; chairman and organizer Lynn Sheffield Simmons; Bible study teacher Delores Greene; and soloist Sandra Boughton. Not shown are Judy Martin and Judy Davenport. (Courtesy of *The Argyle Sun*.)

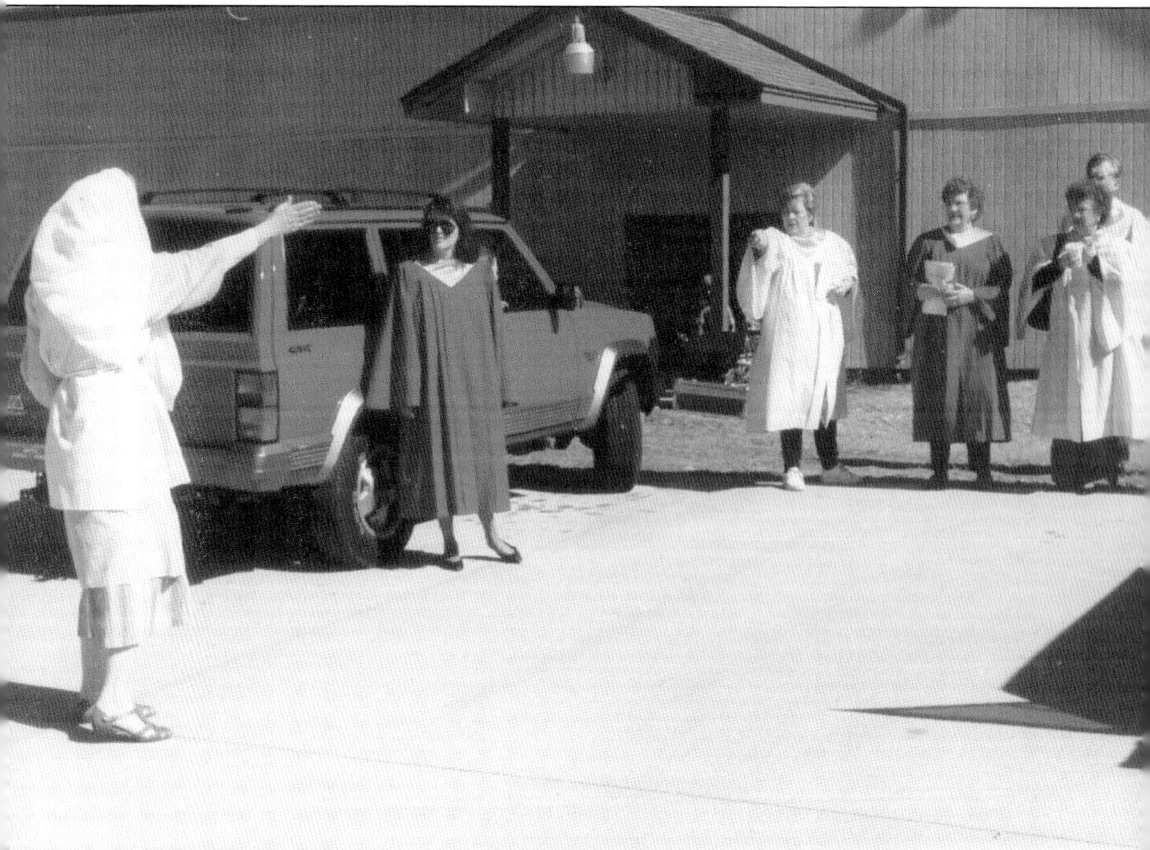

All the Argyle church choirs and ministers participated in the Easter Sunrise pageant, *The Easter Story*. At rehearsal, Lynn Sheffield Simmons shows choir members Kay Teer, Ruth Anderton, Ann Lincoln, Alta Harral, and Dr. Larry Simmons where to stand. Simmons's role was to lead the people of Jerusalem, including pageant cast members Kevin and Vandi Brown, Patrick Fleming, Joel Plangman, Chris Danier, and Cole, Brady, and Clint Brown. (Courtesy of *The Argyle Sun*.)

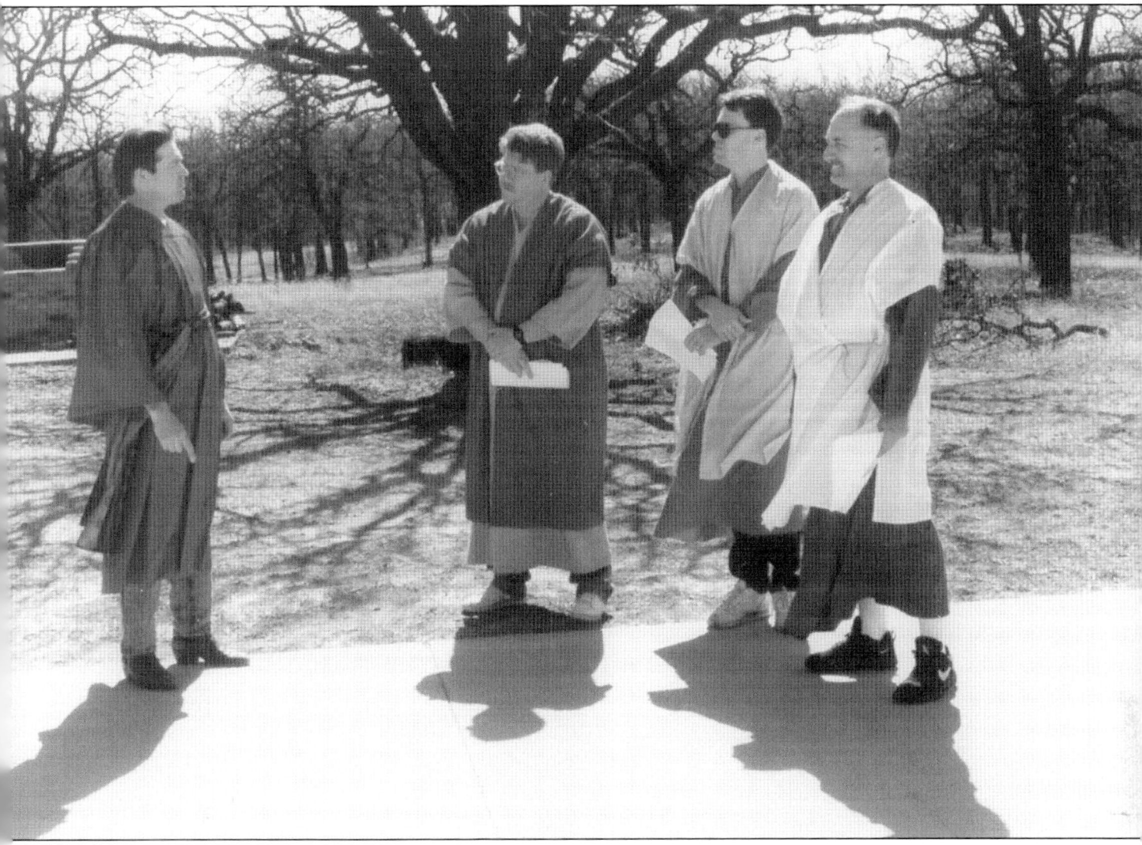

Practicing with Skip Kalb for the April 7, 1996, Easter pageant are Patrick Fleming, Keith Holderman, and Joel Plangman. All of the Argyle church choirs and ministers participated in *The Easter Story*, which was scheduled to be held in the Argyle United Methodist Church's parking lot at 7:00 a.m. Easter morning, but due to the unusually cold weather, the production was rescheduled for inside the church. (Courtesy of *The Argyle Sun.)*

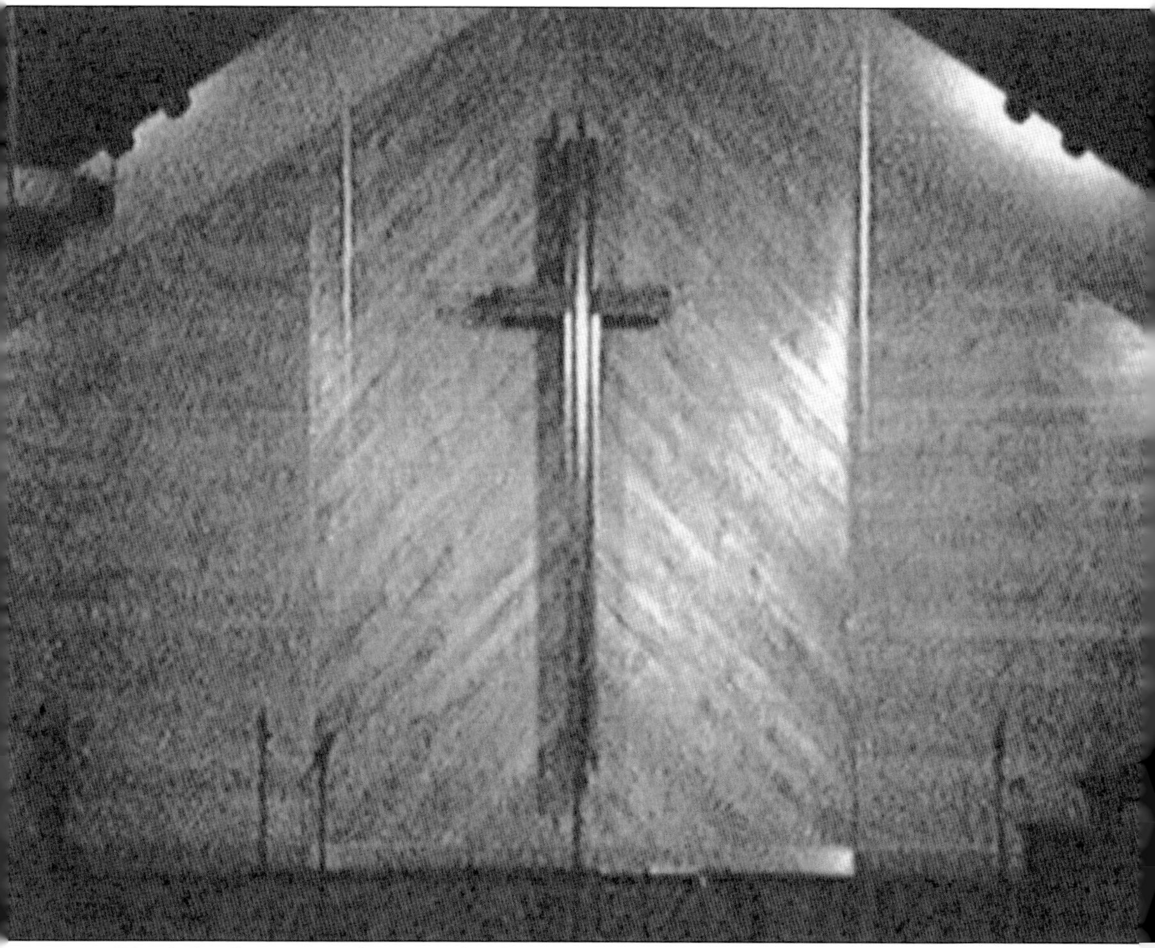

The lighted cross sets the scene for the production *The Easter Story*. The Argyle Community Chorus and Argyle's four churches portrayed Jesus's last week. The narrator was Stacey Beaudine; sound production was managed by Buddy and Carol Mears; the author and producer was Lynn Sheffield Simmons, who was assisted by Bill Smith; the music coordinator was Lynne Tracy; the music director was Bill Smith; the assistant music director was Kay Teer; and the director was Craig Beaudine. (Courtesy by Dr. Allen Buffington.)

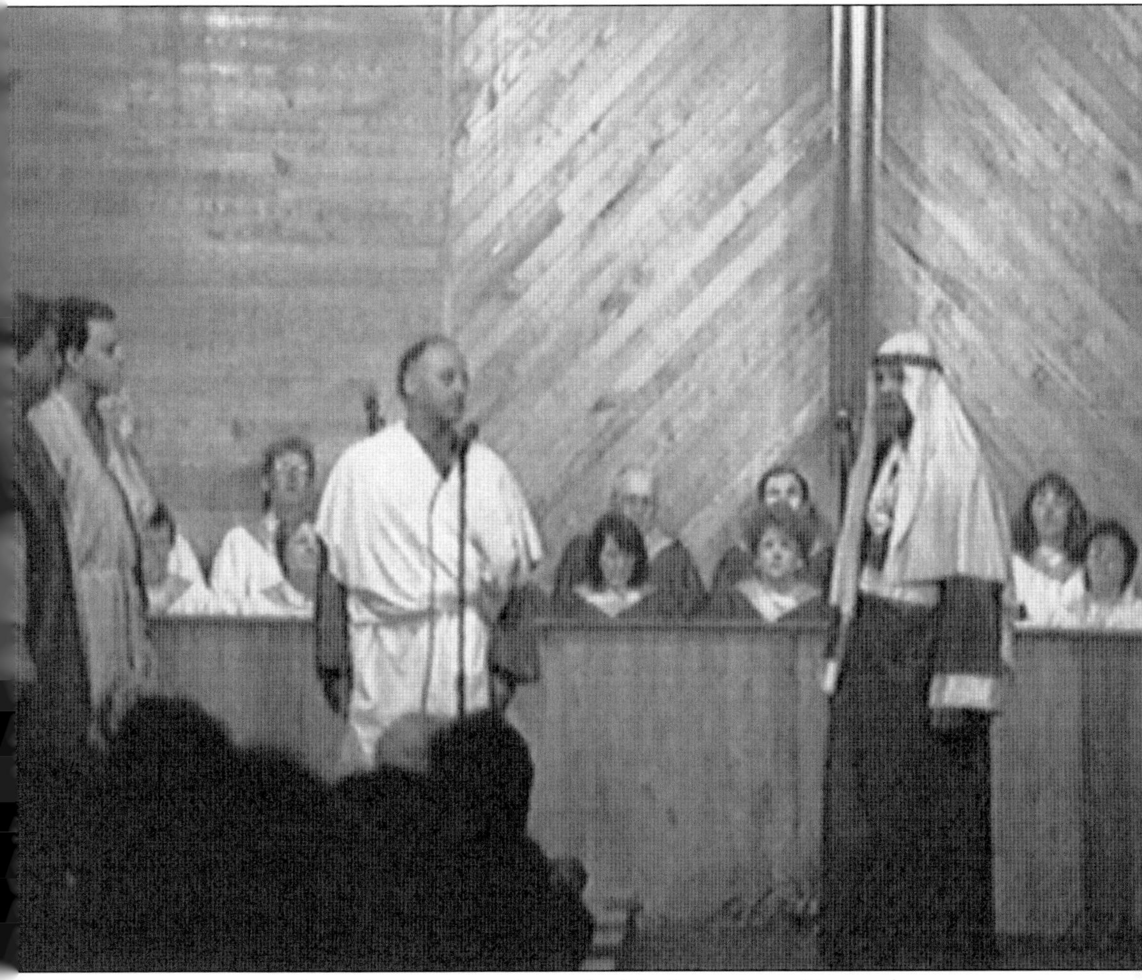

Cast members are seen here playing their roles in the *The Easter Story*. Due to the newspapers' widespread coverage, the church's sanctuary was overflowing with spectators. Following the pageant, an Easter breakfast buffet was served to the public in the Argyle United Methodist Church Community Room. (Courtesy by Dr. Allen Buffington.)

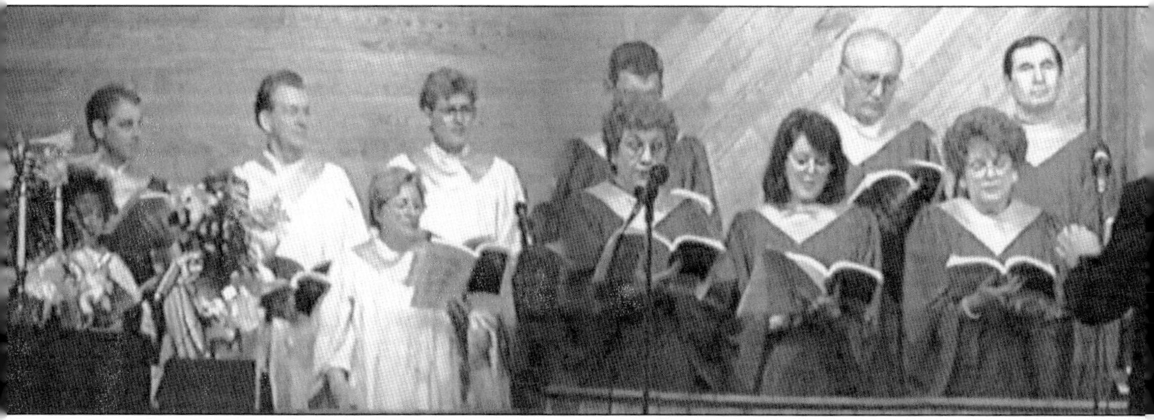

The Easter Story, written and produced by Lynn Sheffield Simmons with Bill Smith assisting, was directed by Kay Jenkins Teer, narrated by Stacey Beaudine, and Bill Smith was the music director. The Argyle Community Chorus included Ruth Anderton, Elsie Barrow, Ken Capelle, Lee Cole, Lorie Cooper, Melinda Crisp, Kathy Emery, Janice Fleming, Gloria Glass, Gwen Goff, Ruth Greene, Delores Greene, Alta Harral, Daniel Humbert, Kay Humbert, Skip Kalb, Dick Kerr, Beverly Lau, Gayle Lewis, Ann Lincoln, Hollie McGalliard, Sandy McLendon, Carol Mears, Doyle

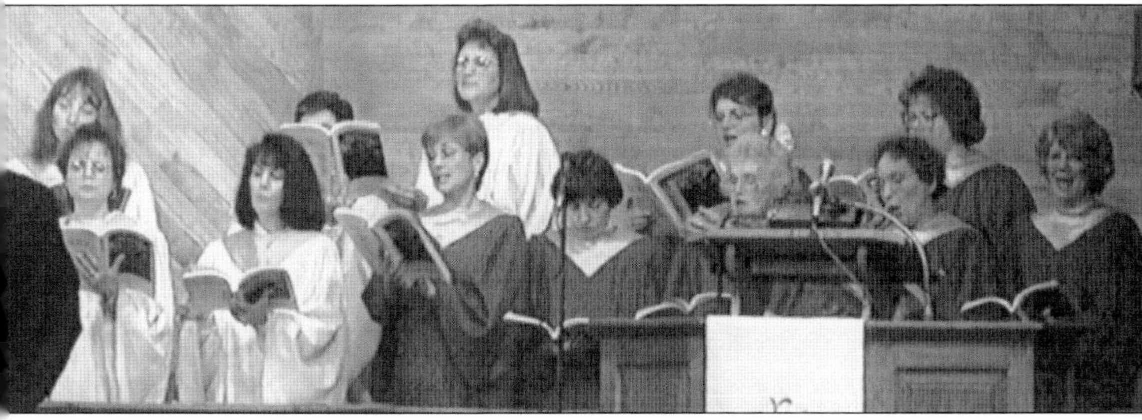

Murray, Janet Newsome, Kenna Rowe, Dr. Larry Simmons, Lynn Sheffield Simmons, Bill Smith, Kay Teer, Lynne Tracy, Mariam Wagner, and Sherry York. Church representatives were Daniel Humbert, pastor of Argyle United Methodist Church; Dick Kerr, pastor of the Argyle Church of Christ; Bill Pritchett, pastor of First Baptist Church of Argyle; and Keith Holdman, of Oak Hills Community Church. (Courtesy of Dr. Alan Buffington.)

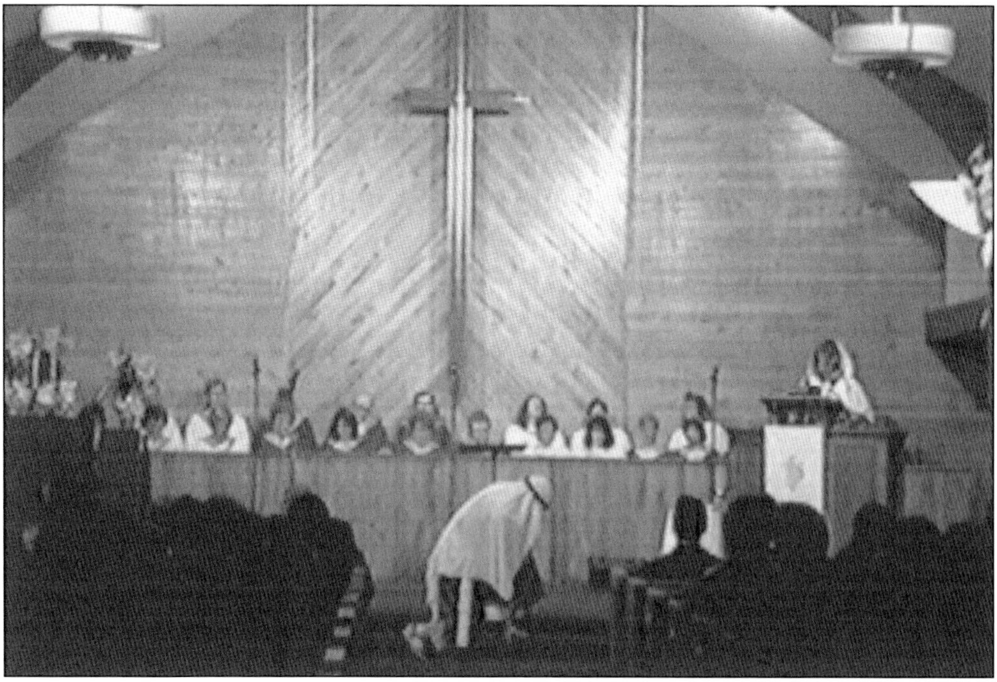

Skip Kalb, portraying Jesus in *The Easter Story,* kneels and prays: "My Father, if it is possible, may this cup be taken from me. Yet not as I will, but as You will." As soldiers lead him away, he says, "In the future you will see the Son of Man sitting at the right hand of the Mighty One and coming on the clouds of heaven." (Courtesy by Dr. Allen Buffington.)

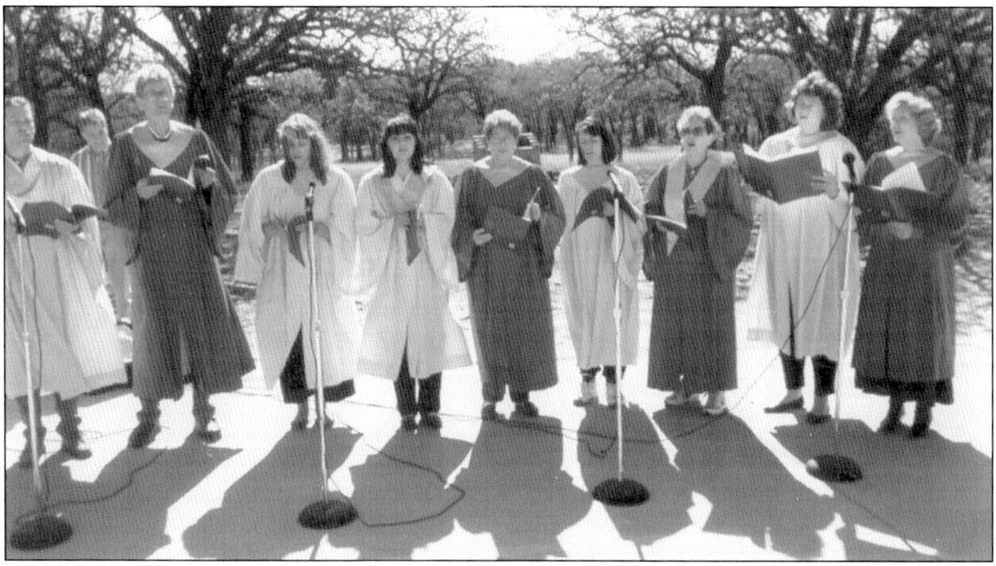

Argyle Community Chorus members practice for the March 30, 1997, Easter Sunrise pageant, *Argyle's Easter Story,* held outside the Argyle United Methodist Church. The production was written and produced by Lynn Sheffield Simmons, directed by Kay Teer, and the music director was Bill Smith. Pictured are Daniel Humbert, Doyle Murray, Delores Green, Kay Teer, Kathy Emery, Gwen Goff, Lorie Cooper, Janet Newsome, and Lynn Sheffield Simmons. (Courtesy of *The Argyle Sun.*)

Three

Business and Municipals
The Backbone of the Town

Most of Argyle's first businesses were destroyed when fire swept through the town in 1895, but rebuilding quickly started and by early 1900 the town was operating again. Postal service came to Argyle after Emily Wilson received her commission as postmaster on July 24, 1878. She ran the post office from a log cabin on what is now C. Taylor Road, and the mail arrived by stagecoach. When the town was settled, the post office moved to the drugstore at the east end of the Argyle State Bank building. Mail was delivered by trains four times a day. The post office then moved to different locations in Meadows Store, eventually taking the north side of the building that was owned by former mayor Yvonne A. Jenkins's grandfather B.W. Meadows, who became postmaster in 1919.

By the turn of the 20th century, Argyle had a bank, cotton gin, blacksmith shops, barbershop, telephone company, and grocery store, to name a few. In 1909, when Dr. M.D. Fullingim donated land to build the First Baptist Church of Argyle, on that same land he dug a water well and piped water to outside faucets of the homes in Old Town Argyle. In 1962, the Argyle Water Supply Corporation was organized, which brought water to many households and kept newcomers from having to dig water wells. The Argyle Volunteer Fire Department was organized in 1963 and women were trained in firefighting in 1973 to assist in fighting fires when the men were at work.

Businesses have come and gone, but the citizens of Argyle continue to work at improving their town and making it even better for generations to come.

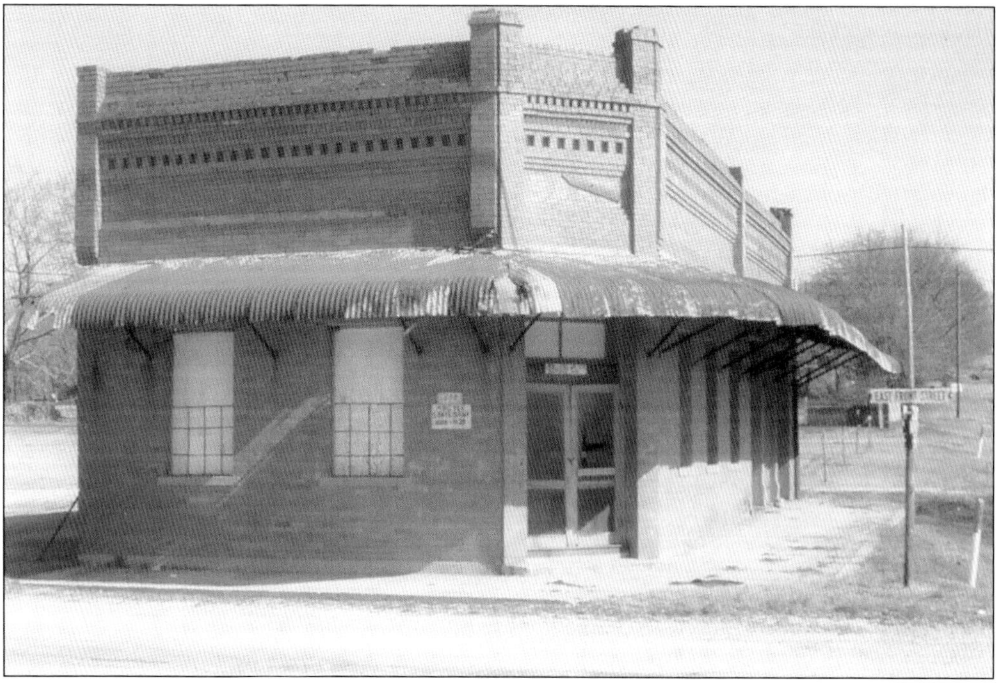

The Argyle State Bank, built in 1888, is at the corner of US Highway 377 and Denton Street. On February 14, 1912, the bank was robbed of $1,700. The robbers avoided capture due to the Denton County sheriff's car having a flat tire on the way to the scene. The bank closed in 1928 after it was thought that a cashier was embezzling funds. (Courtesy of Dr. Larry Simmons.)

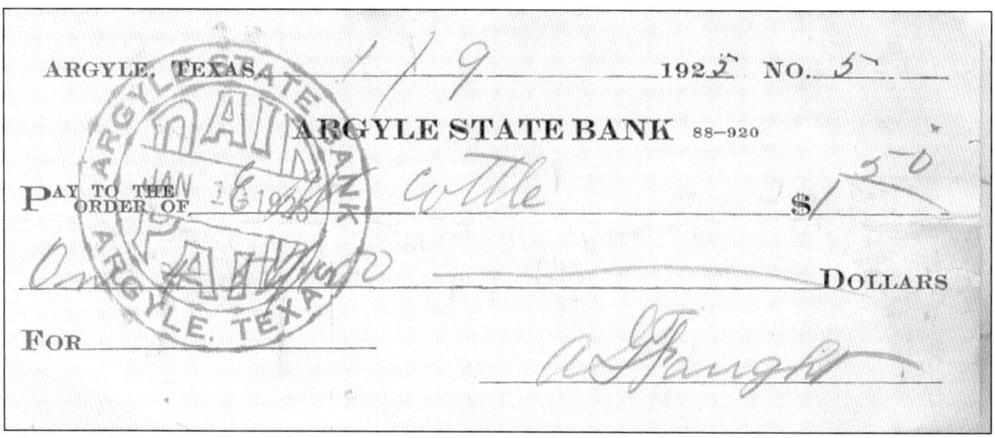

ARGYLE, TEXAS, 1/19 192_ NO. 5

ARGYLE STATE BANK 88–920

PAY TO THE ORDER OF Cottle $1.50

DOLLARS

FOR

This Argyle State Bank canceled check was written by A.G. Faught to E.W. Cottle, who owned a blacksmith shop in Argyle south of Meadows Store. Faught had a farm west of Argyle, and among the different metal works the blacksmith shop did was sharpening plows for farmers. (Courtesy of Wallace Lynch.)

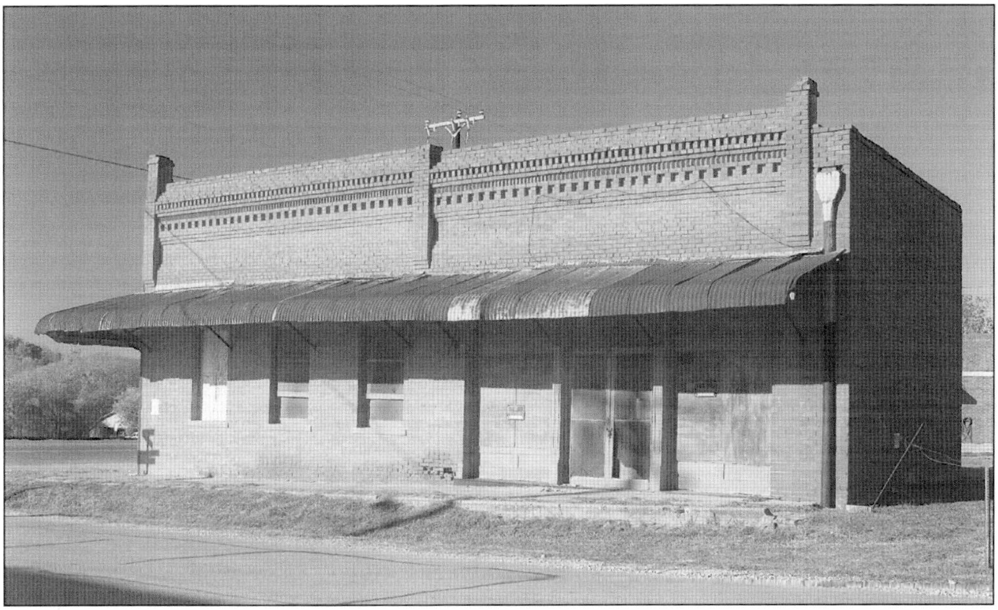

The Argyle State Bank occupied the front of the red brick building, and a drugstore that included the post office was at the back. "After the Argyle Post Office was moved from Miss Emily Wilson's home on C. Taylor Road it became a part of Rock Fenton's drug store," said Jim Heath, rural letter carrier for the Argyle Post Office for 31 years. (Courtesy of Denise Remfert.)

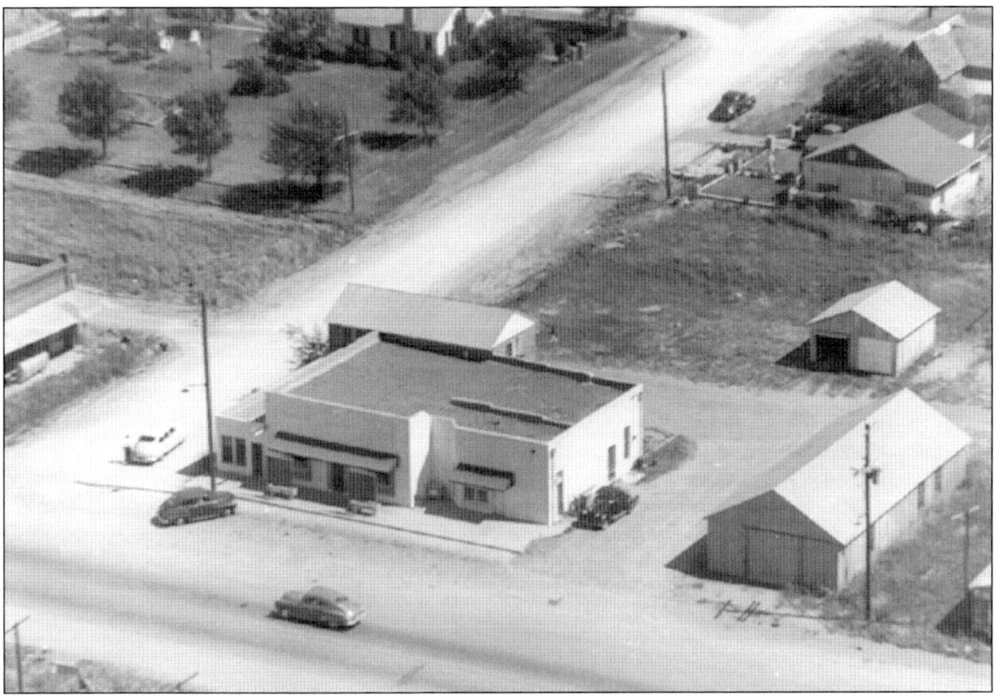

After Bascomb William Meadows bought the R.W. Fenton Hardware Store on US Highway 377, he renamed it Meadows Store. On June 26, 1919, he was appointed postmaster and moved the post office to the store. The building seen to the right of this photograph was a hay barn erected by Murray Johnson. It later became the site for Argyle City Hall. (Courtesy of Kay Teer.)

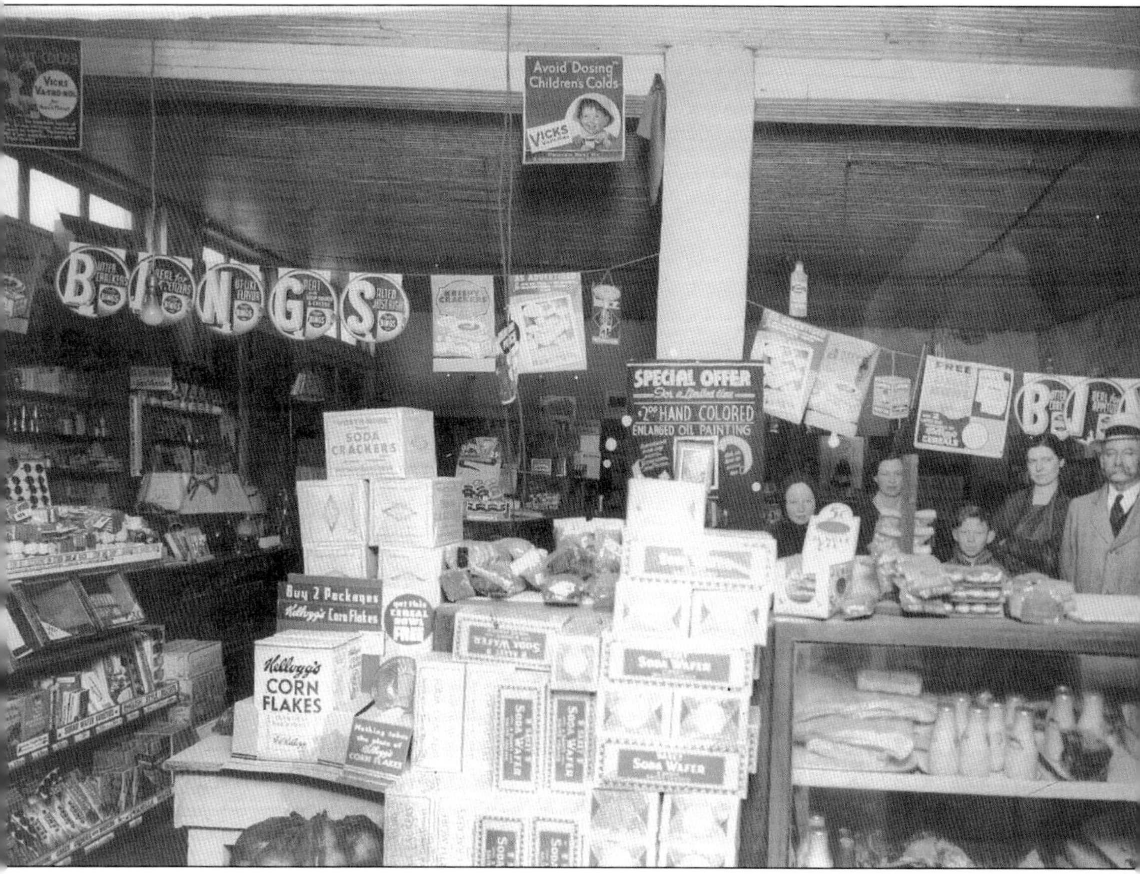

Pictured in 1930, standing behind a showcase in Meadows Store, are Betty Sullivan Meadows and Jewell Morris Meadows. They were the daughters-in-law of Bascomb William Meadows, who owned the store. Meadows Store carried a wide range of items, selling practically everything a person would need. (Courtesy of Kay Teer.)

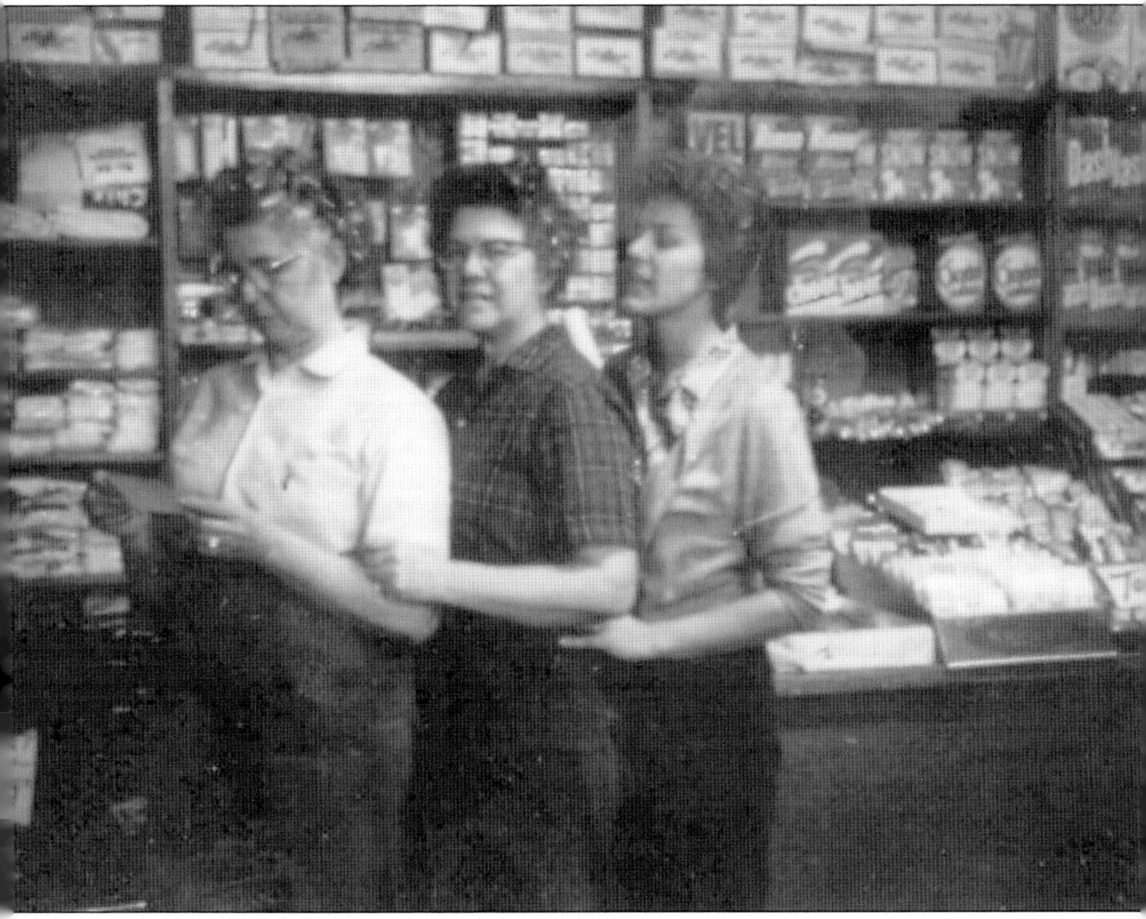

"The Big Three" are pictured in 1963. From left to right, Lillian Meadows Thompson, the Argyle postmaster, helped manage Meadows Store and was former mayor Yvonne Allen Jenkins's aunt. Georgia Belle Meadows Allen was clerk and assistant postmaster, managed Meadows Store, and was Mayor Jenkins's mother. Yvonne Allen Jenkins helped run the store and assisted in the management of the Argyle Water Supply Corporation. (Courtesy of Kay Teer.)

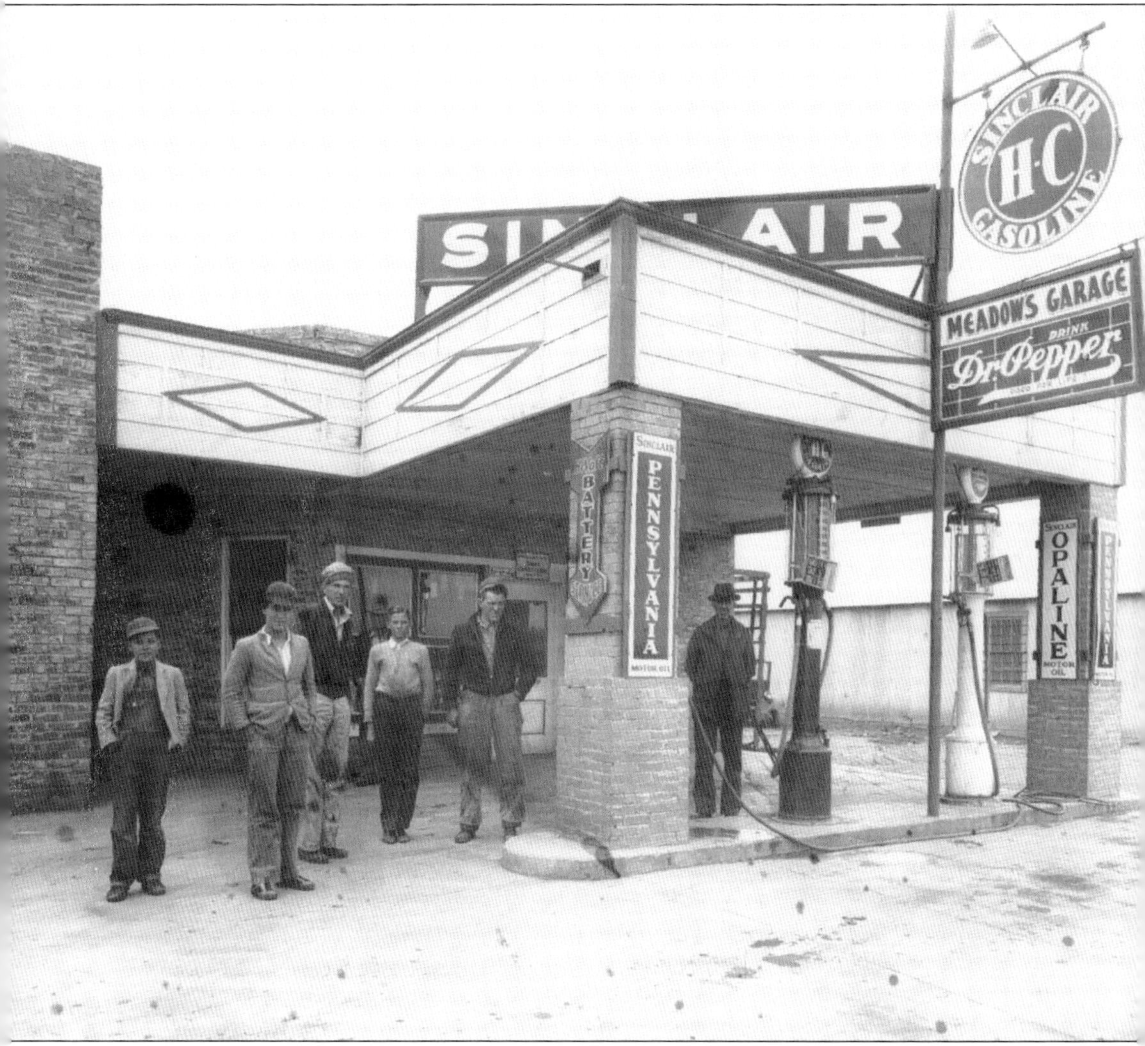

This 1920 photograph of Meadows Garage, located next to Meadows Store on Highway 377, shows Tom Spencer, Red Allen, Ben Davis, and Bill Meadows in the picture. Another service station, owned by Chester Horton, was located on Dallas Street and US Highway 377. It was later owned and operated by Elmo Smith. Inside the service station was a telephone exchange operated by Smith's wife, Muriel Jennings Smith. (Courtesy of Kay Teer.)

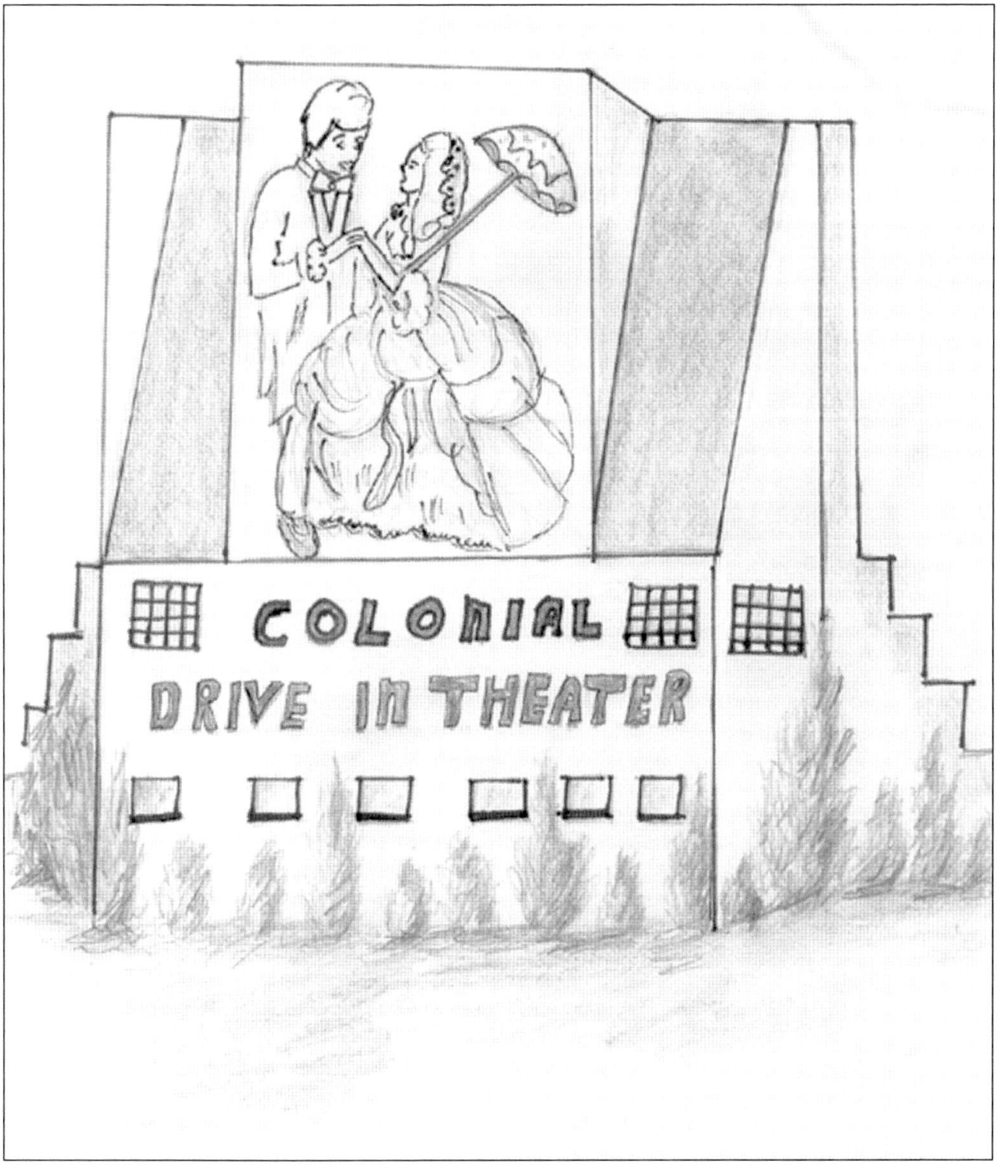

The Colonial Drive-in Theater, built in 1949 on US Highway 377, had twin screens. The multicolored sign showed a gentleman dressed in formal attire holding the hand of a lady wearing a hoop skirt. A number of Argyle teenagers worked there. On March 25, 1954, high winds blew down the screens, killing owner George D. Franklin as he tried to brace them up. This image is a drawing from a 1950 newspaper advertisement. (Courtesy of Pat Brown.)

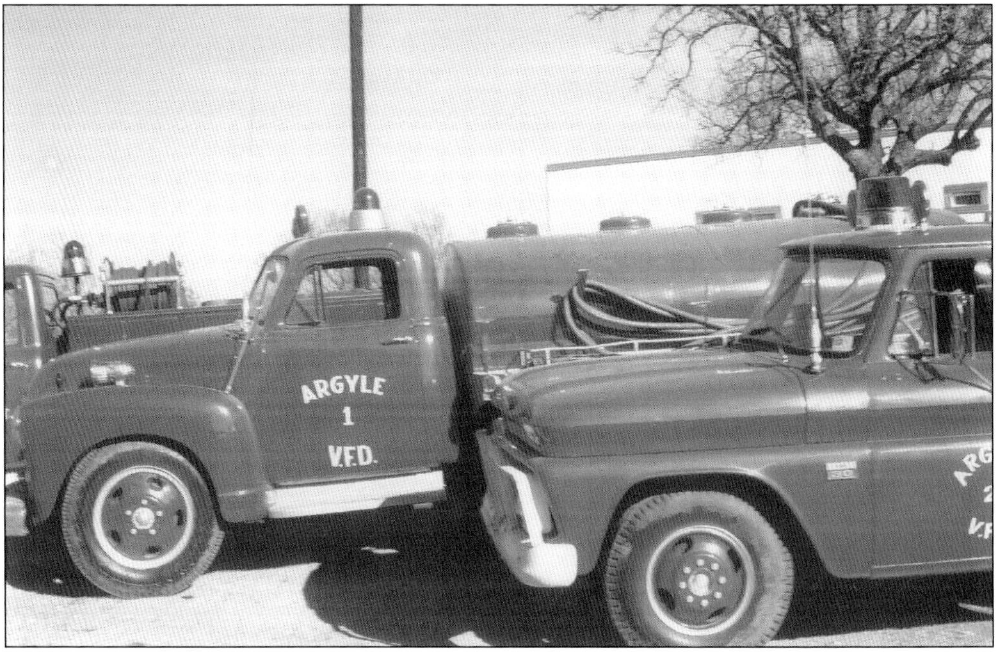

The Argyle Volunteer Fire Department was organized in 1963 by Elmo Smith, Elwood Harrell, Grover Wallace, Wallace Lynch, Earl Cochran, Mr. and Mrs. Charles Jenkins, and Mr. and Mrs. C.A. Whisenhunt. The old Argyle Baptist Church on Dallas and Mesquite Streets became the Argyle community Center and AVFD fire hall. The fire trucks were housed in the basement. This photograph of "Argyle 1 AVFD" is the old pumper truck. Whenever a fire truck pulled out of the basement of the old Baptist Church with a full water load, it could not go down "Baptist Hill" on Dallas Street. The hill was too steep, making the truck go too fast, and prompting the driver to ride the clutch, causing it to burn out. Therefore, the driver had to cross over to "Methodist Hill" on Denton Street, where the hill was not so steep. (Courtesy of AVFD.)

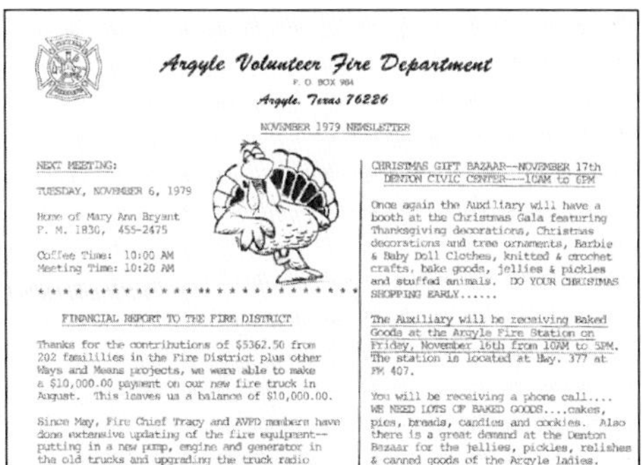

Argyle Volunteer Fire Department
P. O. BOX 984
Argyle, Texas 76226

NOVEMBER 1979 NEWSLETTER

NEXT MEETING:

TUESDAY, NOVEMBER 6, 1979

Home of Mary Ann Bryant
P. M. 1830, 455-2475

Coffee Time: 10:00 AM
Meeting Time: 10:20 AM

* *

FINANCIAL REPORT TO THE FIRE DISTRICT

Thanks for the contributions of $5362.50 from 202 famillies in the Fire District plus other Ways and Means projects, we were able to make a $10,000.00 payment on our new fire truck in August. This leaves us a balance of $10,000.00.

Since May, Fire Chief Tracy and AVFD members have done extensive updating of the fire equipment--putting in a new pump, engine and generator in the old trucks and upgrading the truck radio systems. Total investment...$2400.00.

As most of you know, we are not collecting newspapers for "rolling"...we lost our market. However, The Paper Place, 525 S. Locust, Room 107, Denton (Pho:566-2528) will accept papers for the AVFD. Have the papers labeled for AVFD. They are open Monday thru Friday. Also there is some thought to discontinuing the sale of Fireworks as a Ways and Means project. The Newpapers and Fireworks brought in over $5000.00 to our Treasury. We need your ideas and help to offset these projects.

CHRISTMAS GIFT BAZAAR--NOVEMBER 17th
DENTON CIVIC CENTER---10AM to 6PM

Once again the Auxiliary will have a booth at the Christmas Gala featuring Thanksgiving decorations, Christmas decorations and tree ornaments, Barbie & Baby Doll Clothes, knitted & crochet crafts, bake goods, jellies & pickles and stuffed animals. DO YOUR CHRISTMAS SHOPPING EARLY......

The Auxiliary will be receiving Baked Goods at the Argyle Fire Station on Friday, November 16th from 10AM to 5PM. The station is located at Hwy. 377 at FM 407.

You will be receiving a phone call.... WE NEED LOTS OF BAKED GOODS....cakes, pies, breads, candies and cookies. Also there is a great demand at the Denton Bazaar for the jellies, pickles, relishes & canned goods of the Argyle ladies.

Baked goods & homemade goodies can be brought to the Fire Hall (10-5,Friday) or if more convenient, deliver to the Bartonville Store or Meadows Store. For more information, please call Louise Moore at 464-3138.

* * * * * * * * * * * * * * * * * * * *

With HALLOWEEN just around the corner, we urge you to exercise caution with Jack-O-Lanterns and to take care with the little ones are out "trick or treating".

* *

MISS FLAME CONTEST

Joint efforts of the AVFD, the community, business and the Argyle School, the Annual Miss Flame Contest will net $1300.00 for the department. Our sincere appreciation to all who assisted. Our congratulations to our new royalty...MISS FLAME--MARY ANN MOON; LITTLE MISS FLAME--CRISTINE WEEKS and FIRE CHIEF MASCOT--SHAWN BALDWIN. Runner-ups were Lisa Mills, Dorene Lacey and Addy Yeck. Grand prize Fire Prevention Poster winner was SHARI KOLTES and Essay winner was DAWNAE BOOK.

This November 1979 Argyle Volunteer Fire Department Women's Auxiliary newsletter, written by former mayor Yvonne A. Jenkins, is an example of the monthly newsletters sent out to remind members of the latest fundraising events. After the AVFD Women's Auxiliary began, the leadership was provided by early presidents Edith Sheely, Sylvia Barnard, Yvonne Jenkins, Marcia Savage, and Doryece Cochran. Each year, during Fire Prevention Week, the AVFD and the AVFD Women's Auxiliary sponsored a Fire Prevention Poster and Essay Contest for the schoolchildren in combination with the Miss Flame, Little Miss Flame, and Fire Chief Mascot contests. (Courtesy of Mary Ann DeBerry.)

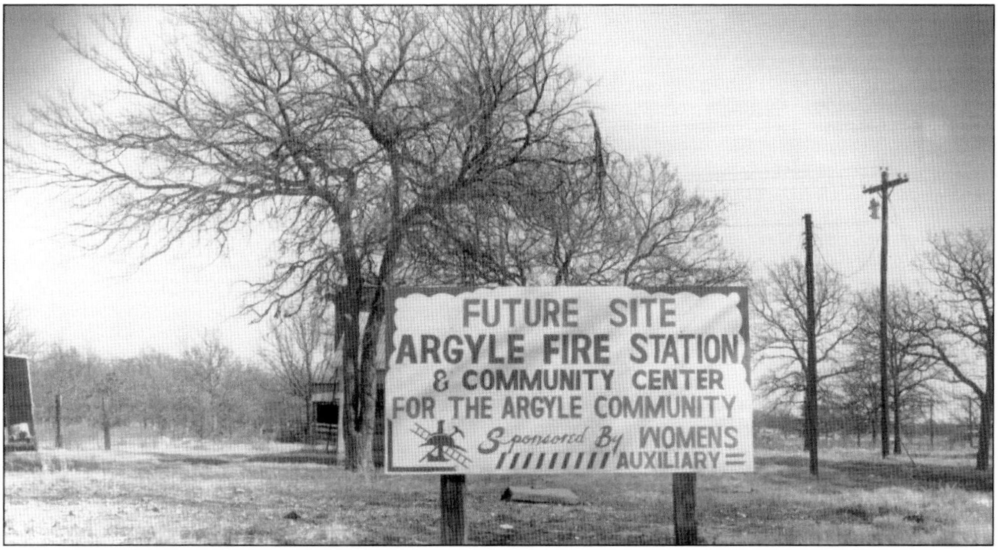

To provide financial support for the Argyle Volunteer Fire Department, the AVFD Women's Auxiliary was organized in 1971. It raised funds through chili suppers, talent shows, barbecue dinners, raffles, garage sales, pet vaccinations, domino tournaments, direct solicitation, and other events in order to purchase two acres on Highway 377 at F.M. 407 to build the fire station. (Courtesy of AVFD.)

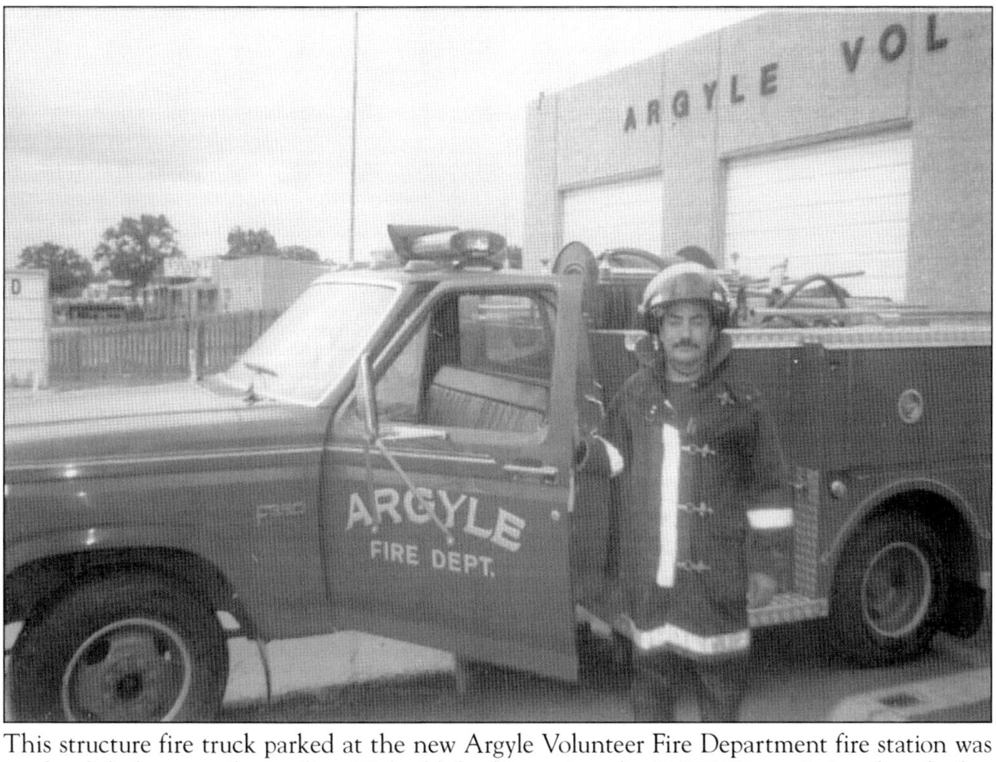

This structure fire truck parked at the new Argyle Volunteer Fire Department fire station was used to fight house and grass fires. To build the fire station, the AVFD Women's Auxiliary had so many fundraising projects that one *Denton Record-Chronicle* headline read, "Those Little Ladies are at it again." (Courtesy of AVFD.)

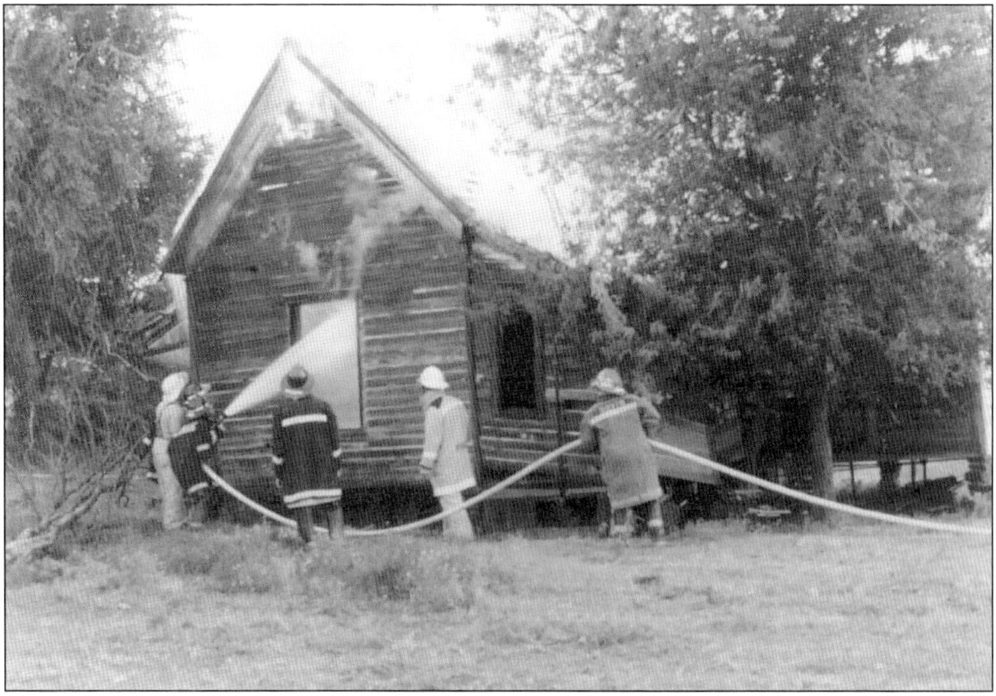

The owner of this old house consented to let the Argyle Volunteer Fire Department firemen burn it down as a practice exercise. Members of the AVFD in 1976 were fire chief Richard Hensley, assistant chief Ray Stefl, fire marshal Ben Brown, and captains Bobby Anderson, John Hanson, Wriley Robbins, James Price, Sam Carroll, Billy Carl Robbins, T.E. Beavers Jr., Foster Long, Odis Fuller, Jr., and Robert Tracy. (Courtesy of AVFD.)

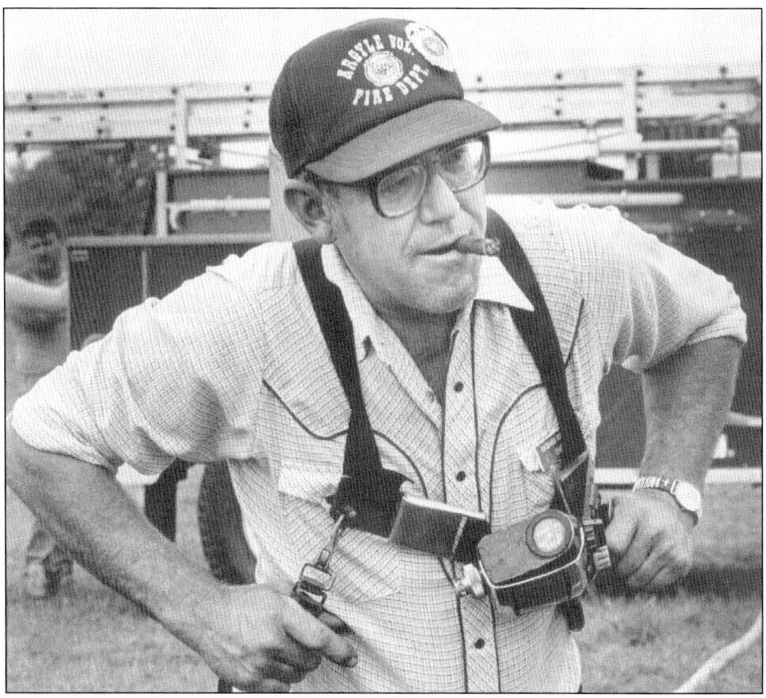

Argyle Volunteer Fire Department fire chief Richard Hensley is shown here demonstrating to new members of the department how to put on an air tank. The new Argyle firefighters were trained at a center in Lewisville, Texas. During Hensley's 21 years serving as AVFD fire chief, he took time out to serve on the Argyle City Council and to be the Argyle mayor. (Courtesy of DRC.)

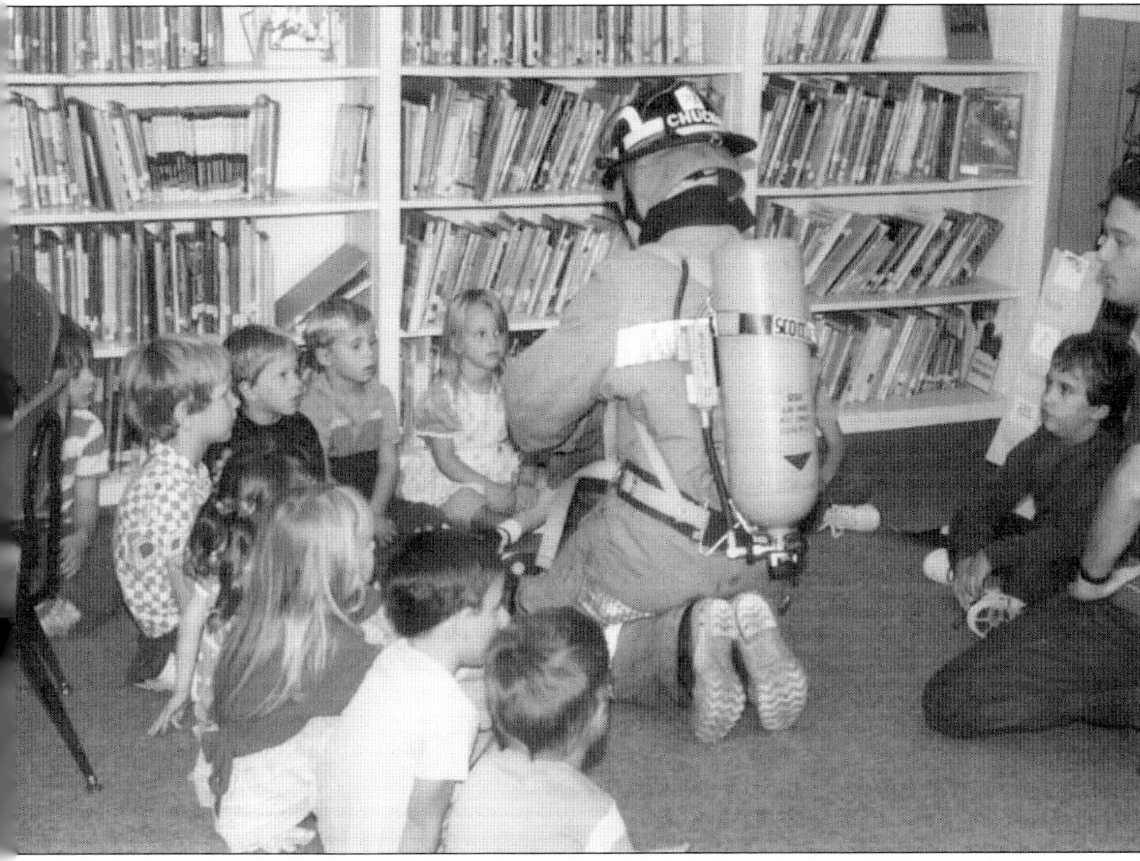

In the 1970s, the AVFD gave presentations at Argyle schools to acquaint children with the firefighters' gear and equipment. After the motion picture *Star Wars* was filmed, some children became afraid of the firemen's outfits because it reminded them of the villain Darth Vader. Children needed to know firemen were there to rescue them if they were involved in a fire. (Courtesy of AVFD.)

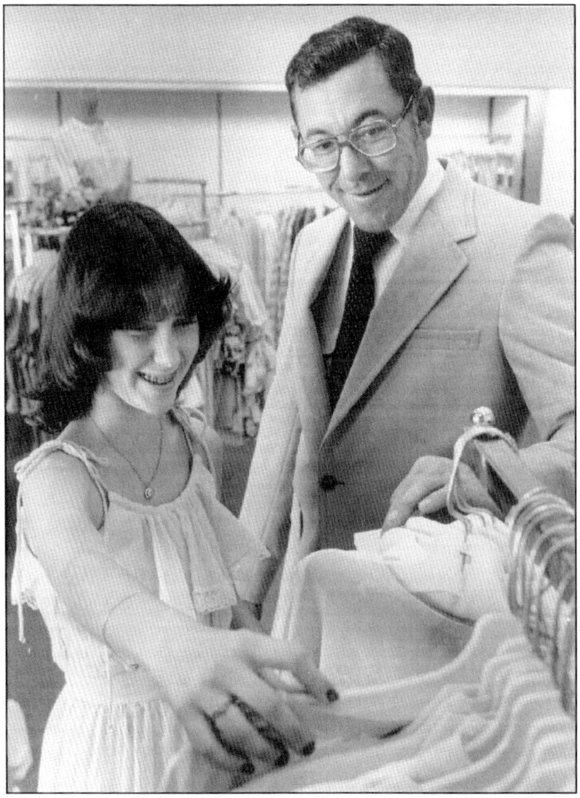

In March 1979, Argyle's Miss Flame, Jamie Magee, and AVFD fire chief Richard Hensley are seen in Russell's Department Store picking out the dresses Miss Magee would wear in the AVFD fashion show. Funds raised from the ticket sales for the fashion show went to the financial support of the fire department. (Courtesy of DRC.)

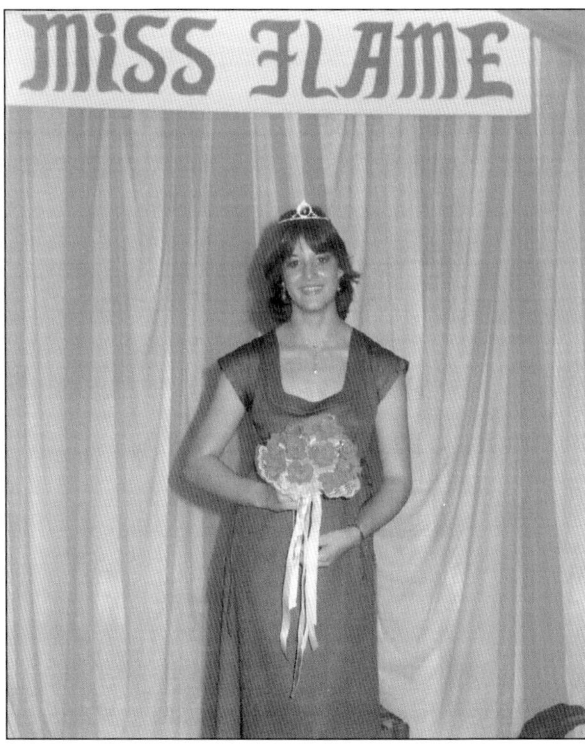

Mary Ann Moon (DeBerry) was the winner of the 1980 Miss Flame contest sponsored by the Argyle Volunteer Fire Department. The funds raised from this and other events were instrumental in helping to build the new AVFD building, buy firefighting equipment, and purchase fire trucks. (Courtesy of Mary Ann DeBerry.)

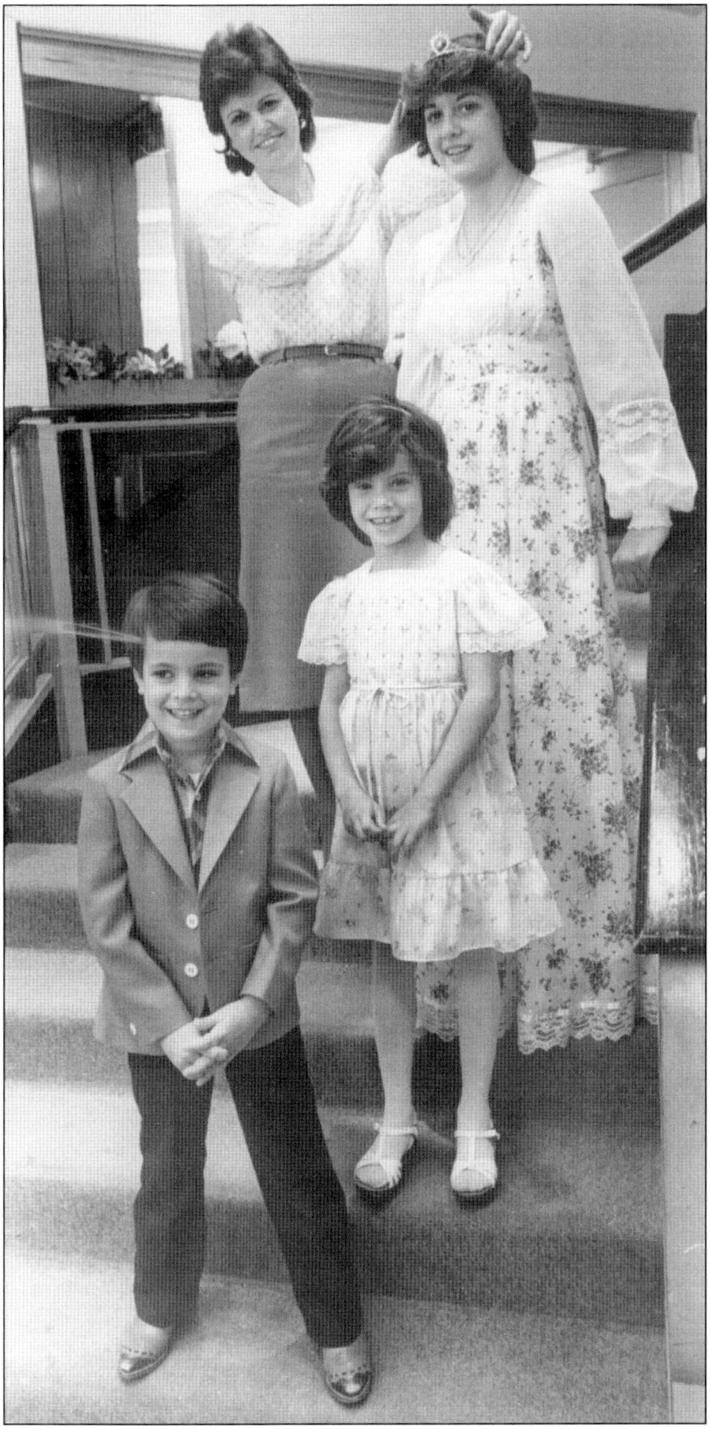

The Easter Fashion Fling and Bake Sale models are the 1980 winners of the Miss Flame contest: Fire Chief Mascot Shawn Baldwin, five, son of the Rev. and Mrs. Gary Baldwin; Miss Flame Mary Ann Moon (DeBerry), 15, daughter of Mr. and Mrs. L.F. Moon; and Little Miss Flame Christine Weeks, six, daughter of Mr. and Mrs. Don Weeks. (Courtesy of DRC.)

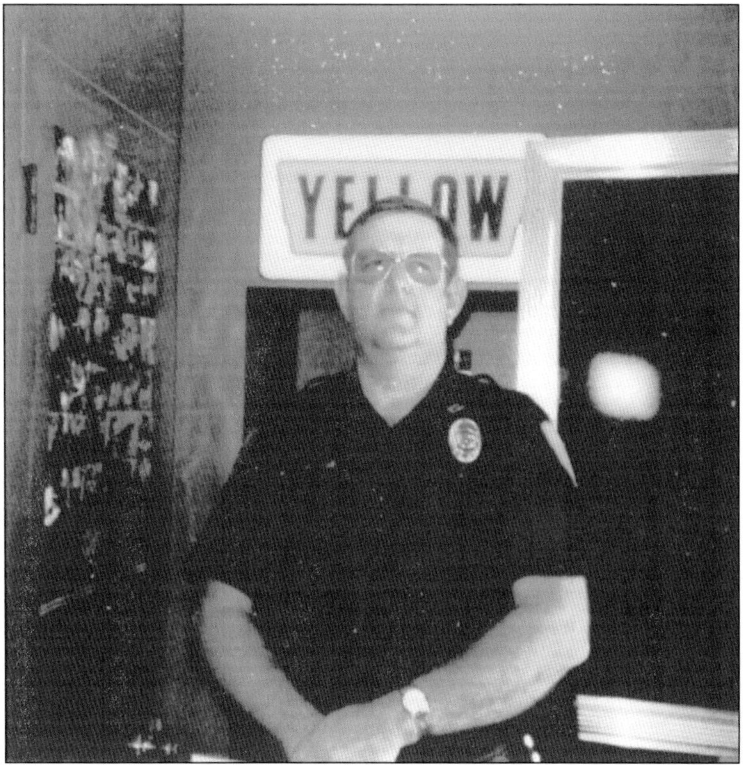

Kim Taylor was chief of police in the late 1980s and early 1990s. In 1976, H.O. Franks Jr. was appointed the first police chief. Mayor Marvin E. Dillard was judge of the corporation court, Nellie Carty was city secretary, and council members were Joseph Hilger, James Bickley, Vergie Nimmo, Myrtle Lee Lynch, and Gary Cunningham. (Courtesy of APD.)

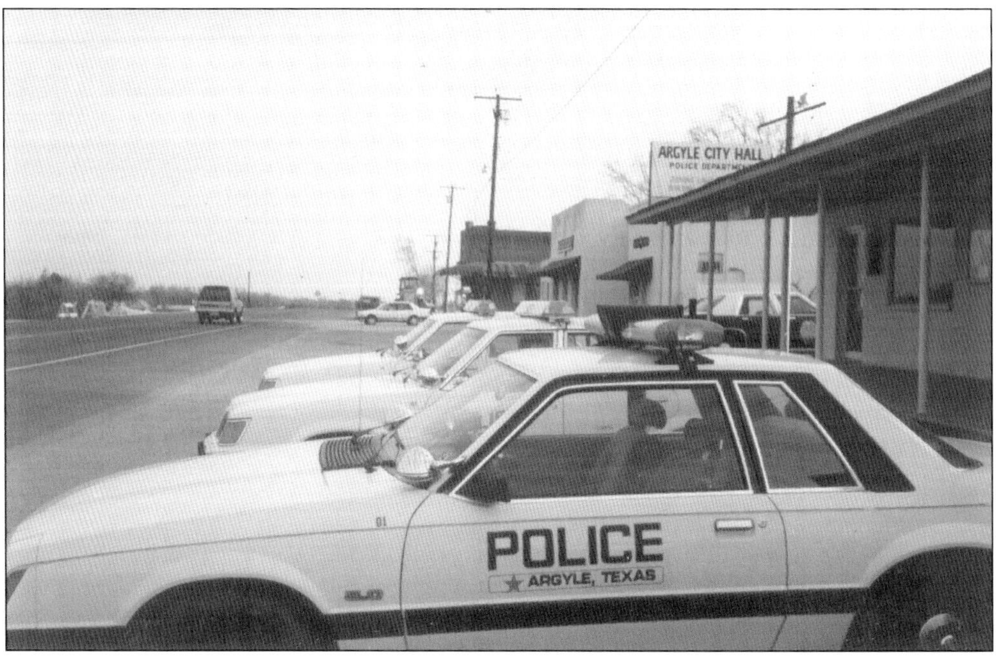

This 1985 picture shows Argyle police cars lined up in front of the Argyle City Hall on US Highway 377. The city offices were at the front of the building and the Argyle Police Department was at the back. A historical marker was placed on the building when it opened in 1981. The Argyle area was settled in the 1850s by members of the Peters Colony. (Courtesy of APD.)

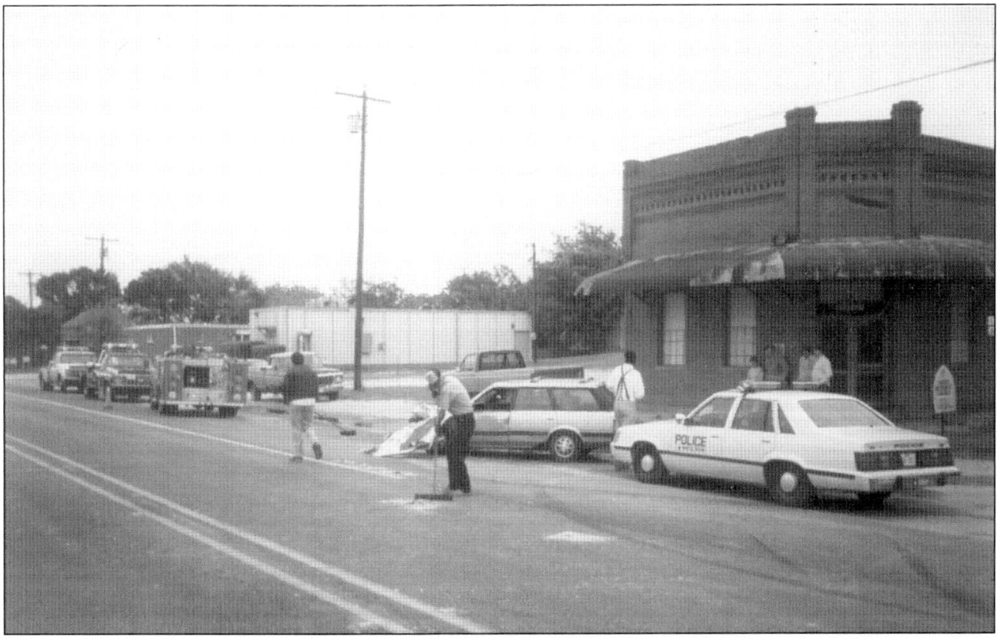

When this car accident took place on US Highway 377 in front of the old Argyle State Bank building in the 1980s, it shows how the Argyle Police Department and the Argyle Volunteer Fire Department worked together. Both departments responded to mishaps and disasters quickly to offer aid and assistance. Working together has been a part of Argyle's history. (Courtesy of APD.)

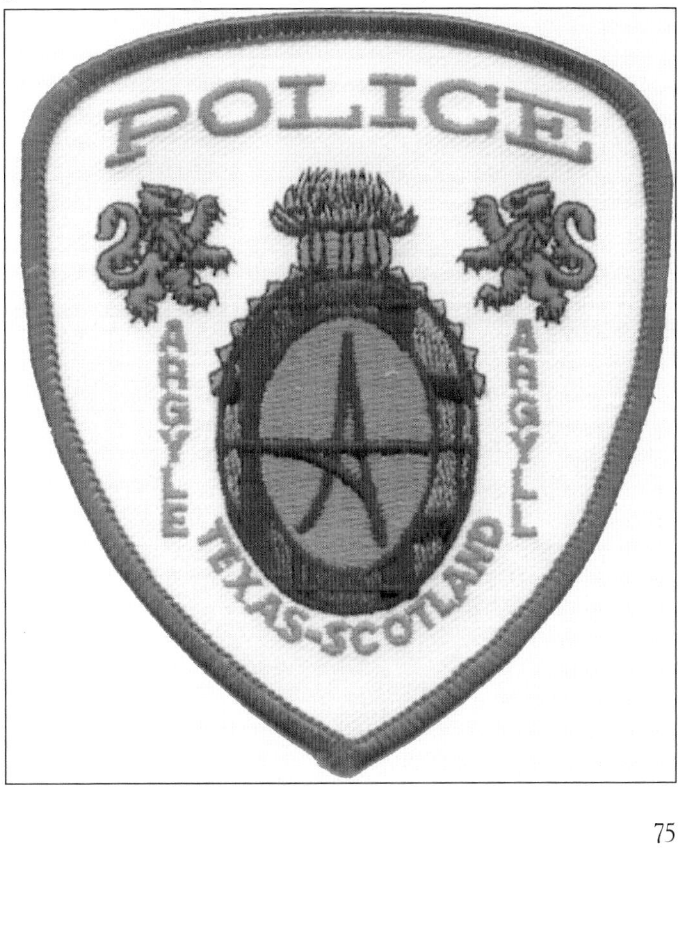

This is the patch worn on the sleeve of Argyle policemen between 1995 and 2006. It shows the Argyle–Argyll connection between Argyle, USA, and Argyll, Scotland. During the 1990s, Mayor Yvonne Jenkins went to Argyll, Scotland, on a fact-finding tour to learn how the city got its name. While she was there, she visited with the Duke of Argyll. (Courtesy of APD.)

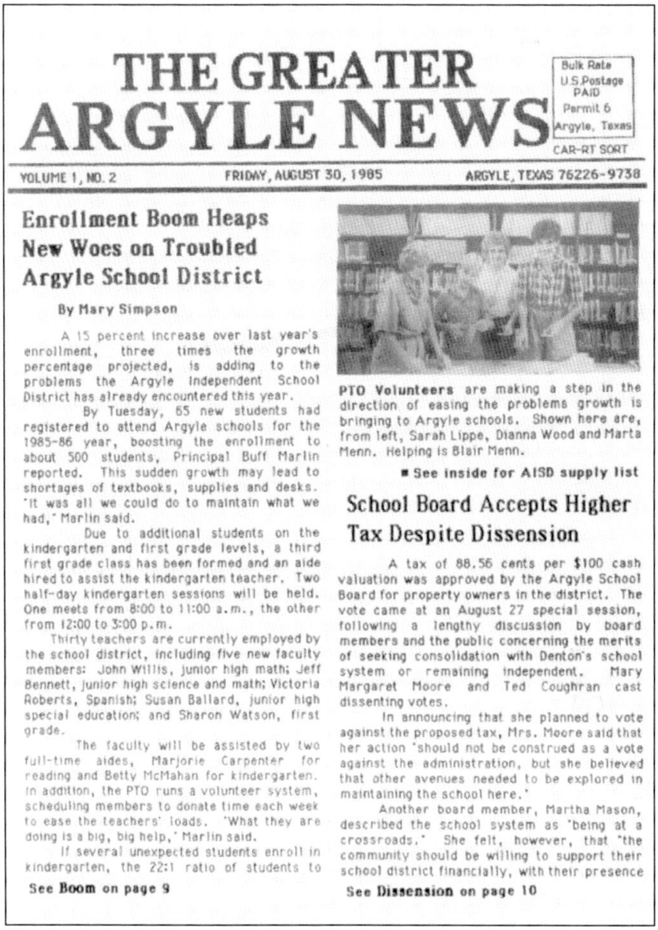

THE GREATER ARGYLE NEWS

Bulk Rate
U.S.Postage
PAID
Permit 6
Argyle, Texas
CAR-RT SORT

VOLUME 1, NO. 2 | FRIDAY, AUGUST 30, 1985 | ARGYLE, TEXAS 76226-9738

Enrollment Boom Heaps New Woes on Troubled Argyle School District

By Mary Simpson

A 15 percent increase over last year's enrollment, three times the growth percentage projected, is adding to the problems the Argyle Independent School District has already encountered this year.

By Tuesday, 65 new students had registered to attend Argyle schools for the 1985-86 year, boosting the enrollment to about 500 students, Principal Buff Marlin reported. This sudden growth may lead to shortages of textbooks, supplies and desks. "It was all we could do to maintain what we had," Marlin said.

Due to additional students on the kindergarten and first grade levels, a third first grade class has been formed and an aide hired to assist the kindergarten teacher. Two half-day kindergarten sessions will be held. One meets from 8:00 to 11:00 a.m., the other from 12:00 to 3:00 p.m.

Thirty teachers are currently employed by the school district, including five new faculty members: John Willis, junior high math; Jeff Bennett, junior high science and math; Victoria Roberts, Spanish; Susan Ballard, junior high special education; and Sharon Watson, first grade.

The faculty will be assisted by two full-time aides, Marjorie Carpenter for reading and Betty McMahan for kindergarten. In addition, the PTO runs a volunteer system, scheduling members to donate time each week to ease the teachers' loads. "What they are doing is a big, big help," Marlin said.

If several unexpected students enroll in kindergarten, the 22:1 ratio of students to

See **Boom** on page 9

PTO Volunteers are making a step in the direction of easing the problems growth is bringing to Argyle schools. Shown here are, from left, Sarah Lippe, Dianna Wood and Marta Menn. Helping is Blair Menn.

■ **See inside for AISD supply list**

School Board Accepts Higher Tax Despite Dissension

A tax of 88.56 cents per $100 cash valuation was approved by the Argyle School Board for property owners in the district. The vote came at an August 27 special session, following a lengthy discussion by board members and the public concerning the merits of seeking consolidation with Denton's school system or remaining independent. Mary Margaret Moore and Ted Coughran cast dissenting votes.

In announcing that she planned to vote against the proposed tax, Mrs. Moore said that her action "should not be construed as a vote against the administration, but she believed that other avenues needed to be explored in maintaining the school here."

Another board member, Martha Mason, described the school system as "being at a crossroads." She felt, however, that "the community should be willing to support their school district financially, with their presence

See **Dissension** on page 10

This Friday, August 30, 1985, edition of *The Greater Argyle News*, copublished by Jeanie and Don Edwards, was a weekly newspaper mailed to Argyle box holders. Earlier, *The Quad-Town Community News*, known as "the most widely circulated 'little' weekly newspaper in Denton County," published by Rosemary and Hershel Parker, began in September 1962, to let people know what was going on in Argyle, Roanoke, Justin, and Keller. (Courtesy by Mary Ann DeBerry.)

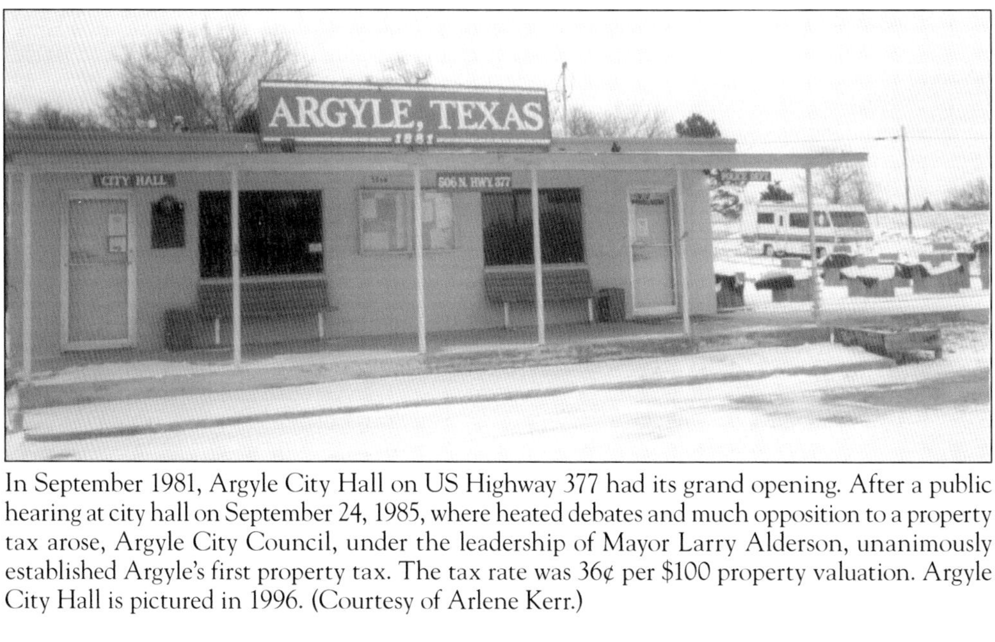

In September 1981, Argyle City Hall on US Highway 377 had its grand opening. After a public hearing at city hall on September 24, 1985, where heated debates and much opposition to a property tax arose, Argyle City Council, under the leadership of Mayor Larry Alderson, unanimously established Argyle's first property tax. The tax rate was 36¢ per $100 property valuation. Argyle City Hall is pictured in 1996. (Courtesy of Arlene Kerr.)

Four

Disasters and Celebrations

The Stamina of the Town

Some of Argyle's first businesses were a grocery store, a dry goods store, a blacksmith shop, and a building that included a bank, post office, and general store. In 1895, a fire that began in the dry goods store swept through town and destroyed most of the buildings.

The town was rebuilt, but it soon faced another catastrophe in 1910 when a tornado tore through town and demolished a number of the brick buildings and sent people running to their storm cellars. On Valentine's Day, 1912, the Argyle State Bank was robbed. J.B. Baker, manager of the Argyle-Justin telephone line, who was on duty that night, telephoned the sheriff's office in Denton at 2:00 a.m. after hearing the dynamite blasts. On the way to Argyle, the sheriff's car had a flat tire, and when the officers arrived, the bank robbers were gone, taking with them $1,700. Then, in 1985, a Missouri-Kansas-Texas Railroad train derailed, dumping all of its cargo in the heart of town.

Along with its disasters, Argyle has also had times to rejoice. Those celebrations include the Community Tree Lighting, the Argyle Centennial Celebration, the Texas Sesquicentennial Celebration and Wagon Train Parade, Argyle Pride Days, Argyle Pride Day Parades, Argyle's Birthday Celebrations with parades, and the performances of the historical drama *The Place Is Argyle*.

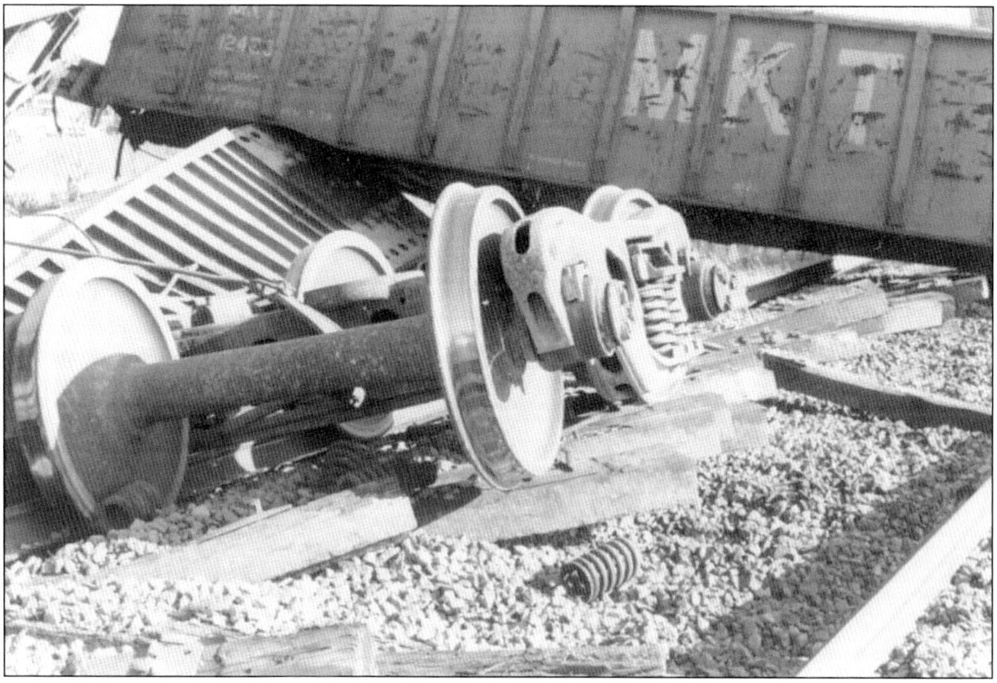

On May 26, 1985, a railroad train car repair may have caused the derailment of 15 railroad cars that wrecked on West Front Street beside US Highway 377 across from the Argyle City Hall. A company brakeman on the train said that the recently repaired air hose may have broken, causing the brakes to lock and forcing the cars off the track. (Courtesy of AVFD.)

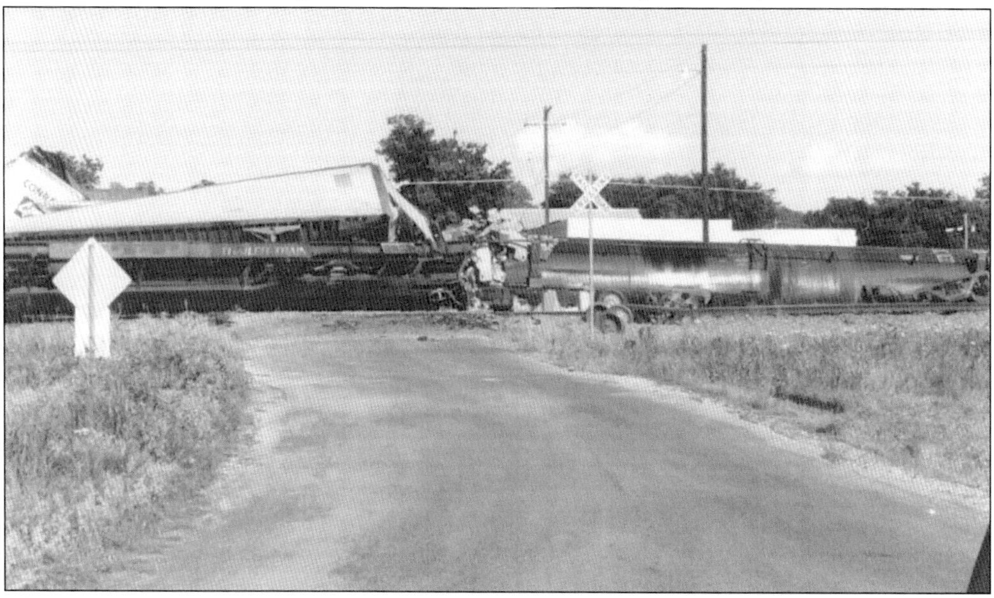

The train wreck occurred two months after Argyle city officials received a letter from railroad officials agreeing to slow down the train's speed to 40 miles per hour through Argyle during school hours. Access to the Argyle School is on West Front Street that runs beside the railroad tracks where the wreck occurred. The Missouri-Kansas-Texas Railroad train was northbound to Denison when it derailed at 3:00 p.m. (Courtesy of AVFD.)

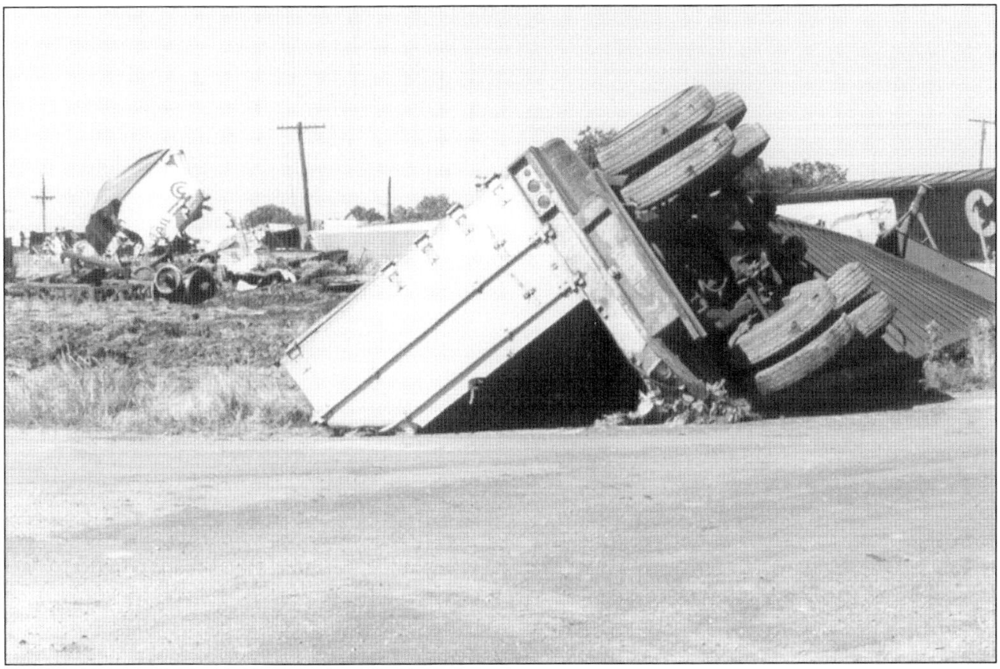

A woman and her baby suffered minor injuries when a semitrailer on one of the railroad cars slid off and hit their station wagon as they waited at the railroad crossing. It shoved the car about 75 feet. The six-engine train was pulling 79 empty cars and 21 loaded cars when the 15 cars derailed. No other injuries were reported. (Courtesy of Joan Delashaw.)

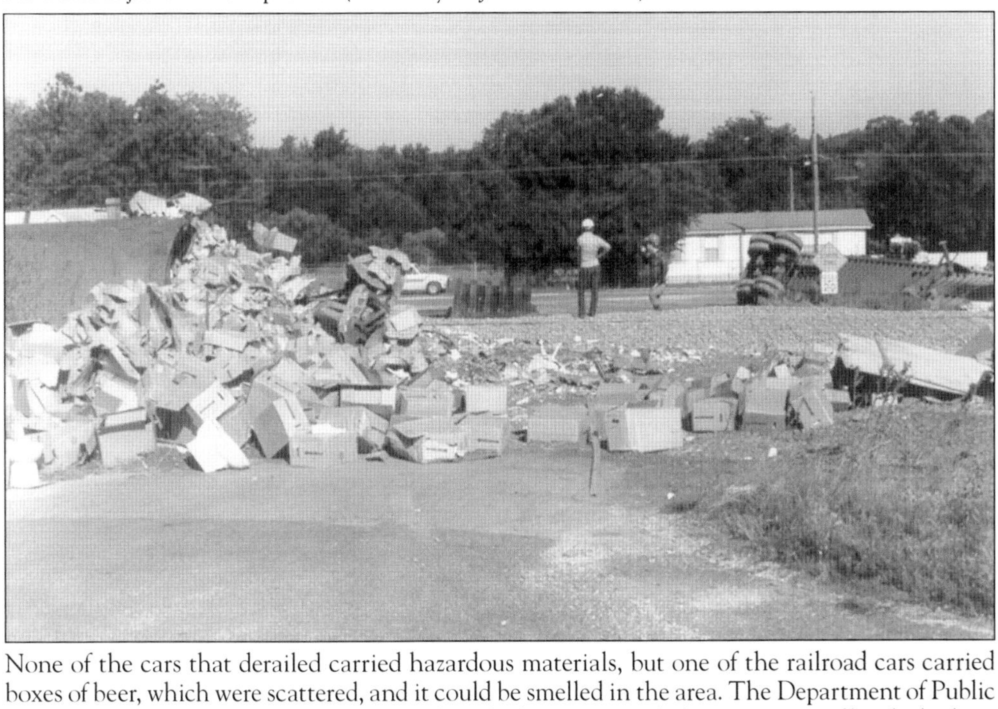

None of the cars that derailed carried hazardous materials, but one of the railroad cars carried boxes of beer, which were scattered, and it could be smelled in the area. The Department of Public Safety officers and Argyle police officers thought keeping people from running off with the beer would be the biggest security concern. (Courtesy of Martha Beavers.)

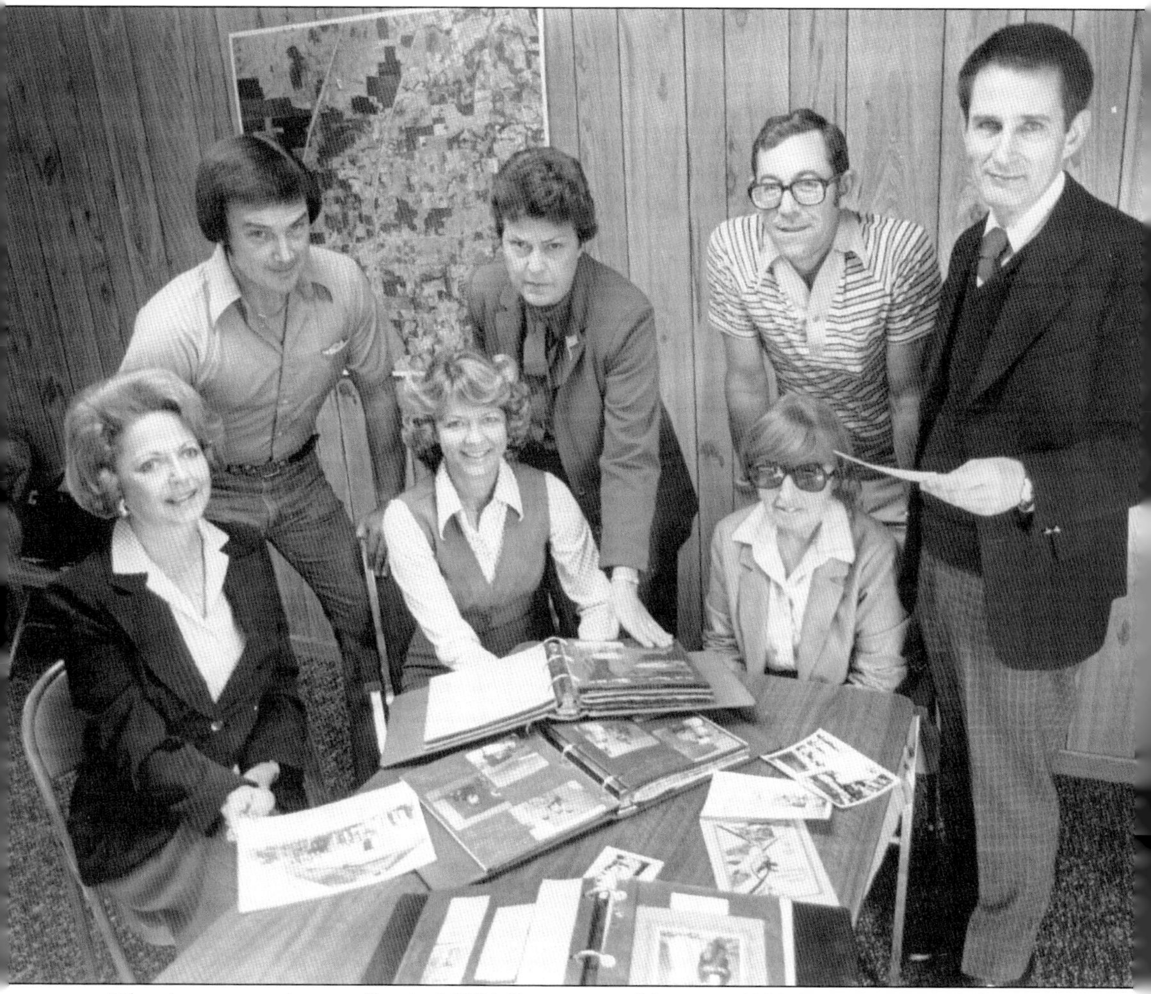

The three committees—Festival 1981 Committee, Horizons 1981 Committee, and the Heritage 1981 Committee—met on March 22, 1980, to plan for Argyle's 100th birthday celebration. Standing, from left to right, are Bill Carpenter, Yvonne Jenkins, Richard Hensley, and George Lewis. Seated, from left to right, are Mimi Denning, Lynn Sheffield (Simmons), and Lee Judy. The centennial committee, led by cochairman Yvonne Jenkins and the Rev. George Lewis, secretary-treasurer Lee Judy, and publicity chairman Lynn Sheffield (Simmons), was divided into three project groups. The Heritage 1981 Committee Chairmen were Geraldine Foster and Mimi Dinning. They researched the documentation for historical markers at the Argyle Methodist Church, Argyle Baptist Church, Prairie Mound Cemetery, and Johns' Well and Campgrounds. The Festival 1981 Committee included the goals for the homecoming at the Argyle Centennial and plans for raising funds. The leaders were chairmen W.P. Carpenter Jr. and Sue Anderson. Mayor Richard Hensley and Lewis Boyles were in charge of the Horizons 1981 Committee that was responsible for restoring Johns' Well and building a tabernacle at the Graham-Argyle Cemetery. (Courtesy of DRC.)

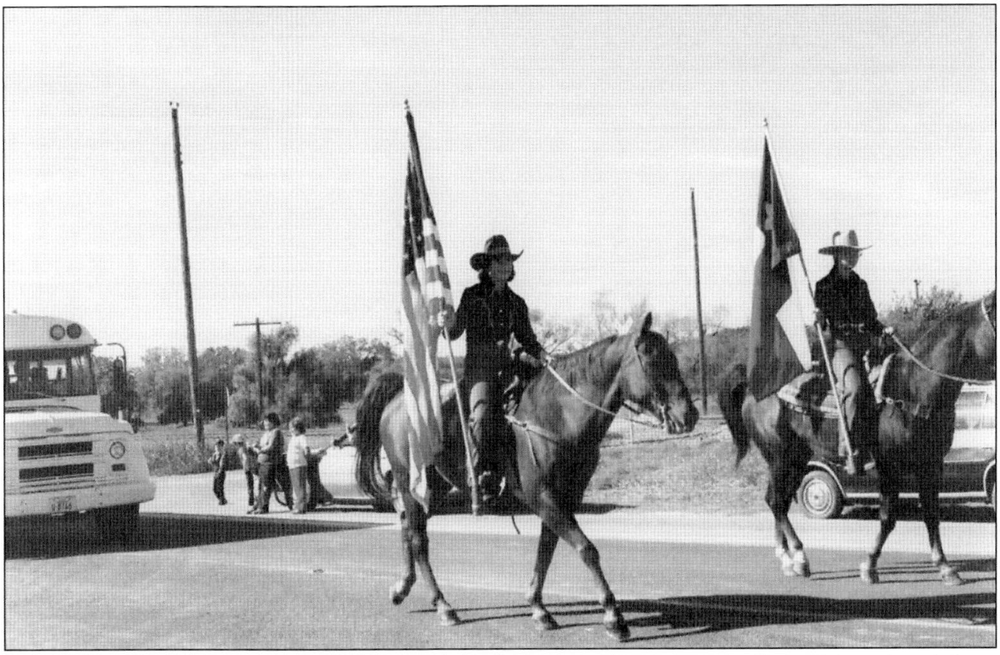

Leading the 1981 Argyle Centennial Parade and carrying the American flag is Mary Ann Moon (DeBerry) riding Smoky. Her sister Lisa Moon (Tilton) is carrying the Texas flag and riding Dodger. An estimated 1,500 people from Argyle and surrounding towns showed up for the event-packed celebration. (Courtesy of Martha Beavers.)

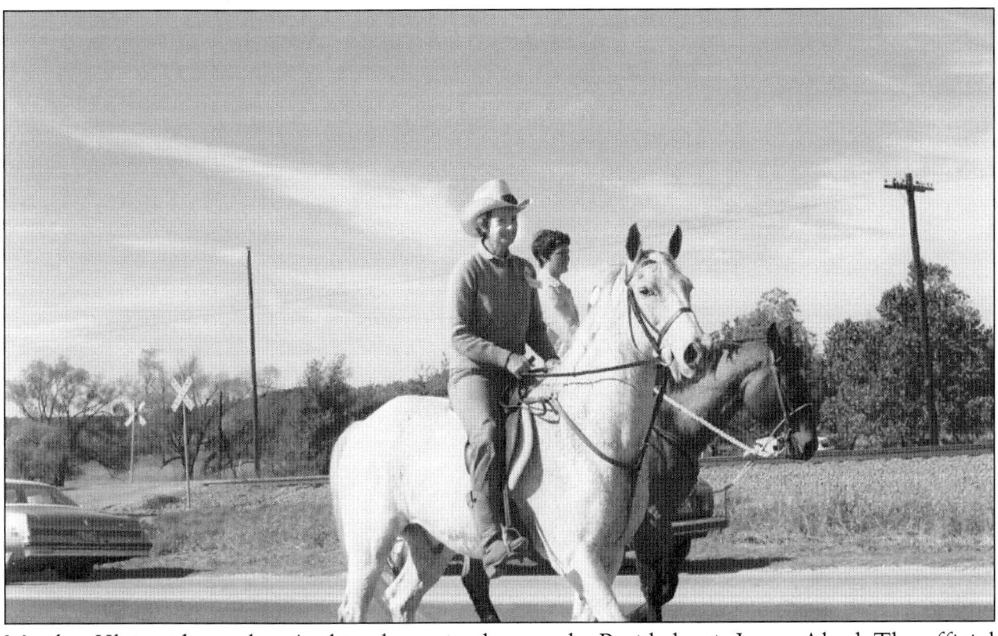

Marilyn Klein rides on her Arabian horse in the parade. Beside her is Jenny Alred. The official T-shirt for the Argyle Centennial was red with white lettering inquiring "Where is Argyle?" Below the question was a map showing Argyle's location in relationship to Denton, Dallas, and Fort Worth. The T-shirt was designed by Argyle resident Tread Sheffield, a Josten's yearbook representative. (Courtesy of Martha Beavers.)

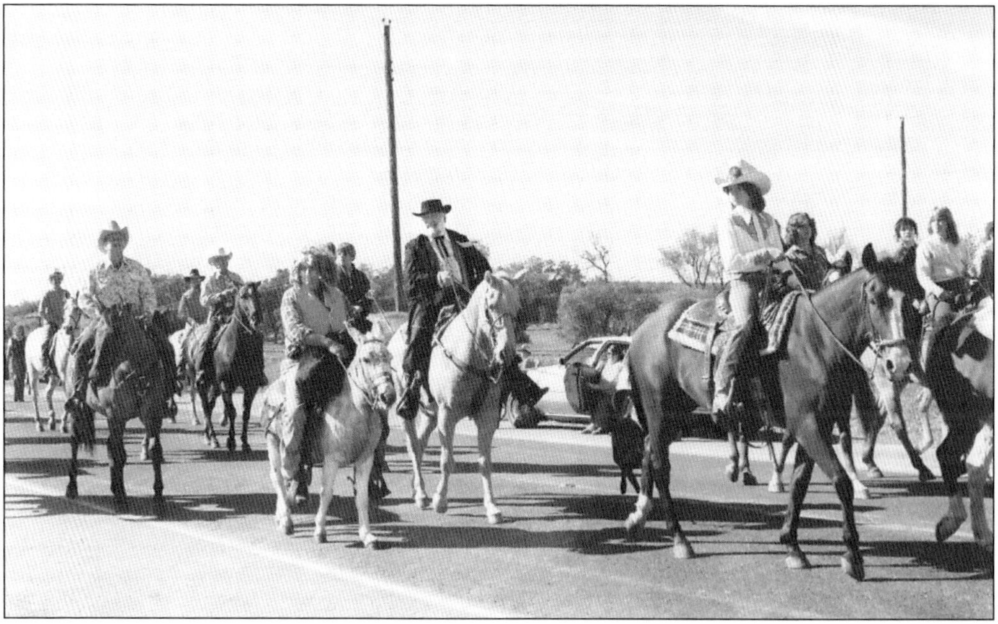

Leading this group of participants in the Argyle Centennial Parade is Argyle resident Sherrill Dianne Barrow, wearing a cowboy hat and jeans and riding her chestnut horse Stu. She appears amused at Argyle Centennial committeeman Floyd Kerr, who is wearing a wig and riding his little white donkey Sally. Behind him is Andy Moon, riding Red. Argyle residents, along with people from other towns, participated in the parade. (Courtesy of Martha Beavers.)

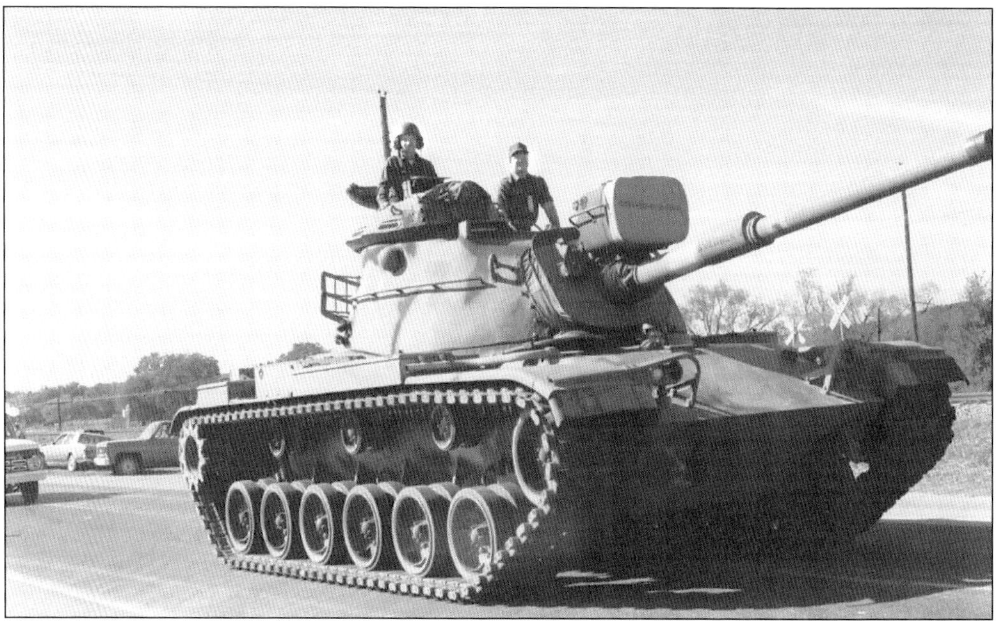

Argyle resident Sgt. John Sheffield, at the right, takes turns with Sgt. Tim Kelly, below, driving a Texas National Guard tank. Sheffield, owner and chef at Sheff's Place, a restaurant south of town on US Highway 377, was recognized by a little boy watching the parade. The youngster waved and then shouted to his father, "Dad, I didn't know Argyle had its own Army!" (Courtesy of Martha Beavers.)

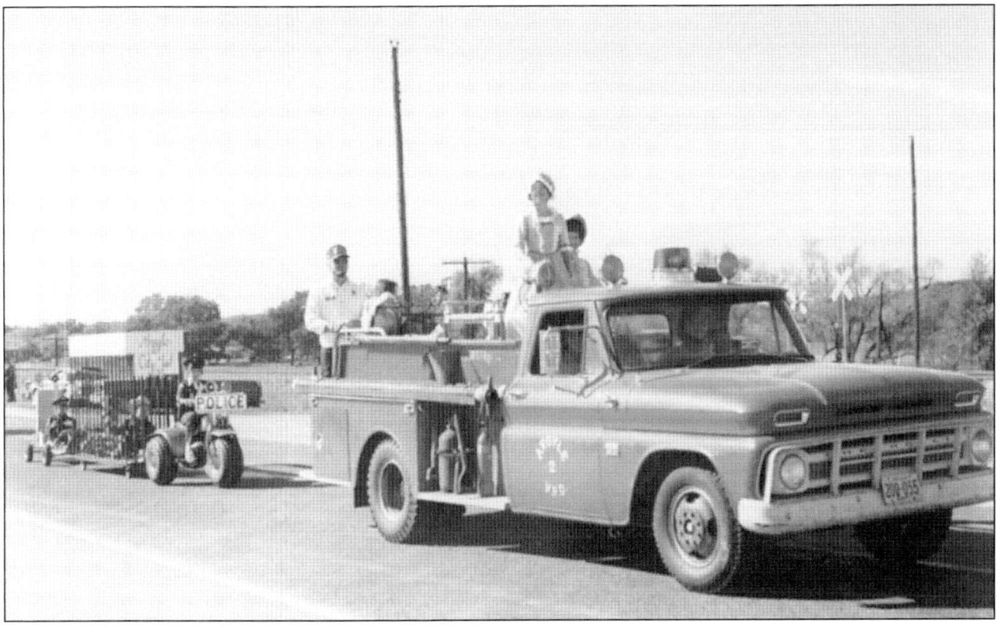

In the Argyle Centennial Parade was the Argyle Volunteer Fire Department fire truck driven by AVFD fireman Sam Carroll. At the back of the truck is firefighter James Price, and riding on top is AVFD fire chief Richard Hensley's daughter Sharon Hensley and wife, Wilda "Tootsie" Smith Hensley. Their prairie dresses and bonnets were designed and made by Chief Hensley's mother, Marie Hensley. (Courtesy of Martha Beavers.)

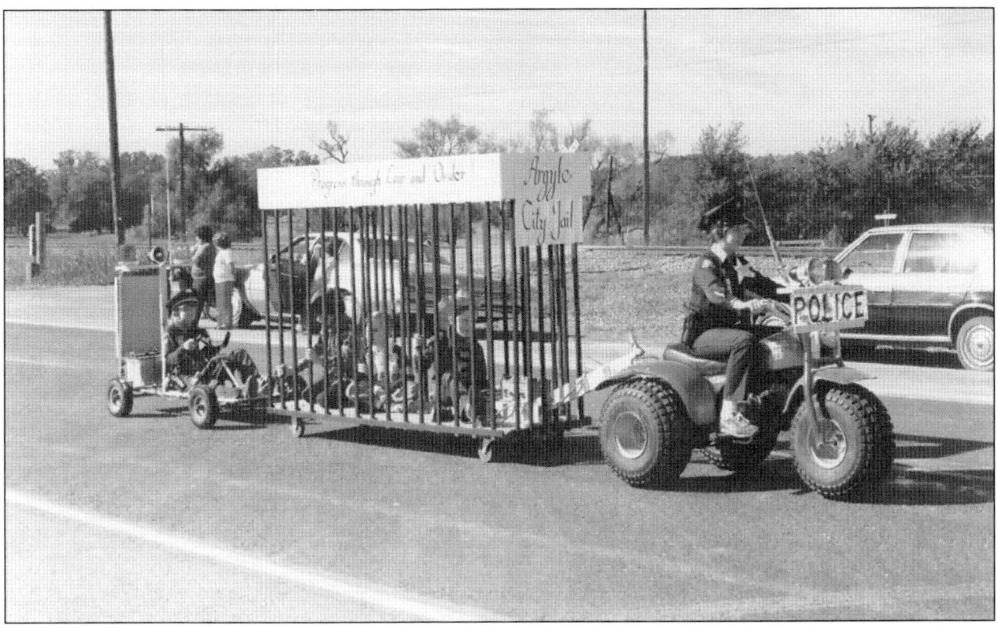

Children rode bicycles or walked and some were enclosed in the "Argyle Jail." Anyone could participate in the Argyle Centennial Parade, and most did. One newspaper reported there were more people in the parade than on the sidelines watching it. This group of participants had the Argyle Jail as its distinctive theme. Their style of travel was also unique. (Courtesy of Martha Beavers.)

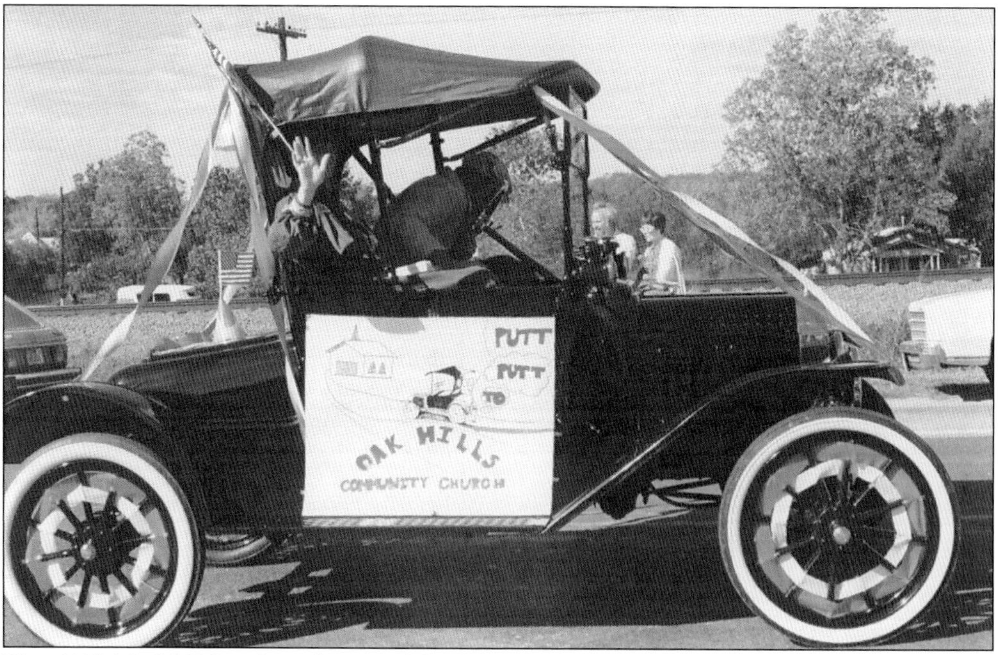

This 1915 Model T Roadster decorated for the Argyle celebration bears the sign "Putt, Putt to Oak Hills Community Church." The automobile was owned and driven by Dick Emery, one of the founders of the church. His wife, Kathy, who was also an Oak Hills Community Church founder, is sitting beside him waving to the public. (Courtesy of Martha Beavers.)

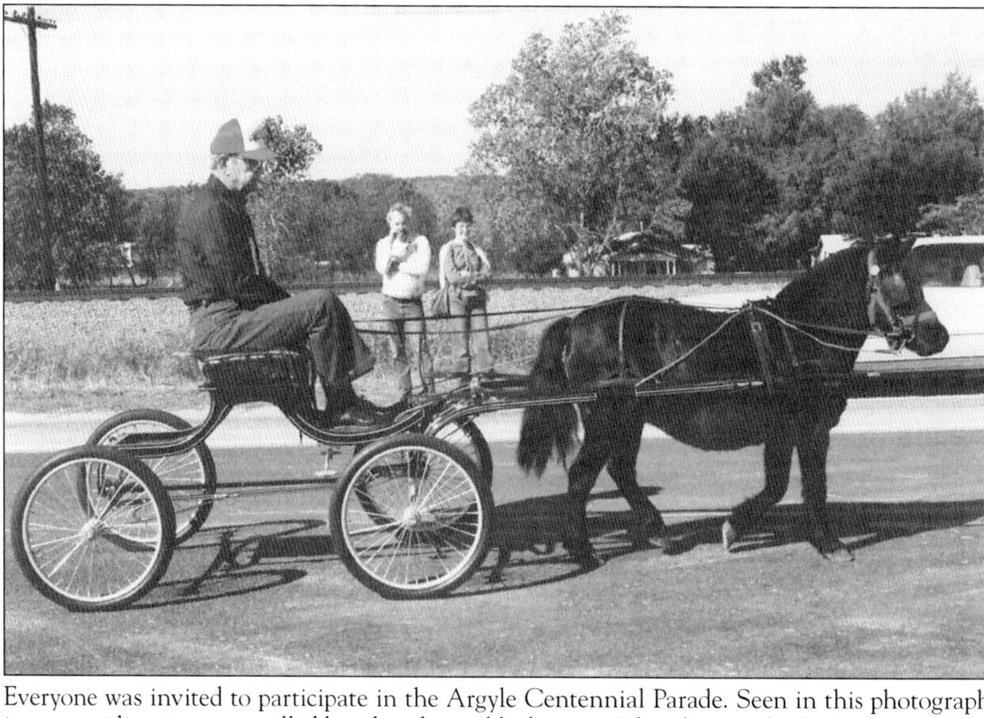

Everyone was invited to participate in the Argyle Centennial Parade. Seen in this photograph is a man riding in a cart pulled by a handsome black pony. After the parade, food was served on the grounds of the Argyle United Methodist Church. (Courtesy of Martha Beavers.)

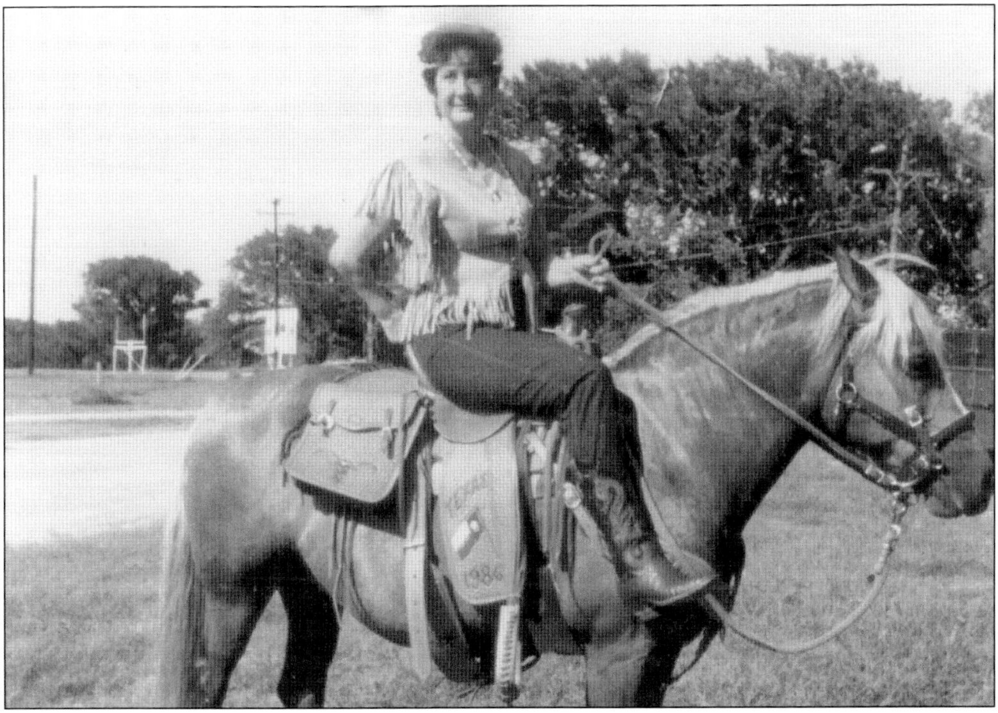

Edwinna Kerr rode her horse Lemon in the Argyle Centennial Parade. Her saddle was from Foster's Western Wear and made by Tim Tiaiad. Kerr served on the Argyle City Council in the mid-1980s. (Courtesy of Edwinna Kerr.)

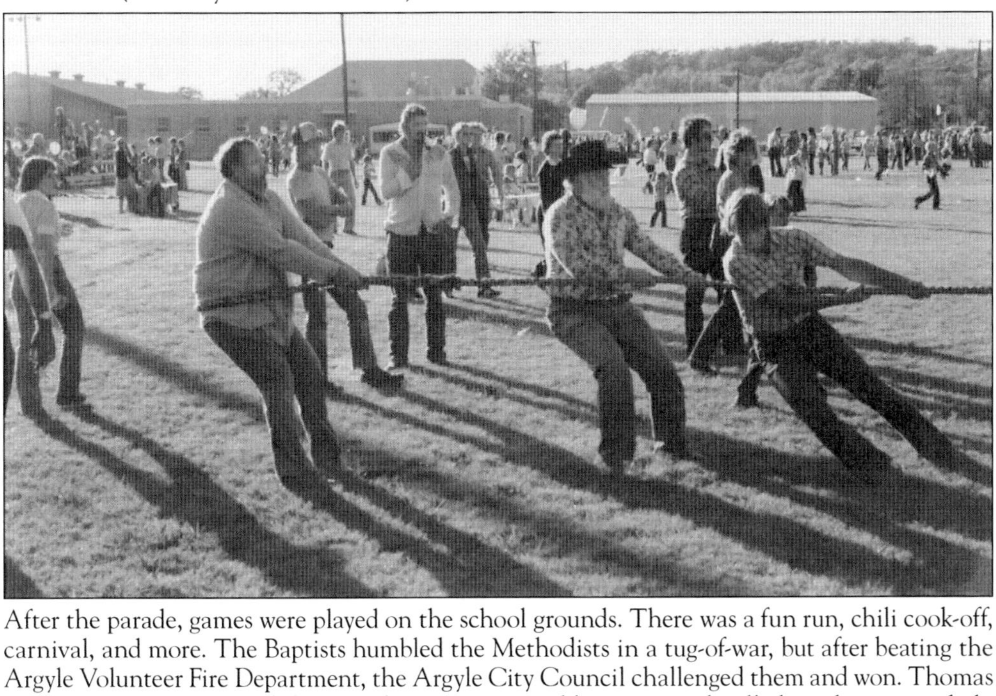

After the parade, games were played on the school grounds. There was a fun run, chili cook-off, carnival, and more. The Baptists humbled the Methodists in a tug-of-war, but after beating the Argyle Volunteer Fire Department, the Argyle City Council challenged them and won. Thomas "Tooter" Beavers wrapped the tug-of-war rope around his waist and pulled on the rope to help his team win. (Courtesy of Martha Beavers.)

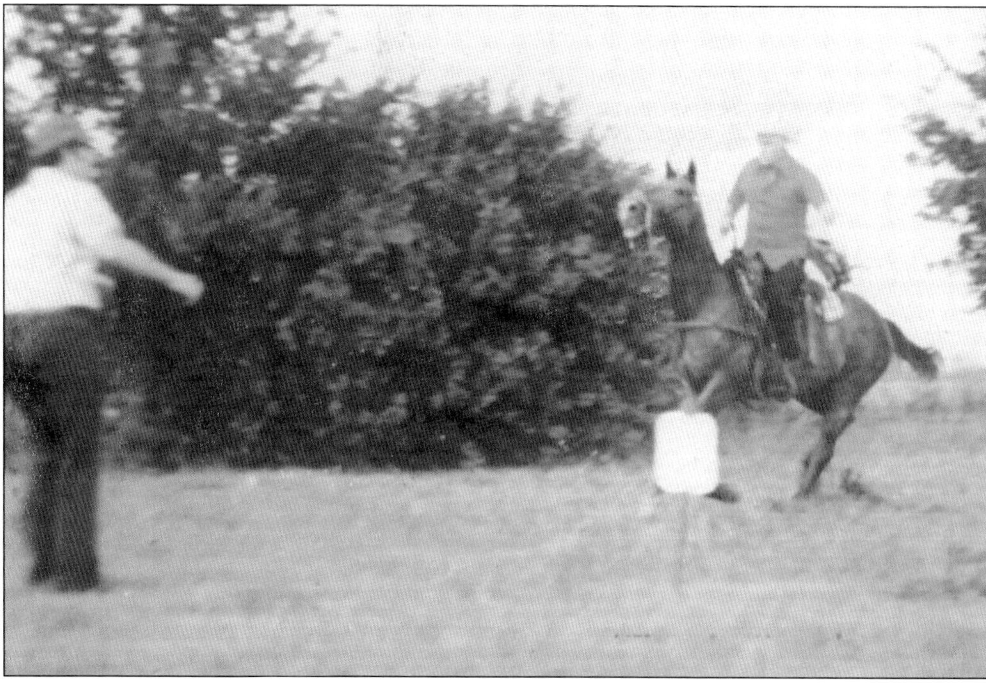

Floyd Kerr is seen riding his horse Dan as he wins a relay contest at the Argyle Centennial Celebration. Kerr was helpful in getting people to participate in the parade and the celebration. He was the owner of the first sanitation service in Argyle. (Courtesy of Edwinna Kerr.)

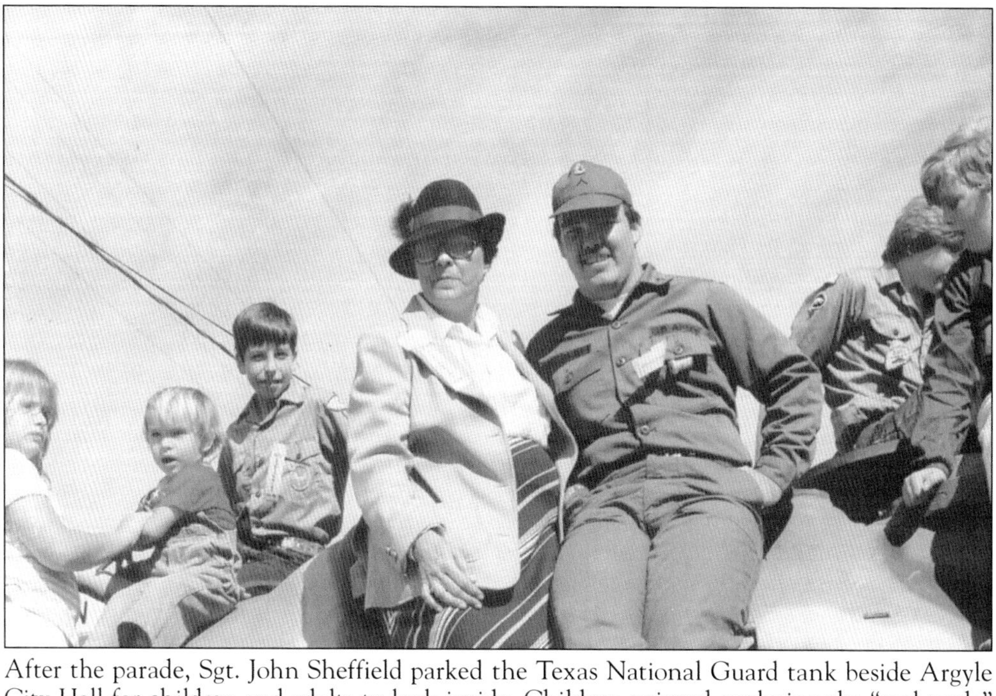

After the parade, Sgt. John Sheffield parked the Texas National Guard tank beside Argyle City Hall for children and adults to look inside. Children enjoyed exploring the "real tank." Mayor Yvonne Jenkins is pictured wearing her costume of the day and standing on the tank beside Sheffield. (Courtesy of Martha Beavers.)

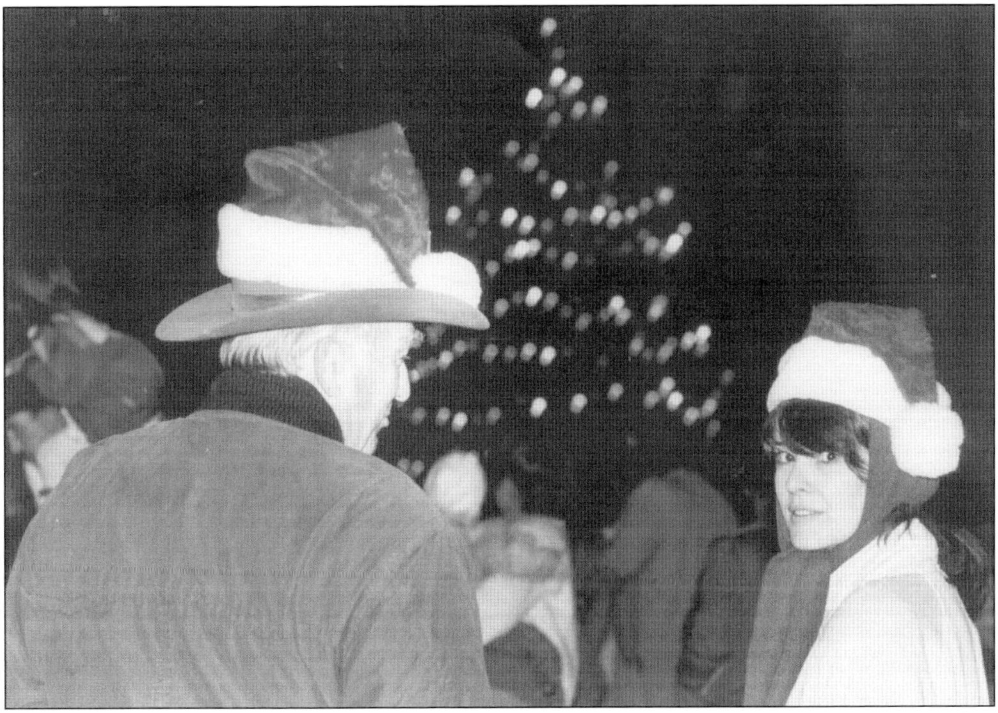

Seen in this photograph at the 1992 Annual Tree Lighting Ceremony at the Argyle Post Office are Argyle City Council members Don Wood and Kay Teer. To bring the community together, Mayor Yvonne A. Jenkins began an Annual Tree Lighting Ceremony. At the event, there was a lot of fanfare when the tree lights came on, illuminating the big cedar trees south of the Argyle Post Office. The Argyle church choirs, along with members of the Argyle Community Chorus, sang carols. Santa Claus threw candy to the children as he rode in on an Argyle Volunteer Fire Department fire truck. It was a joyous time for everyone. Pictured below is Sgt. William T. Tackett of the Argyle Police Department getting ready for the 1996 Annual Tree Lighting Ceremony. (Above, courtesy of DRC; below, courtesy of APD.)

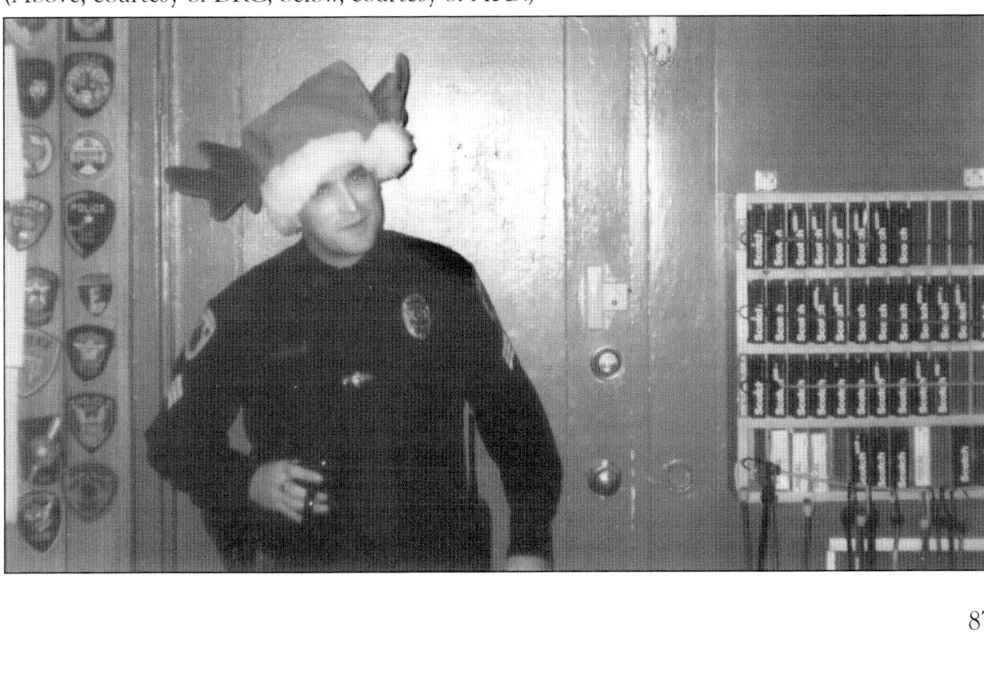

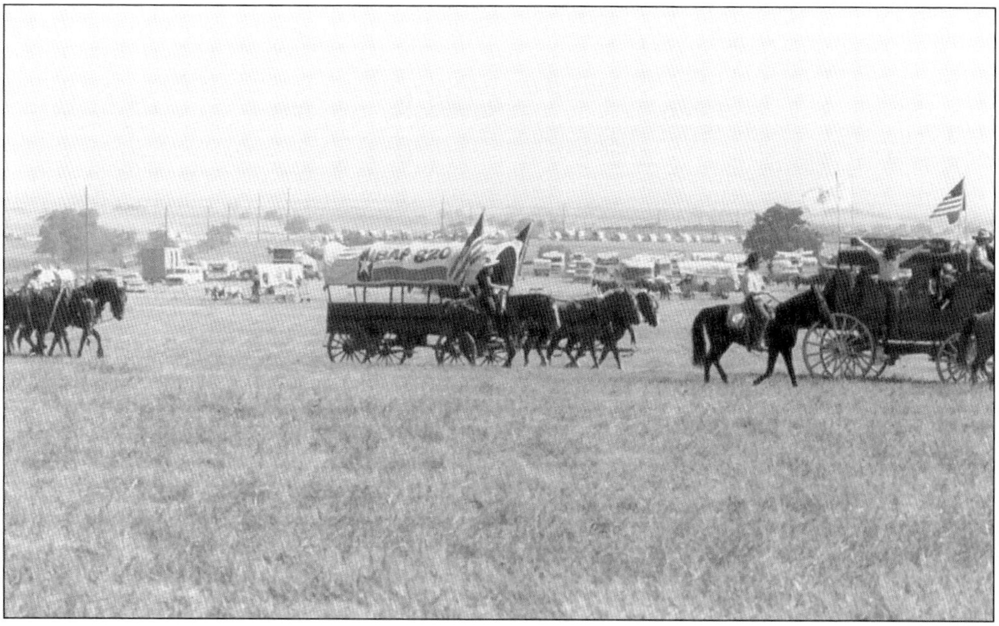

On Thursday, June 26, 1986, wagons in the Texas Sesquicentennial Wagon Train pulled into Pilot Knob Ranch in Argyle to spend the night. Local citizens went to the site to greet and visit with the campers. By the time the wagon train reached Denton County, it had swelled to 150 wagons and 450 people on horseback. The Texas Sesquicentennial Wagon Train toured the state on a 3,000-mile trek celebrating Texas's 150th birthday. (Courtesy of Pat Brown.)

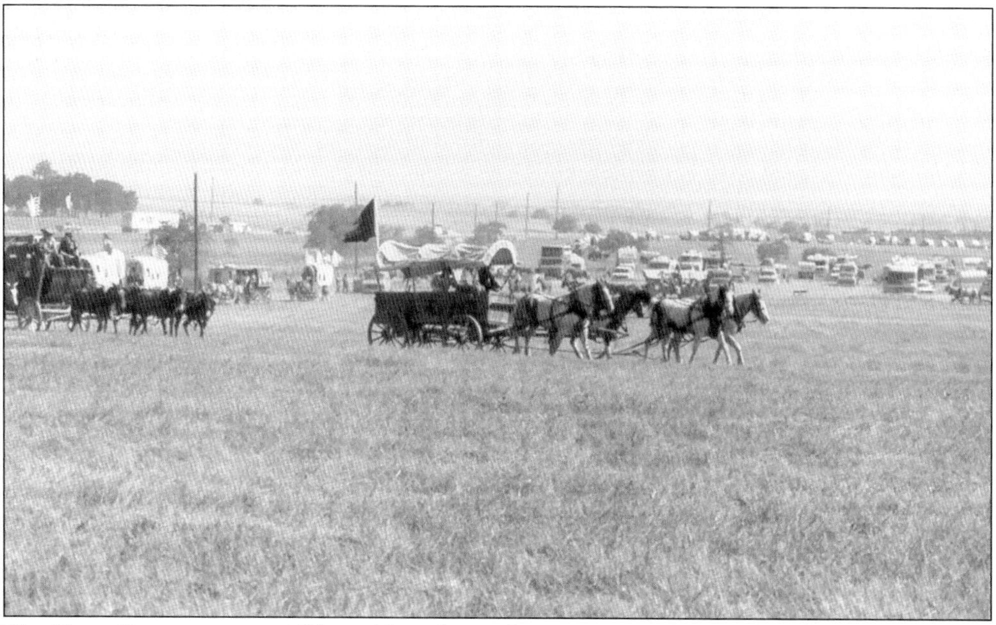

The Texas Sesquicentennial Wagon Train began January 2, 1986, in Sulphur Springs with about 400 wagons. A route was planned for the wagons to come within 100 miles of every Texas city for all Texans to have a chance to see the train. The wagon numbers fluctuated during the journey, but a few dozen wagons made the entire trip, which ended at the Fort Worth stockyards on July 3, 1986. (Courtesy of Pat Brown.)

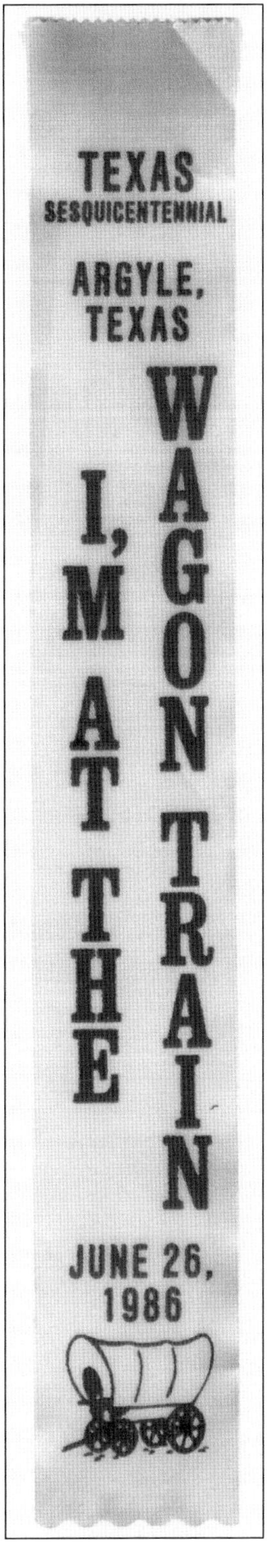

This ribbon was worn by Argyle citizens notifying people they visited the Texas Sesquicentennial Wagon Train. On Thursday, June 26, 1986, to coincide with the arrival of the wagon train camping out at Pilot Knob Ranch, the Argyle Sesquicentennial activities began at 5:30 p.m. People mounted their horses and climbed into their wagons to travel on Old Justin Road to Johns' Well and Campgrounds. The well once provided a 50-gallon barrel of cold water for 10¢, and years before, the campgrounds were a two-week religious camp held every July. At 6:30 p.m., a program for the dedication of the Official Texas Historical Marker for Johns' Well and Campgrounds began. It included pledging allegiance to the US and Texas flags, a prayer, hymns, the history of Johns' Well and Campgrounds, the unveiling of the historical marker, an unveiling of a wagon train plaque, a closing prayer, and refreshments. (Courtesy of Mary Ann DeBerry.)

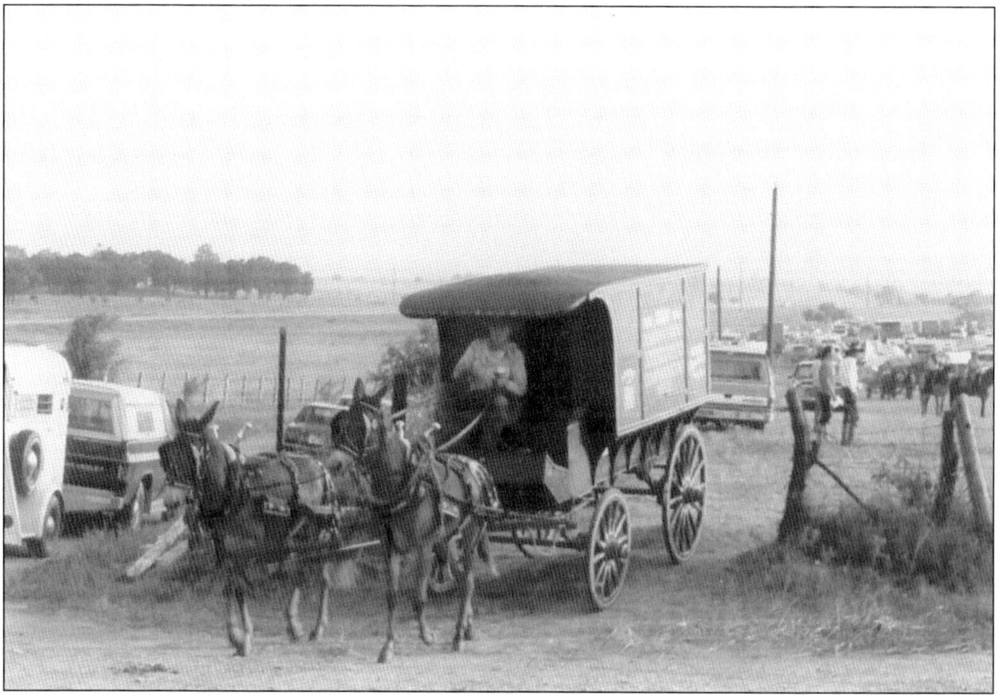

On Friday, June 27, 1986, at 7:00 a.m., the Texas Sesquicentennial Wagon Train pulled out of Pilot Knob Ranch and rolled south on US Highway 377. A group of Argyle citizens on horseback followed with those in the lead carrying the US flag, the Texas flag, and the Argyle flag. They traveled with the wagon train east on F.M. 407 through Bartonville, Highland Village, and Flower Mound. The wagon train continued to the Lewisville State Park, where it camped Friday night. The wagon train's route bypassed large cities like Houston and Dallas, traveling instead through the smaller Texas towns. (Above, courtesy of Pat Brown; below, courtesy of Martha Beavers.)

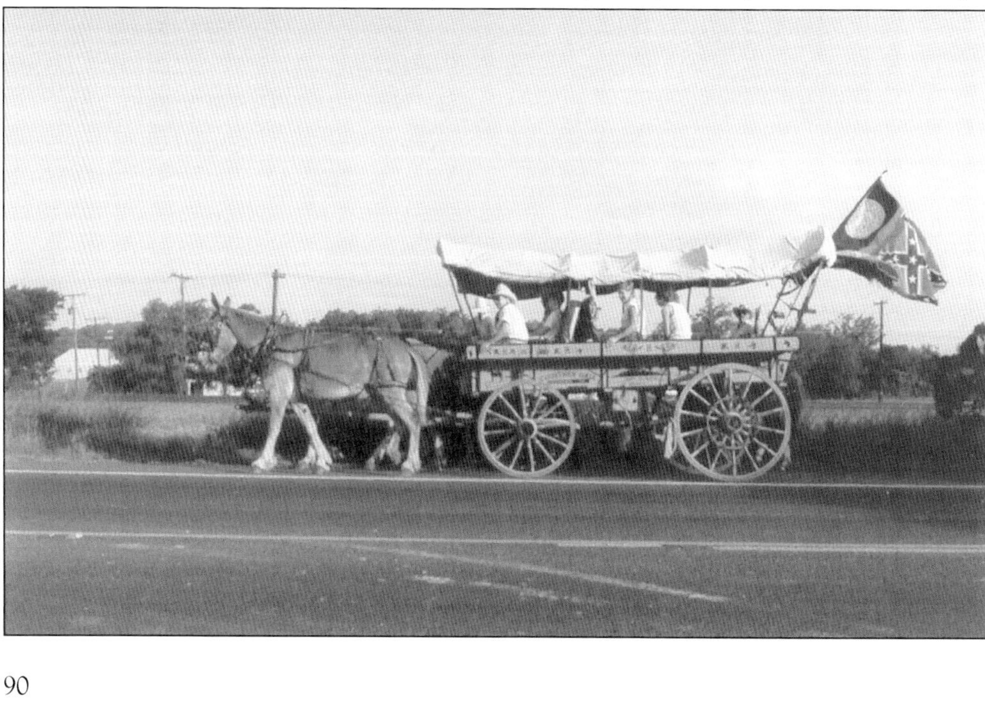

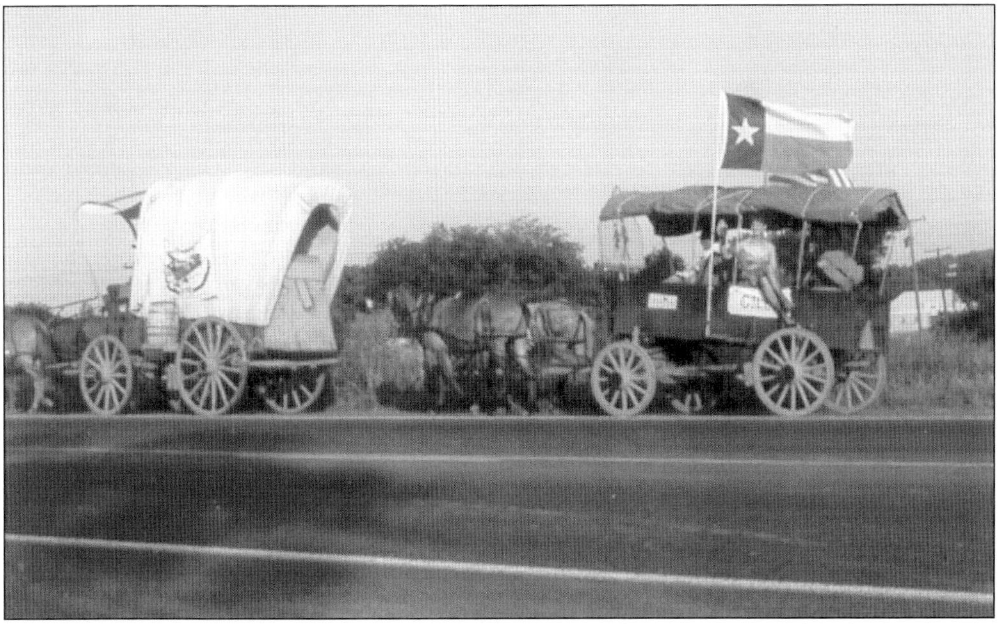

Wagons in the Texas Sesquicentennial Wagon Train are seen here leaving Argyle. The wagon train spent five nights in Denton County, and, while staying in Ponder before traveling to Argyle, it had the graduation of 22 students in the Wagon Train School. Texas Woman's University president Mary Evelyn Blagg-Huey addressed the students including Lori Wagner, a graduating senior from Longview, Texas, who received her diploma. The other students received certificates. Many of the wagons displayed the Texas flag and often had printed on their canopies the names of the towns from where they came. Most of the campers traveling with the wagon train had countless stories to tell about their journey through Texas. (Courtesy of Martha Beavers.)

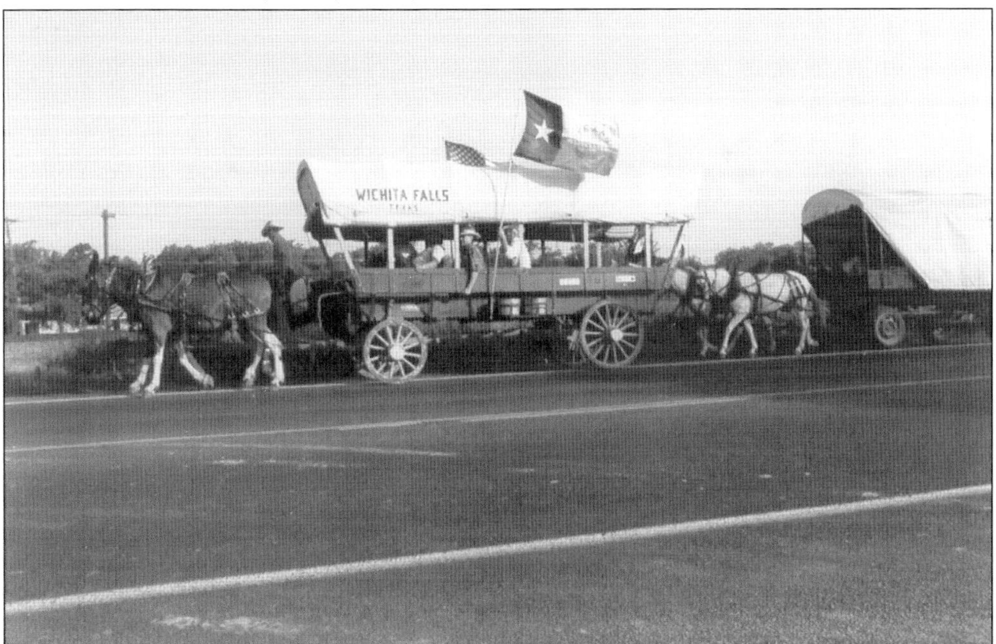

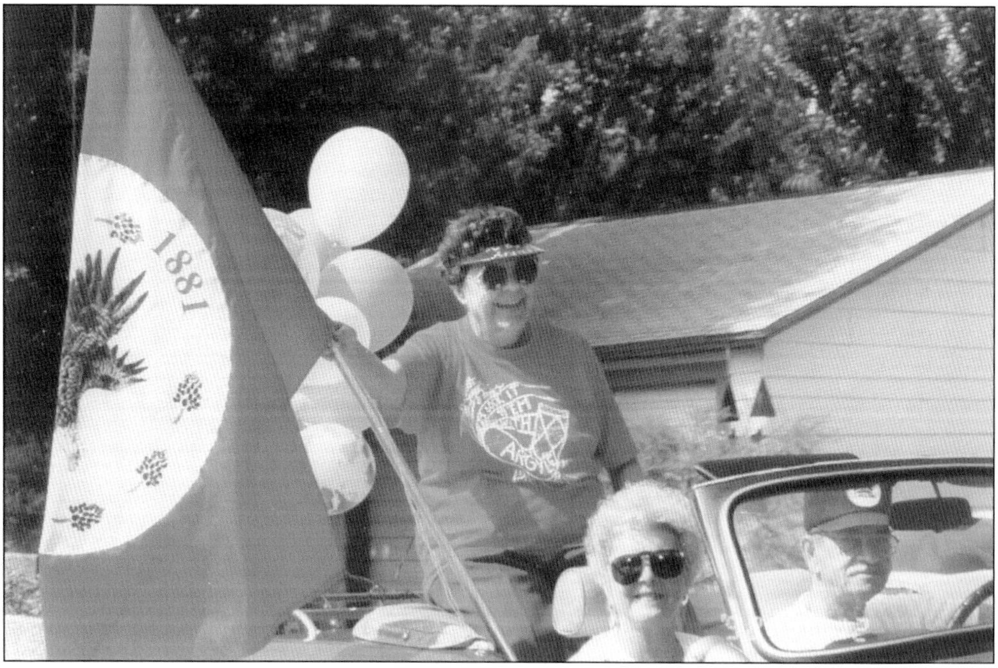

Leading the parade down West Front Street to the Argyle School for the first Argyle Pride Day on September 12, 1992, is Mayor Yvonne A. Jenkins holding the Argyle flag and wearing the official Argyle Pride Day T-shirt of an argyle sock declaring "Sock It To 'Em with Argyle Pride." The T-shirt was designed by Eva Johnson, seen riding in the front seat with her husband, Phil. (Courtesy of Joan Delashaw.)

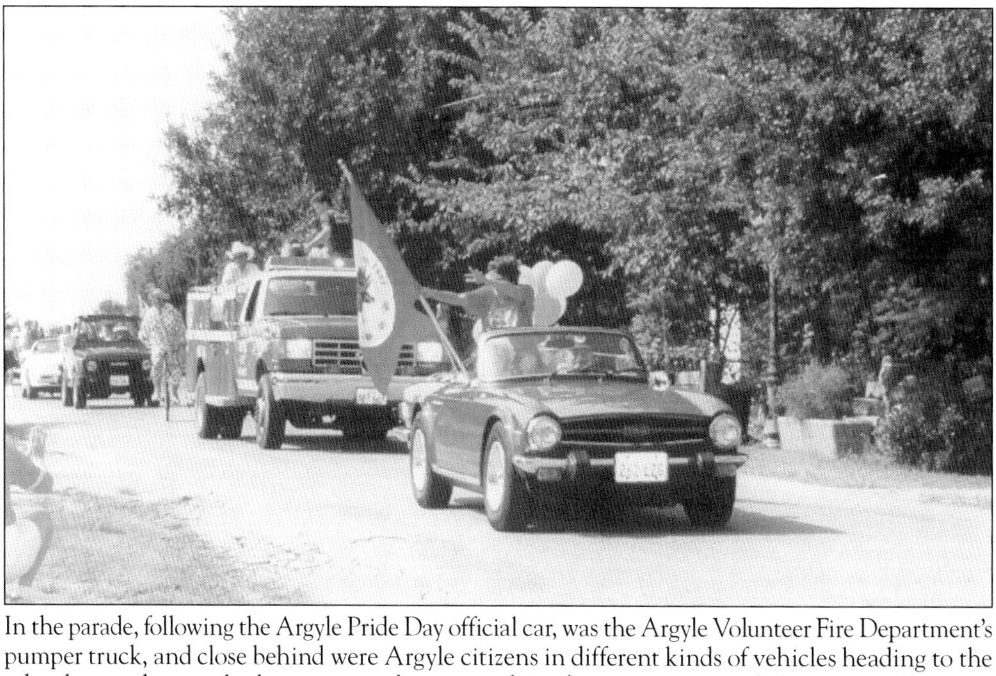

In the parade, following the Argyle Pride Day official car, was the Argyle Volunteer Fire Department's pumper truck, and close behind were Argyle citizens in different kinds of vehicles heading to the school grounds to eat barbecue, enter their animals in the pet contest, and play games. (Courtesy of Joan Delashaw.)

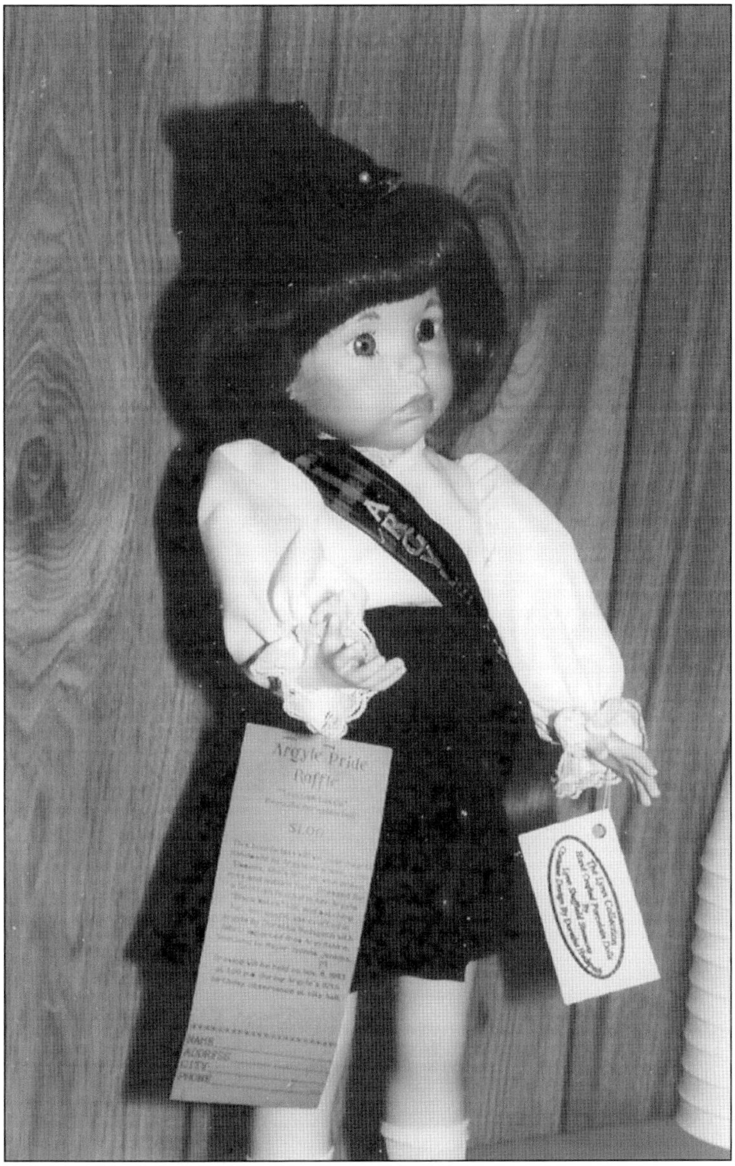

This Scottish lassie porcelain doll wore a Scottish kilt and hat made by Doretha Hudspeth of Denton from the Black Watch material that Mayor Yvonne A. Jenkins bought in Argyll, Scotland. Two dolls were made by Argyle author and porcelain doll maker Lynn Sheffield Simmons, chairman of the Argyle Pride Task Force from 1992 to 1997. One doll was donated to the City of Argyle and one was raffled off to raise funds for the Argyle Pride Task Force, an ad hoc committee appointed by the Argyle City Council to beautify the city. The committee sponsored cleanup days, an Argyle Pride Day and Barbecue, the Argyle Walking and Jogging Path, the Annual Tree Lighting Ceremony, the heritage play *The Place Is Argyle,* the Argyle Community Chorus, the Argyle Community Players, the Argyle Pride Holiday Decorating Contest, and the Argyle Middle School essay contest, "What's Good About America?" On the committee were Lynn Sheffield Simmons, John Tutuni, Dr. Larry Simmons, Donna Durham, Julie Marcum, Janice Freeman, Rick Freeman, Lillian Linebarger, Donna Kahney, Brenda Kerekes Mooney, and Mayor Yvonne A. Jenkins. (Courtesy of *The Argyle Sun.*)

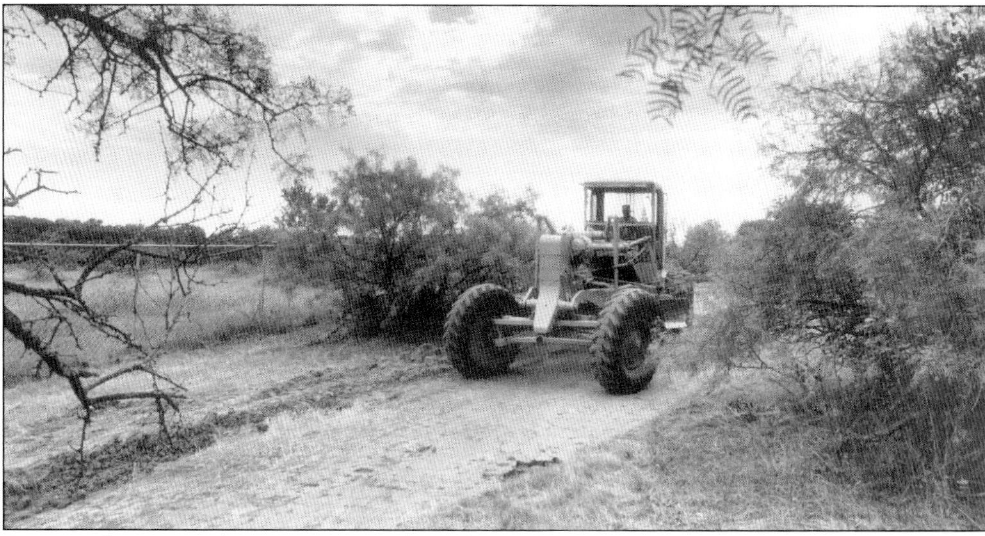

On Saturday, September 11, 1993, Argyle Pride Day began with a parade leaving the First Baptist Church of Argyle to go to the dedication of the Argyle Walking and Jogging Path at the Argyle School. The eight-foot-wide path was built by Reynolds Grader Service of Justin and was paid for with money raised by the Argyle Pride Task Force. Unfortunately, in the spring after a torrential rainfall, the walking and jogging path was washed out. It was repaired but washed out again. Mayor Yvonne A. Jenkins and the Argyle Pride Task Force acquired creosoted utility poles that workers used to shore up the low-lying areas of the path. Unfortunately, the poles damaged the skirting around the Argyle School Administration Building as they were swept to the creek during another downpour. (Above, courtesy of DRC; below, courtesy of Denise Remfert.)

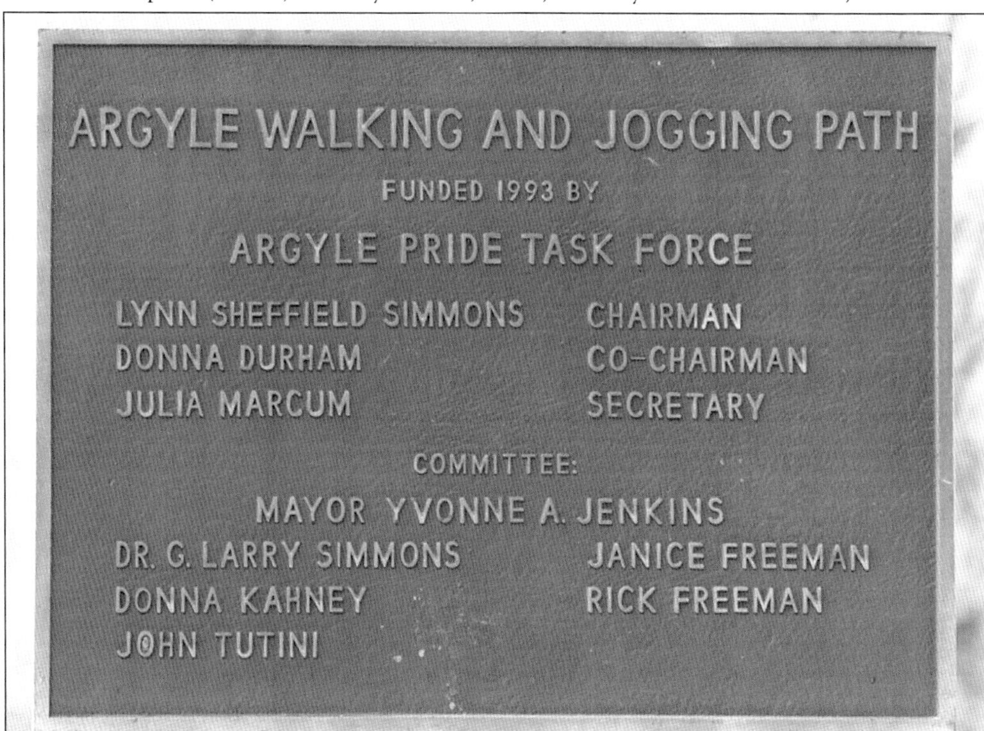

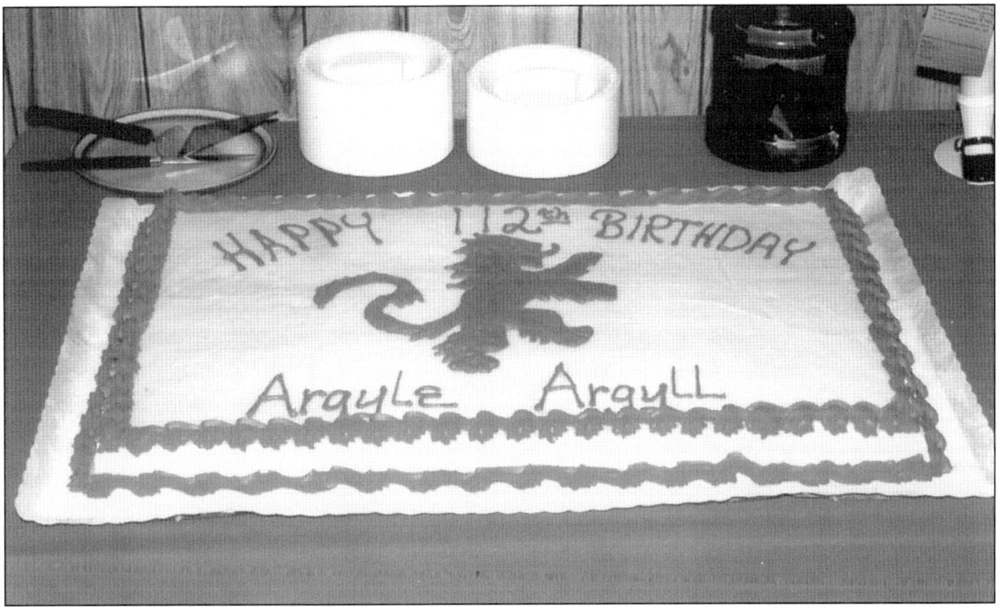

The Argyle "Rampant Lions" helped to celebrate Argyle's 112th birthday. For years, residents thought Argyle was named for a garden in France. However, after Mayor Yvonne A. Jenkins conducted a fact-finding tour in Argyll, Scotland, and additional information was obtained from Denton resident Martha Len Nelson, whose great grandfather was Dr. Daniel McIntire Stewart, it was determined Argyll, Scotland, is the namesake. (Courtesy of Dr. Larry Simmons.)

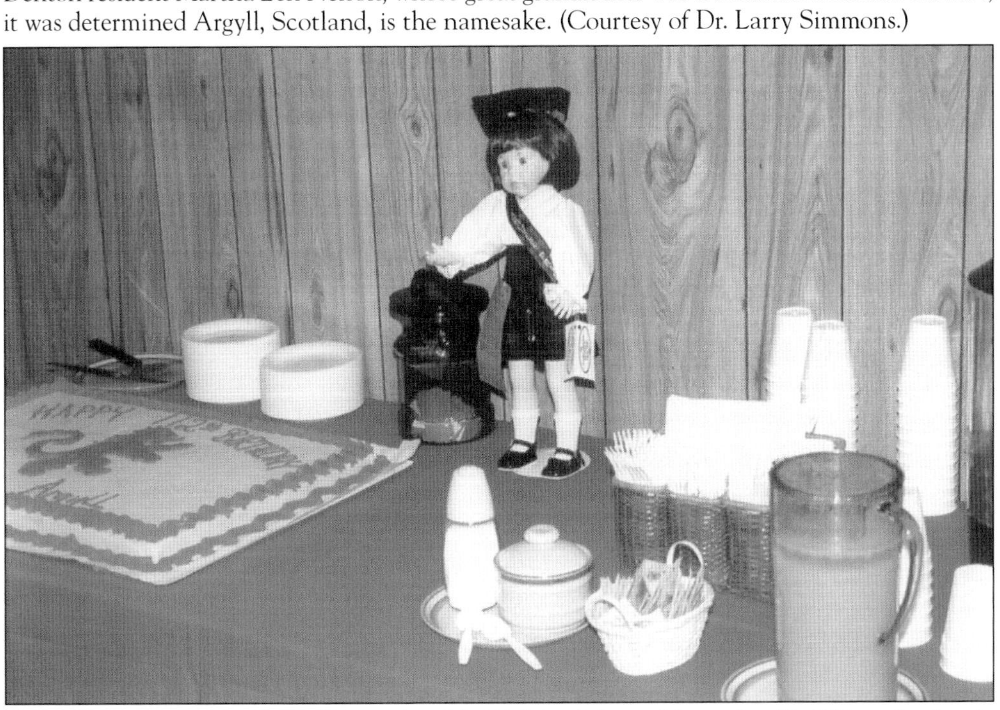

Local citizens were invited to celebrate Argyle's 112th birthday on November 13, 1993, at the Argyle City Hall. The event was sponsored by the Argyle Pride Task Force and the 18-inch Scottish lassie porcelain doll raffle drawing was held. Proceeds from the raffle sales went to the Argyle Pride Task Force to support projects to beautify Argyle. (Courtesy of Dr. Larry Simmons.)

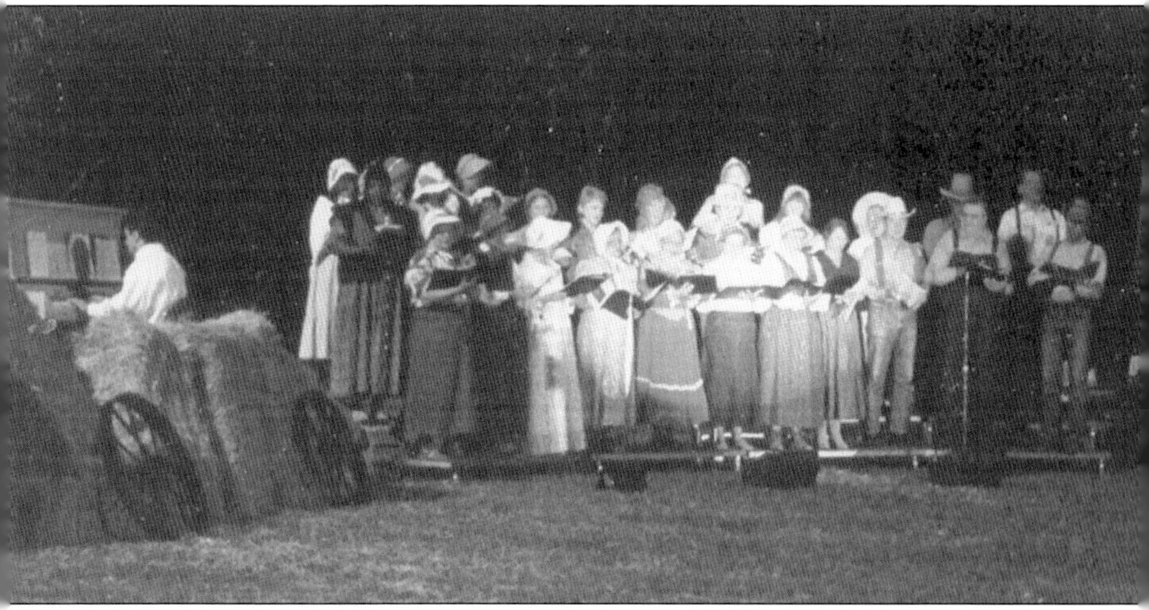

On September 10, 1994, the Argyle Pride Task Force sponsored the historical pageant *The Place Is Argyle*, held on the Argyle School football field at 8:00 p.m. after a parade and barbecue dinner. The pageant was written and produced by Lynn Sheffield Simmons and directed by Craig Beaudine, who was assistant director for the television series *Walker, Texas Ranger*. The assistant director was Councilwoman Kay Teer, and the narrator was former Miss Arizona Stacey Beaudine. The Argyle Community Chorus was directed by Dan Lipford with Lynne Tracy as music coordinator. Those in the chorus were Ruth Anderton, Elsie Barrow, Mikey Bodkin, Sandra Boughton, Ken Capelle, Mary Ann Carroll, Lee Cole, Lorie Cooper, Delores Greene, Gloria Glass, Gwen Goff, Ruth Greene, Mary Hager, Skip Kalb, Lou Kraft, Gayle Lewis, Ann Lincoln, Glendine Lipford, Martha Mason, Carol Mears, Connie Mehos, Janet Newsom, Doug Schema, Kimberly Simmons, Larry Simmons, Bill Smith, Verlene Springer, Kay Teer, Lynne Tracy, Marian Wagner, Donna Williams. Soloists were Bill Smith, Karyl Smith, Skip Kalb, Doug Schema, and Lou Kraft. The Argyle fourth- and fifth-grade elementary school chorus was directed by Kathy Joyner. (Courtesy of *The Argyle Sun*.)

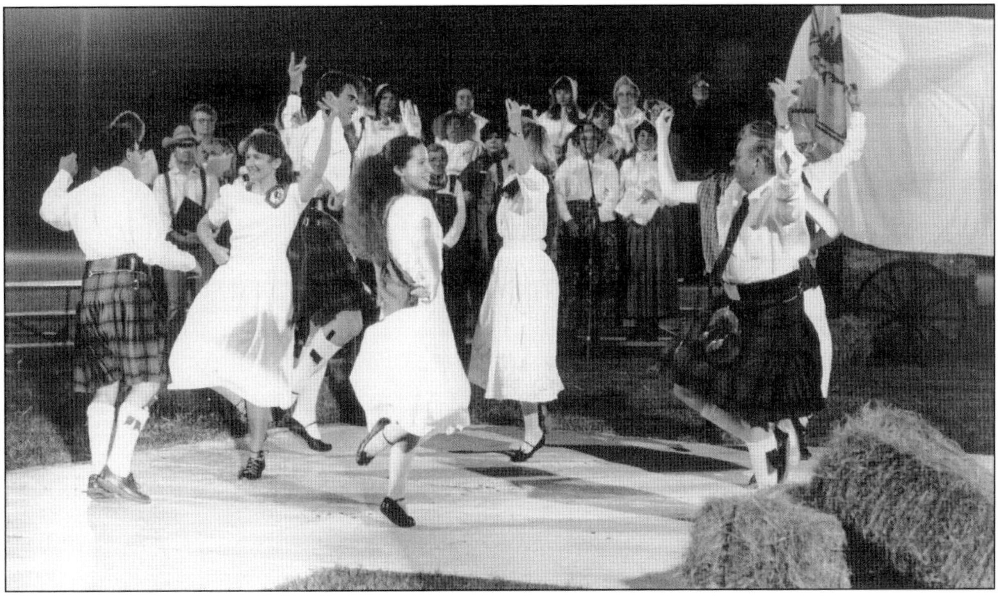

The Denton Celtic Dancers performed in Argyle's historical pageant *The Place Is Argyle*. The Scottish dances symbolized Argyle's connection to Argyll, Scotland. The Argyle Community Players, who performed in the September 9, 1995, pageant were Kyle Beaudine, Horace Glass, Drake Teer, Skip Kalb, Ken Capelle, Larami Crawford, Lorie Cooper, Amy Beaudine, Liesl Lipford, Ann Lincoln, Doug Schema, and Kay Teer. Also on stage in the 1995 presentation were the Argyle Community Chorus, the Highlander Square Dance Club, and the Tweeddale Dancing Twosome. For three years, the pageant performed on the Argyle School football field. Stacey Beaudine is seen here relating to the audience the history of Argyle. A large net full of helium balloons was released as the chorus sang its final song, "This Is My Country." (Above, courtesy of DRC; below, courtesy *The Argyle Sun*.)

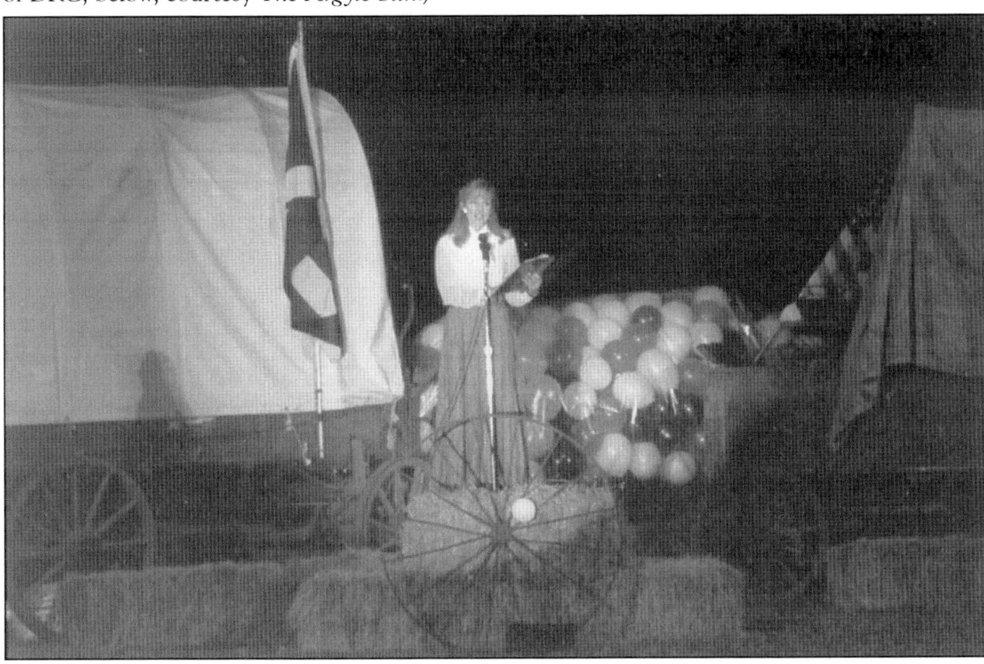

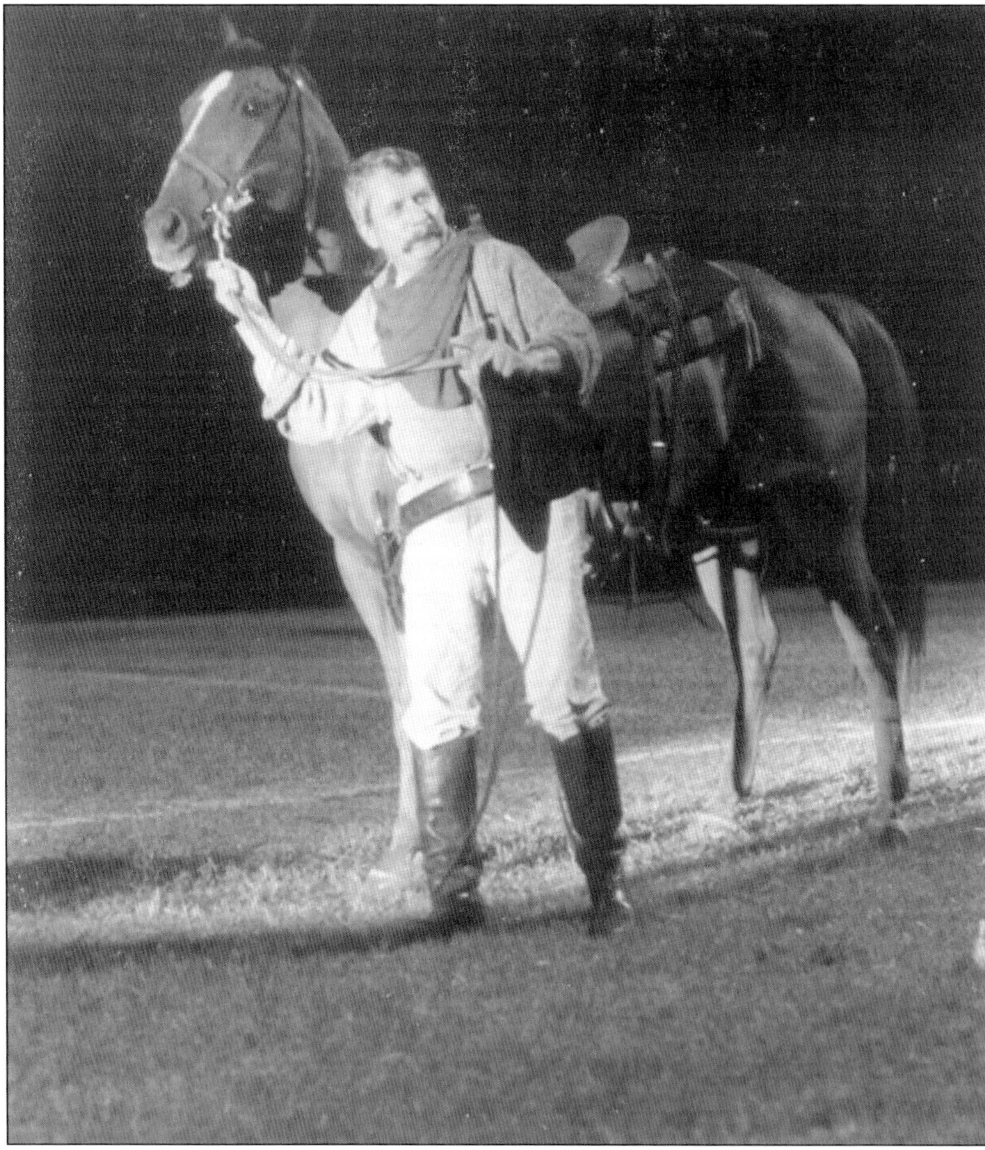

Doug Schema played the role of the outlaw Sam Bass in the historical drama *The Place Is Argyle*. He is seen here clutching the reins to his horse as he recites "The Sam Bass Poem" written by Lynn Sheffield Simmons. The verses in the poem review the life of Sam Bass: "From Indiana I came, a cowboy I wanted to be, I bought a horse and gave her a name, the Denton Mare you see. I was a fine upstanding man, until I ran with the wrong crowd of men, I quit my job as the Sheriff's hand, to become a gambler just like them. I'd bet on the mare when she'd race, and a lot of cash I won, I spent the money not leaving a trace, I liked whiskey, parties, and having fun. I didn't want to have a regular job, I liked to get my money fast, so it was stages and trains I'd rob, until the Texas Rangers got me at last." (Courtesy of *The Argyle Sun*.)

In the 1996 production of *The Place Is Argyle* cowgirls on horseback carrying the US flag, the Texas flag, and the Argyle flag raced across the Argyle School football field in front of the viewing stands as patriotic songs played and the audience cheered. The horseback flag bearers were Mindy Alred, Keri Miller, and Georgia Morris. (Courtesy of *The Argyle Sun*.)

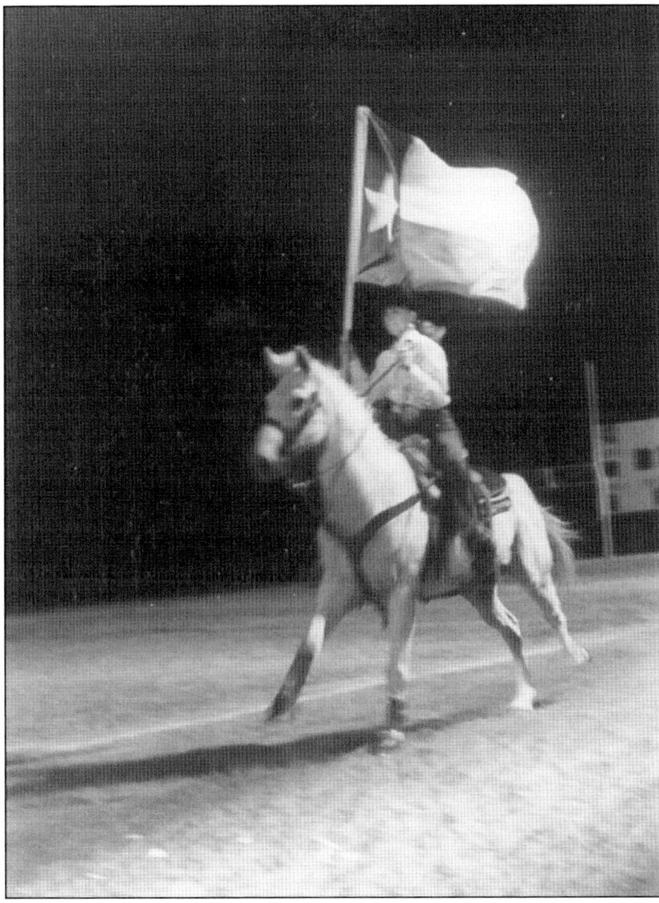

During the 1990s, whenever there were celebrations, Argyle City Hall flew the American flag, the Texas flag, the Argyle city flag, and Scotland's two national flags: the Saint Andrew's Cross flag and the Royal Flag of Scotland. The Argyle Pride Task Force bought American flags to be flown on US Highway 377 on special and patriotic occasions. (Courtesy of Dr. Larry Simmons.)

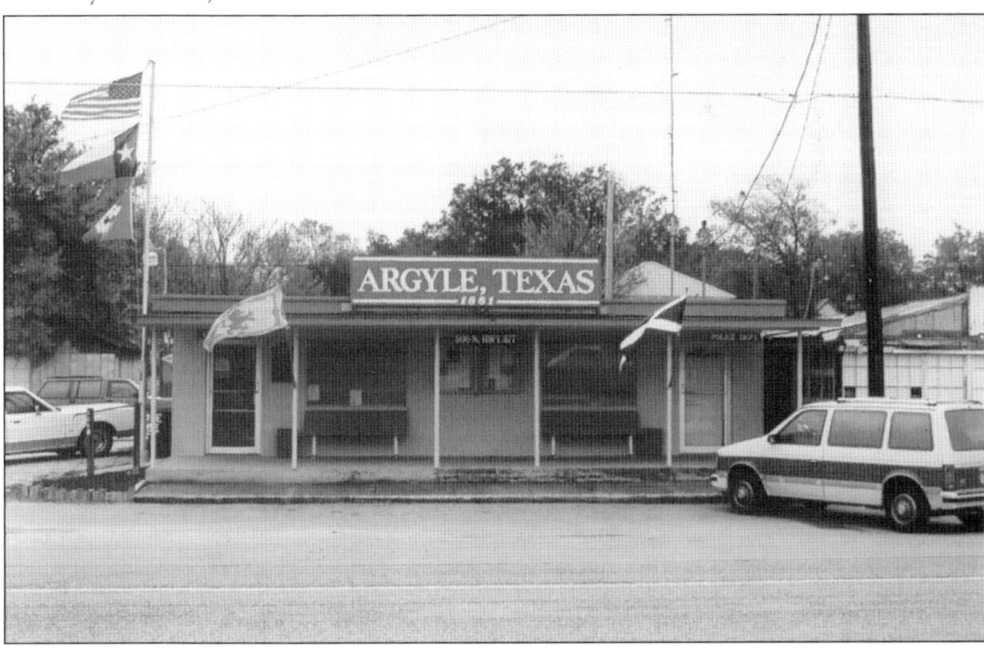

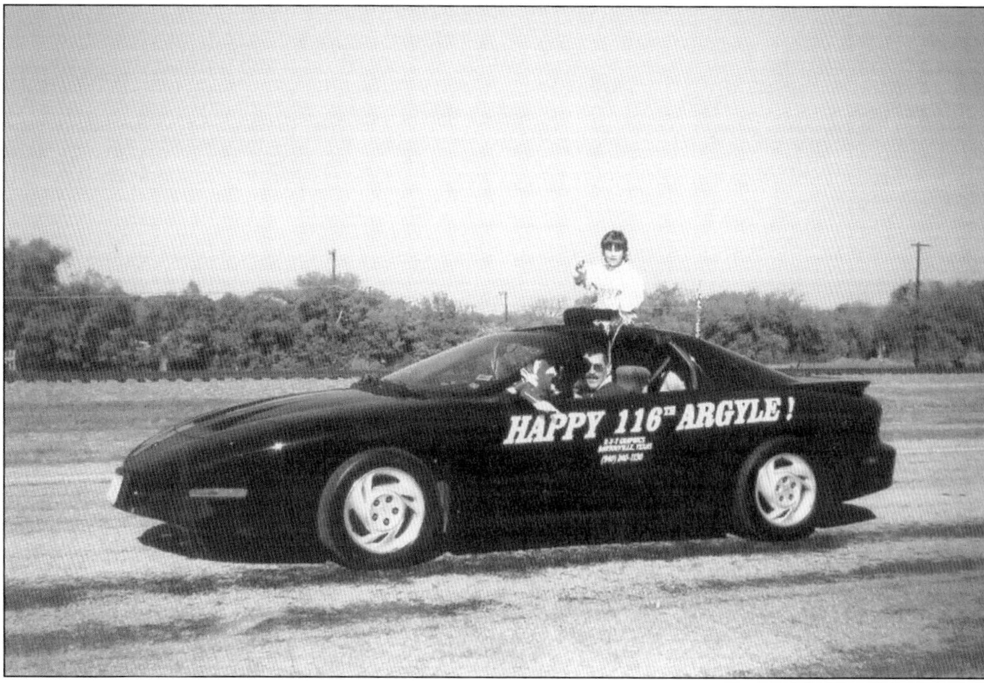

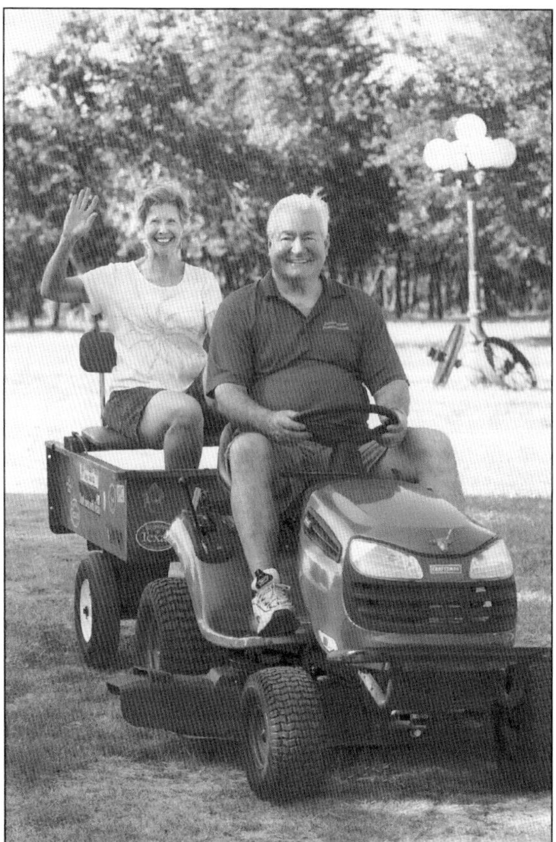

Argyle's 116th birthday celebration in 1997 featured a parade followed by a performance of excerpts from the historical pageant *The Place Is Argyle* that was held at Argyle City Hall. This photograph shows a car in the parade wishing Argyle a happy 116th birthday. (Courtesy of Martha Beavers.)

After a parade, it is nice to stop and visit with friends. Seen here are John and Jody Bellinghausen in the 1990s, calling on neighbors after participating in a fun-filled celebration and traveling in Argyle style. (Courtesy of Denise Remfert.)

Five

The People
The Spirit of the Town

The people of Argyle have a resiliency of overcoming a variety of obstacles, whether it is the general public rebuilding the town after a devastating fire or a disastrous tornado, or residents taking the responsibility to establish a municipal electric utility and form a public corporation such as the Argyle Water Supply Corporation and the Argyle Volunteer Fire Department. Individuals show their community spirit and desire to improve the lives of Argyle residents by forming nonprofit organizations such as Communities Civic League, Inc., and the Argyle Educational Foundation. Perceptive city council members carefully write zoning laws to help Argyle make a smooth transition from being an agricultural community to a place where commuters live.

Argyle's early settlers were farmers and ranchers. Soon after Dr. Daniel McIntire Stewart came to the Argyle area in 1877, he bought the 300-acre Long Point Farm on the south side of Pilot Knob. In 1882, John Cassin Heath bought a 640-acre farm on what is now F.M. 407. By the turn of the 20th century, cotton was Argyle's main crop. In 1930, after the depletion of the soil, cotton farming stopped. Many residents grew peanuts and fruit such as plums, peaches, and pears, selling most of their produce to neighbors.

Argyle's population declined with the advent of the automobile and as employment took citizens to work in the cities. Also, World War II gave residents the opportunity to work and live elsewhere. In the mid-1960s, the population began to grow with people wanting to live in a rural atmosphere and continue to work in the metropolitan area. Therefore, Argyle became known as "a bedroom city," a commuter's delight.

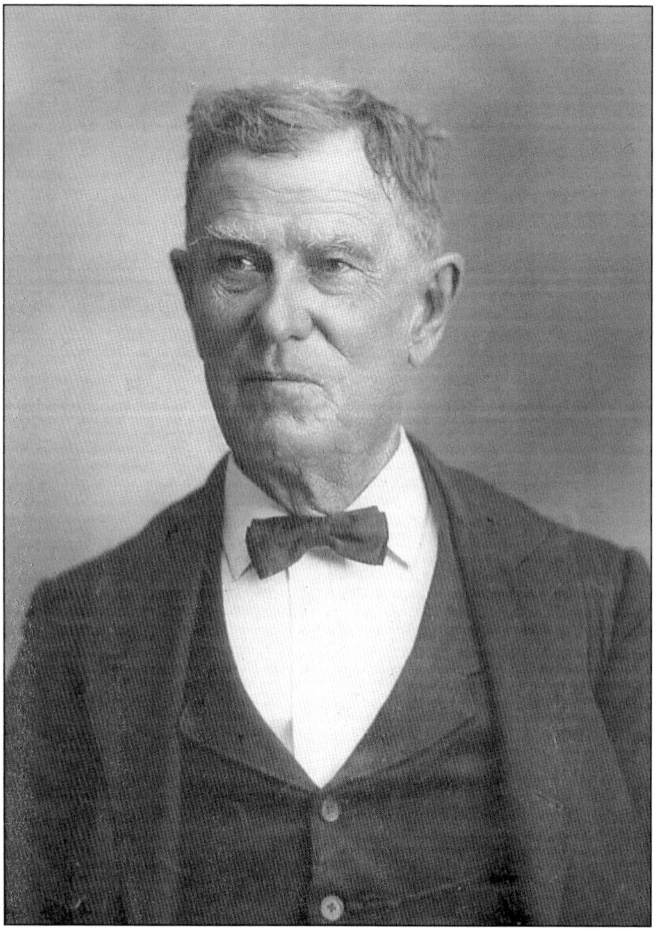

In 1877, Dr. Daniel McIntyre Stewart came to Texas from Lawrenceburg, Tennessee. He settled in "Garden Valley," a small community halfway between Argyle and Roanoke. Within two years he earned enough money to buy 300 acres of land south of Pilot Knob and 2.5 miles northwest of Argyle. On the land Dr. Stewart named "Long Point Farm" grew a line of timber marking the end of the Eastern Cross Timbers and the beginning of the Grand Prairie. The timbers furnished heat for the farmhouse while the flat land to the west grew Bermuda and natural grasses good for grazing livestock. The bulk of the farm lay to the south where oats, wheat, and corn were planted. Besides owning Long Point Farm, Doctor Stewart was the first physician to practice medicine in the Argyle area. (Courtesy of Martha Len Nelson.)

D. M. STEWART M. D.

Practising Physician & Surgeon.

DEAVENPORT'S MILLS, DENTON COUNTY, TEXAS;

Takes pleasure in informing the people of Denton County, that he has permanently located at the above named place, and offers his professional services to the people, as a practising physician of long experience. All classes of diseases skillfully treated; diseases of women and children made a specialty, and special attention given to the minor branches of SURGERY.

REFERENCES.

Dr. C. L. Herbert, Denton, Texas.	Maj. M. W. Deavenport, Deavenport's Mills, Texas.

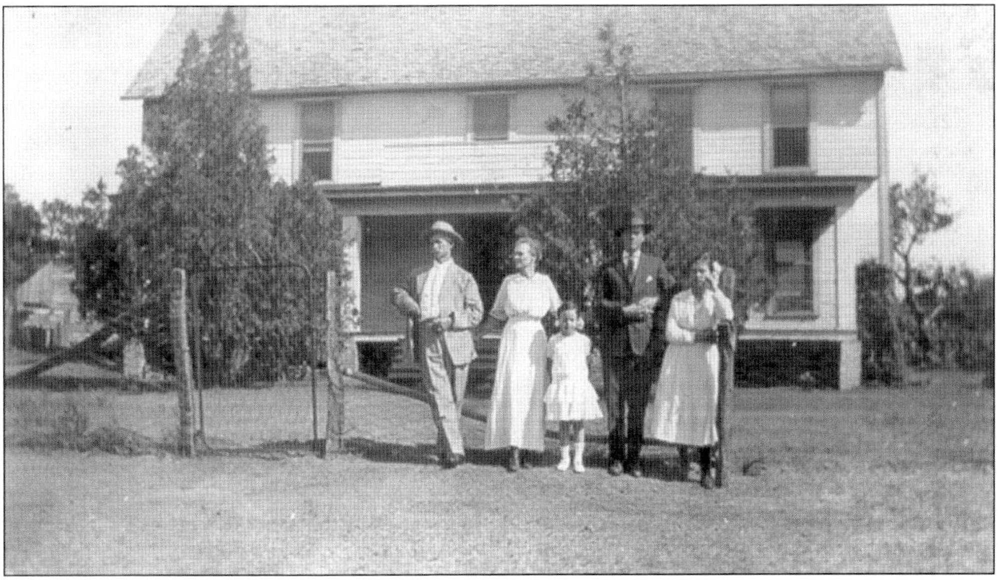

The Stewart family is pictured in front of the farmhouse on Long Point Farm. The house was built from timber brought in from Fort Worth, Texas, after Dr. Daniel McIntyre Stewart bought the farm. Those in the picture are Doctor Stewart's son and daughter-in-law Henry Thomas Stewart and Ina Livey Stewart with their children, Eugenia, John, and Marcella. (Courtesy of Martha Len Nelson.)

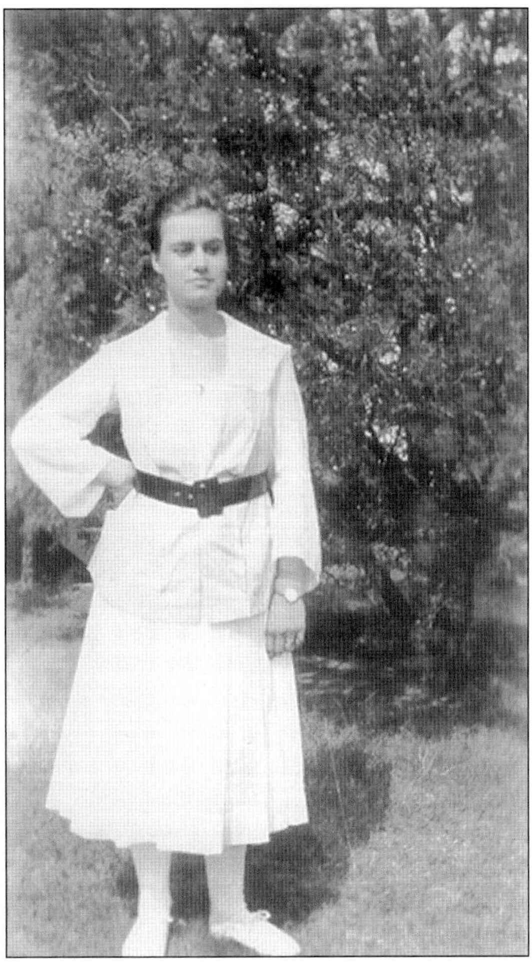

This photograph is of 17-year-old Marcella Stewart (Henderson) taken in 1918. She attended Pilot Knob Elementary School and then went to the Argyle School until she graduated. During her school years, her best friend was Lalla Crawford, whose father, Ish Crawford, was Denton County commissioner for the southwest corner of the county. Crawford Road, where their home was located, was named for him. (Courtesy of Martha Len Nelson.)

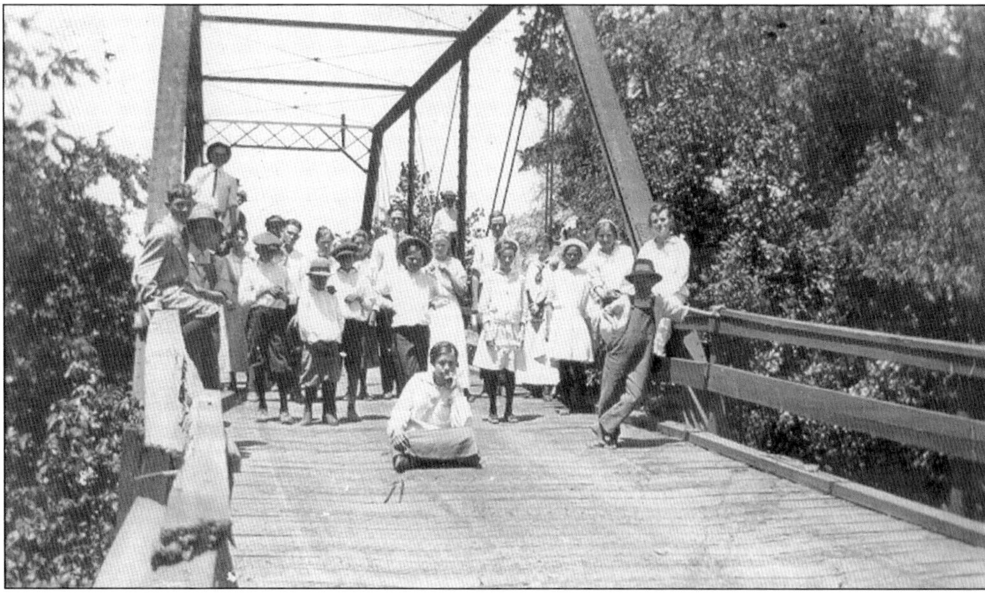

Marcella Stewart (Henderson) is seen sitting in front of some unidentified children socializing on a bridge on a Sunday afternoon. Another way for youngsters to spend their leisure time was to climb Pilot Knob and engrave their initials in the rocks. During the week, children had to do after-school farm chores until suppertime, making these Sunday afternoons very special times. (Courtesy of Martha Len Nelson.)

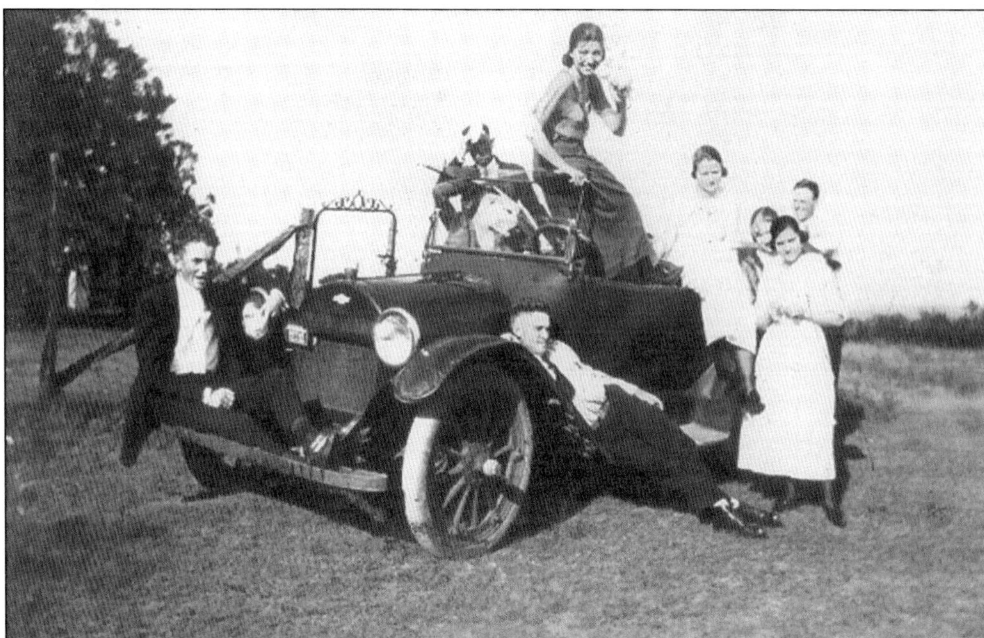

The young people identified in this August 22, 1920, photograph are Billy Cook (sitting on the front bumper), Ray Crawford (sitting on the running board leaning against the fender), and Lalla Crawford, (the dark-haired girl standing beside the back fender). The image is of a Sunday afternoon gathering of friends and classmates enjoying each other's company. (Courtesy of Martha Len Nelson.)

James "Jim" Pennington Heath was in the Texas A&M College Corps of Cadets during his college years until he graduated in 1949. Then he became a military officer in the US Army. In 1953, he received his appointment as rural letter carrier for the Argyle Post Office. He carried mail for 31 years, driving over 1 million miles without an accident. (Courtesy of Jim Heath.)

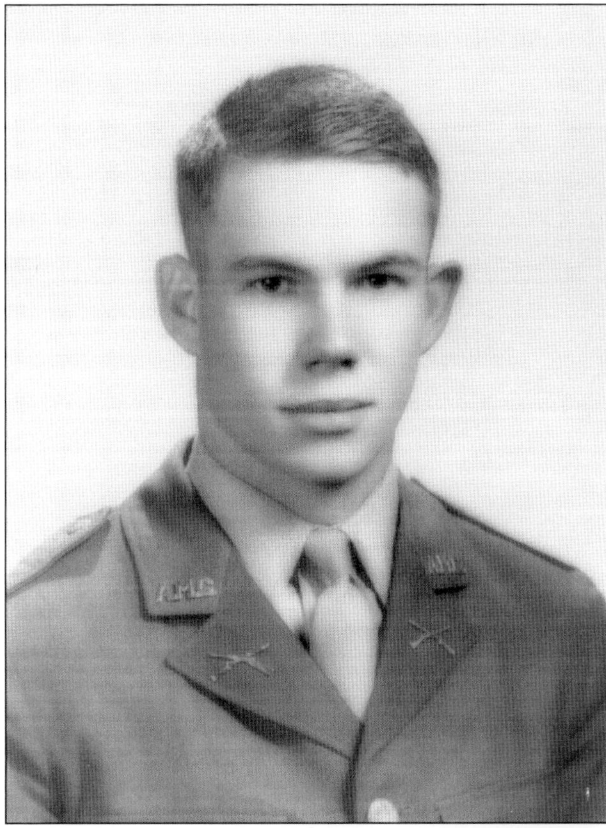

In 1882, John C. Heath migrated to the Argyle area from east Texas and bought 640 acres along what is now F.M. 407. He was a farmer and a cattleman. Pictured are John C. Heath and his family. From left to right are Penn Heath, Lark Heath, John C. Heath (Jim Heath's father, uncle, and grandfather), Dora Heath, Annie Heath, and Emma Donald Heath (Jim Heath's two aunts and his grandmother). (Courtesy of Jim Heath.)

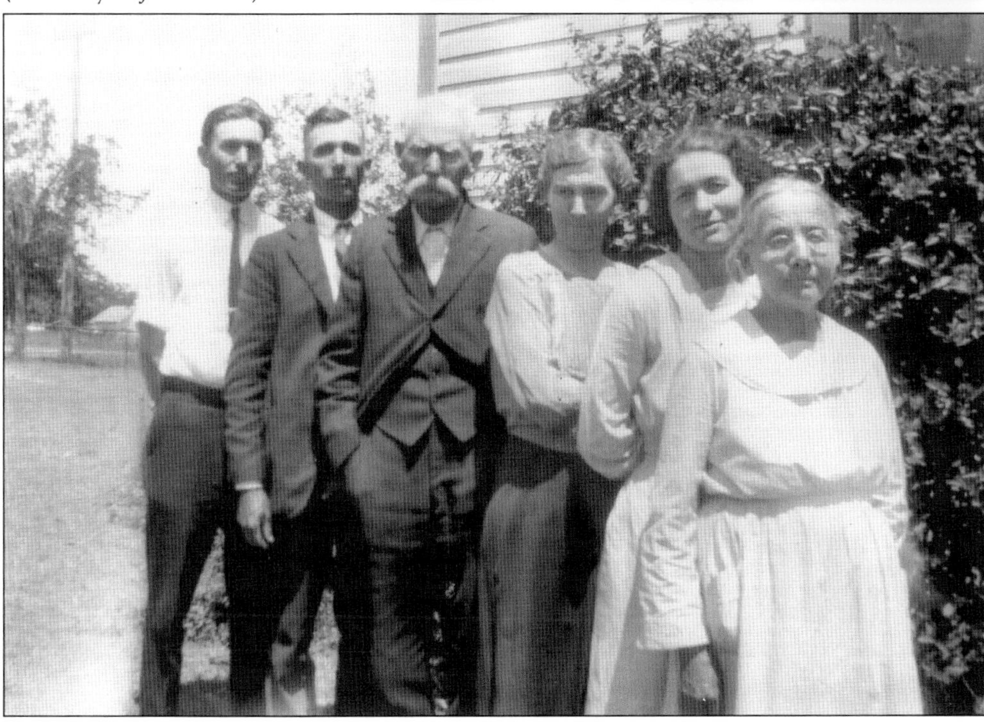

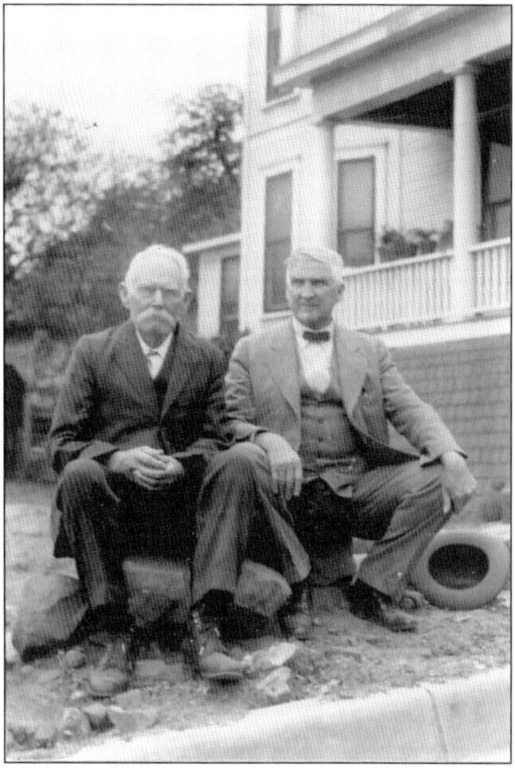

This is a photograph of John C. Heath and Dr. W.H. Pennington. Pennington was the first physician in Justin, Texas, and he organized the Justin State Bank. He was the practicing physician that delivered John Pennington "Penn" Heath, who was named for him. More recent generations of the Heath family have also been named for Doctor Pennington. (Courtesy of Jim Heath.)

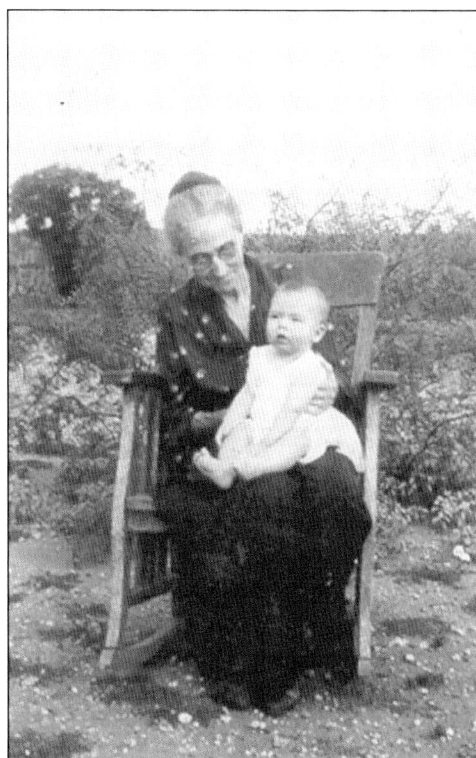

This photograph was taken in 1927 of Cora McMakin holding her grandson Jim Heath. Heath was born on November 22, 1926, on the Heath farm in Argyle. He attended the Argyle School until he was in the eighth grade and then he went to Denton Junior High School. He graduated from Denton High School. (Courtesy of Jim Heath)

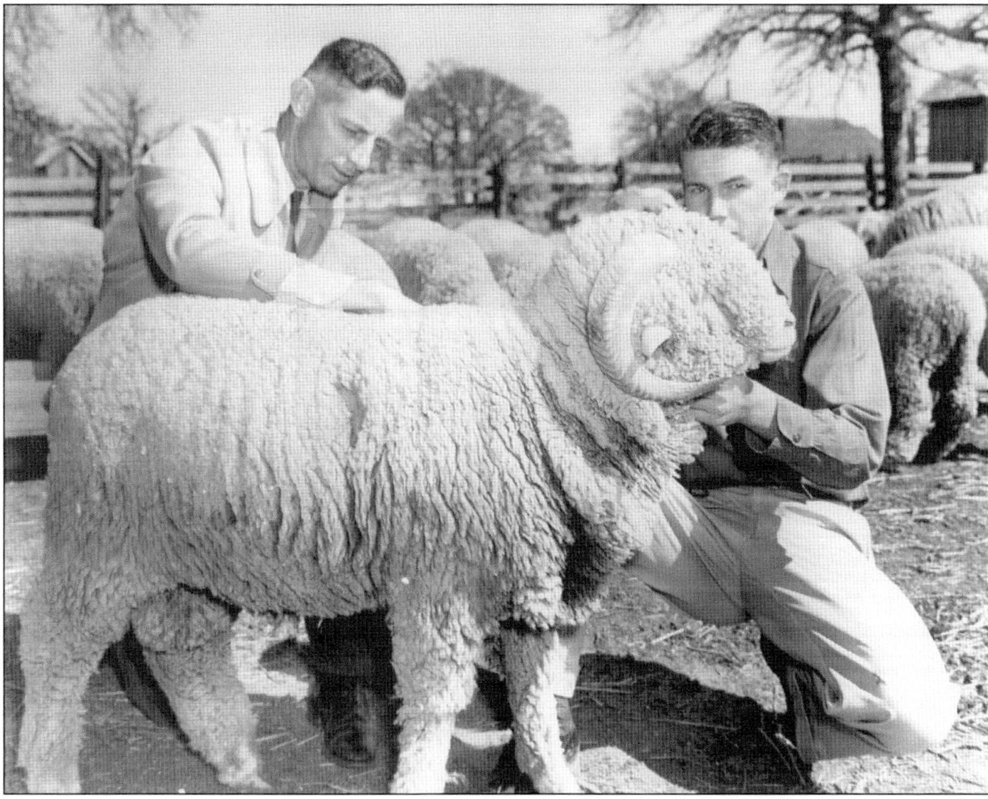

In 1943, Jim Heath was the first to be awarded the Future Farmers of America Lone Star Farmer Degree. He is seen here with his sheep and H.D. Roberts, Denton High School's agricultural teacher. Jim attended Texas A&M College (now University) in 1944 and graduated in January 1949. (Courtesy of Jim Heath.)

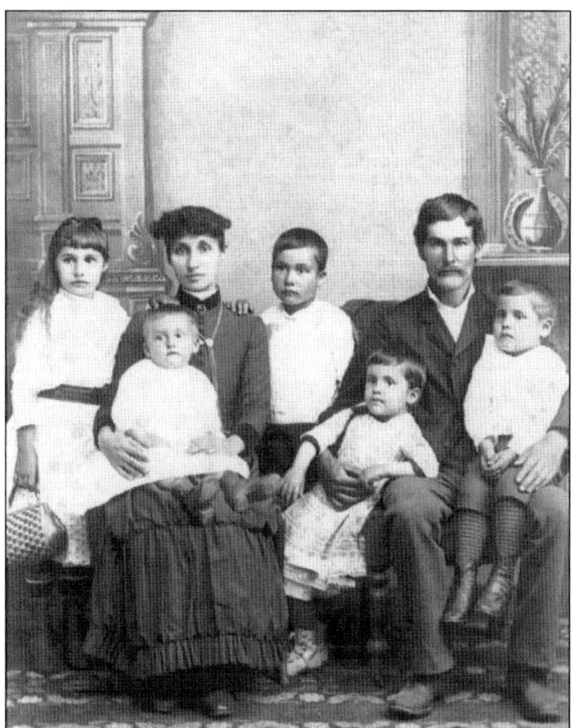

This 1887 photograph is of the first five children of the Alva Byron and Charlotte Johns Horton family. Pictured from left to right are Anna Mary Horton (Cogdell), Rufus Landon Horton, Charlotte Johns Horton, Richmond Harding Horton, Dollie Horton (Thompson), Alva Byron Horton, and Thomas Jefferson Horton. Charlotte Johns Horton was the sister of Sarah Delphia Johns Lynch, who married James Lynch and was the grandmother of Argyle's longtime resident Wallace Lynch. (Courtesy of Thom Horton.)

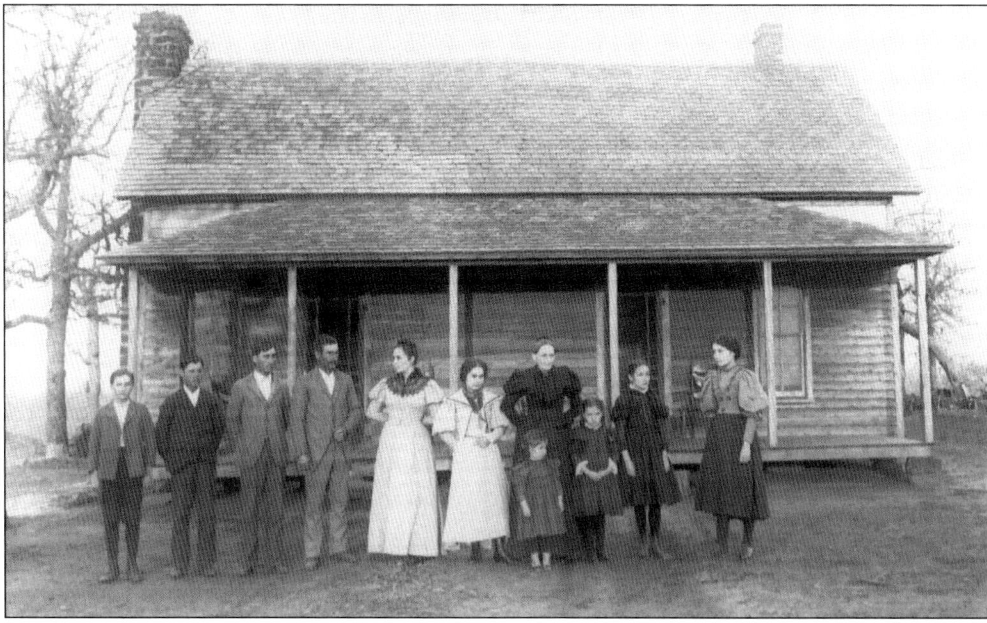

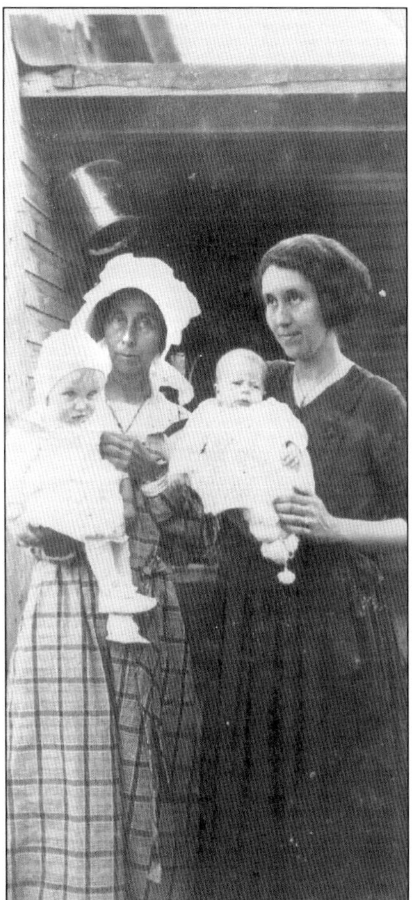

This is a photograph of the Alva Byron and Charlotte Johns Horton family in 1900. Pictured from left to right are Rufus Landon Horton, Thomas Jefferson Horton, Richmond Harding Horton, Alva Byron Horton, Charlotte Johns Horton, Dollie Horton (Thompson), Minnie Chloe Horton (Cauthen), Vonnie Horton (McMakin), Lillie Mae Horton (Young), Anna Mary Horton (Cogdell), and standing at the back is Charlotta Stephenson Johns, mother of Charlotte Johns Horton and wife of Harden William Johns, the owner of Johns' Well. He bought the historical site located on Old Justin Road April 7, 1875, for $2,500. The 10 acres became known as "the Campgrounds" in 1884 when J.A. Mayes sold the land for $60 to the trustees of the Prairie Mound Campgrounds of the Methodist Episcopal Church, South. Families traveled in wagons to the two-week nondenominational summer campground meetings to sing and share the gospel. In 1986, Dr. Eugene and Wanda Wright, the current owners, purchased the Texas Historical Commission marker and consented to have the location dedicated as a historic site. (Courtesy of Thom Horton.)

Wallace Lynch and his nephew Perry Wood were born five months apart. This is a picture of Sally Lynch holding Wallace, the older of the two boys, with her daughter Clela Lynch Wood holding her son Perry. The two boys grew up together and were in the same class at school. (Courtesy of Wallace Lynch.)

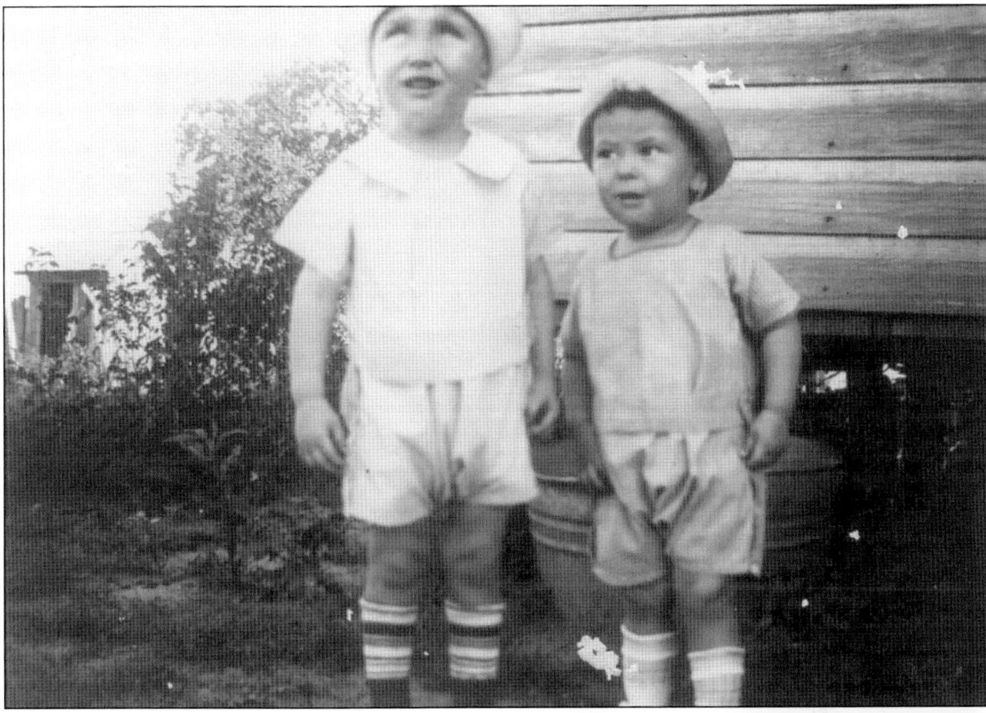

Pictured are Wallace Lynch and Perry Wood when they were young children. Lynch would later help establish the Argyle Water Supply Corporation and retired as vice president of First State Bank in Denton, Texas, after working there for almost 45 years. Wood joined the US Army Air Corps during World War II and then worked for the US Weather Bureau. (Courtesy of Wallace Lynch.)

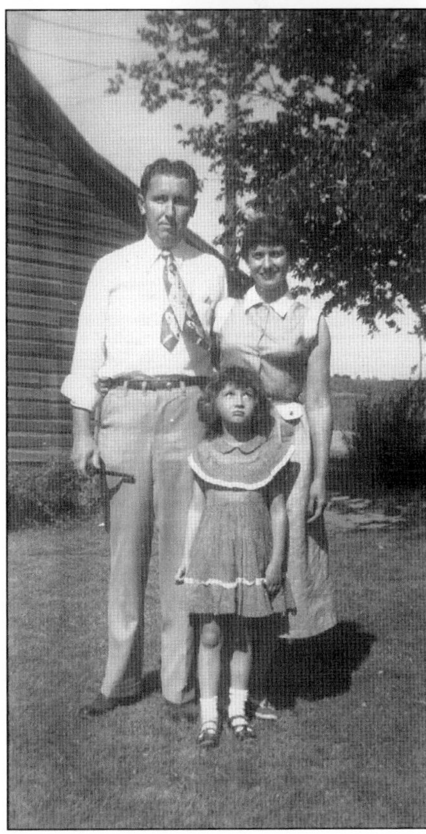

Wallace, Myrtle Lee, and Karyl Lynch are pictured standing beside their home on West Front Street. In 1945, Wallace bought the house from Tom Wingo, a foreman for the Texas and Pacific Railway. At the time, Wallace purchased it, Wingo told him there was a log cabin in the house. He said the one-room log cabin, concealed by sheetrock, was the old Denton County Courthouse moved to Argyle from Alton, Texas. According to the *History of Denton County* by Ed. F. Bates, the old log cabin Denton County Courthouse at Alton burned down. After the sheetrock was recently removed, Karyl said, "We knew a log cabin was in the house because we could see the logs in the closet, and whenever a storm blew in, mother would say, 'Let's go to the log room.'" Her mother, Myrtle Lee, served on the Argyle City Council in 1977 when Argyle's first zoning ordinance, 7-7-77, was passed. (Courtesy of Wallace Lynch.)

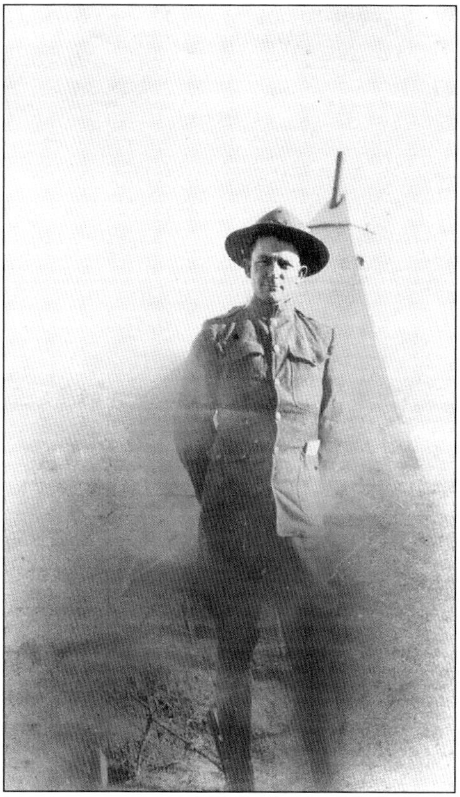

Cpl. Perry Clifton Wood, father of Perry A. and Greta Dean Wood (Garrett), is seen in his World War I US Army uniform. Those in the Argyle area to serve their country during World War I were Allen Arthur, Clifford A. Baker, Ray N. Baker, Roy H. Baker, Edgar W. Ballentin, John C. Bays, Joe Brown, Virgil Brown, Jim C. Cogsdell, Ray Crawford, Newt Fincher, William E. Gibbons, Emory M. Hacker, W. R. Harpole, Richard McMakin, James G. Marsh, Ovie C. Meadows, Olin W. Middleton, Caldwell Price, John Stewart, Walter Thompson, Frank Whitten, Hubert B. Whitten, Luther Wood, and Perry Wood. Below is a picture of Perry Wood with another cook in their US Army World War I cook outfits. (Both courtesy of Greta Garrett.)

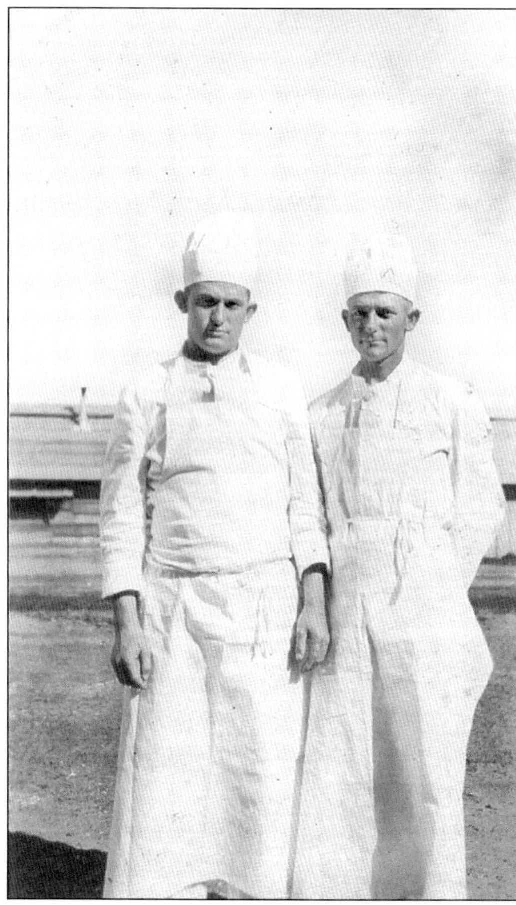

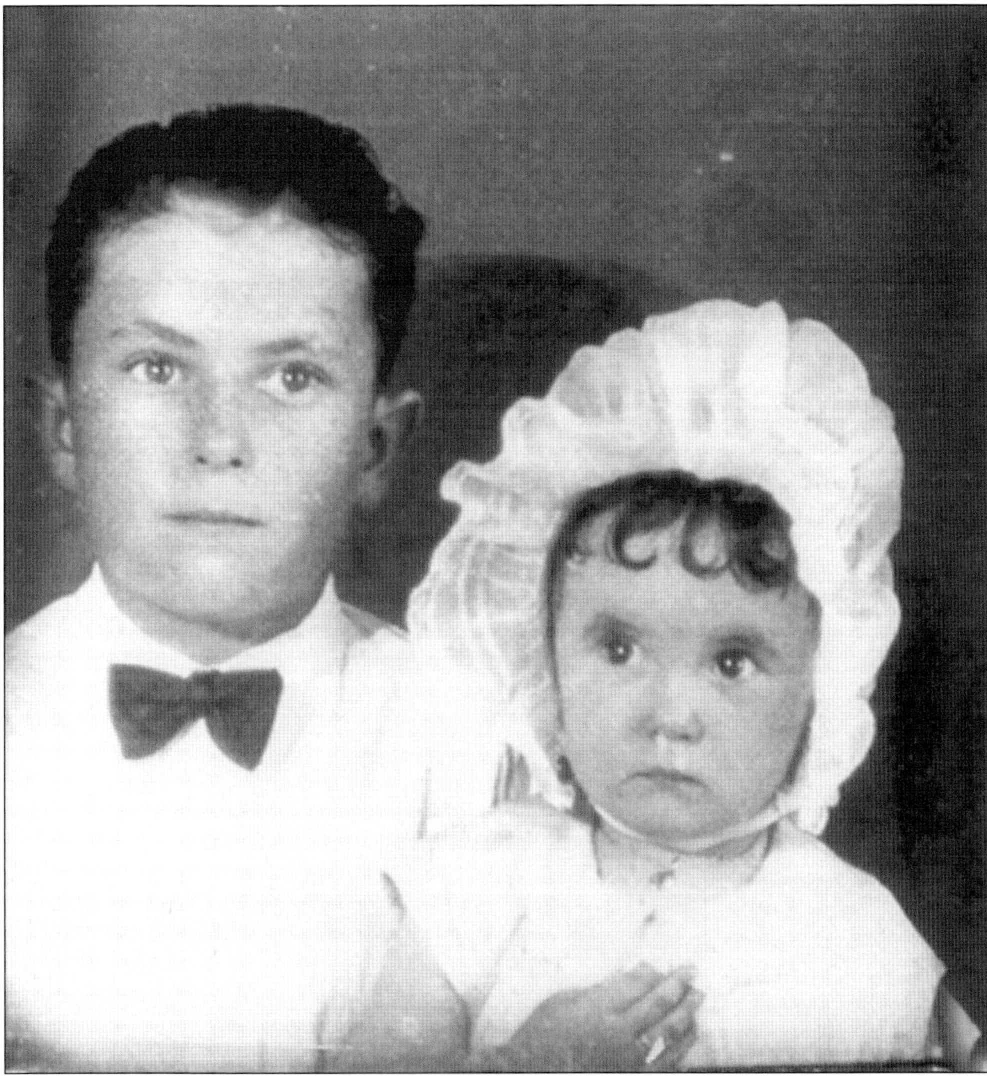

This is a photograph of Perry A. Wood with his sister, Greta Wood (Garrett) when they were children. In 1942, Perry Wood joined the US Army Air Corps and served in World War II along with others from the Argyle area including L.C. Bays Jr., Eugene G. Boyles, Geraldine Crawford, C.A. Cunningham, Roy V. Cunningham, Roy F. Cunningham, Frances Ruth Davis, John Ben Davis, Jack Davis, Frank Davis, Lee Roy Erwin, Grady L. Erwin, H.W. Erwin Jr., Jack Faught, James Faught, Travis B. Faught, Edwin L. Faught, Newton Crawford Fincher, Joe E. Fincher, Herman N. Fincher, Ralph Frasher, Winford F. Grimes, Delbert M. Hacker, Carroll M. Harper, C.B. Harper, Olin T. Hawk, Taylor B. Hawk, Charles M. Hawk, Samuel Lemon Haynes, Felbert Hudson, Miles F. Hurley, Elmer Lee Jennings, J.J. Jennings, Richard C. Jones, Emmett Jones, S. Roy Jones, Otis L. King, Walter R. Madewell, Paul Mata, Ascension Mata, Joe H. McDonald, and Harvey A. McMakin. The list is continued on the next page. (Courtesy of Greta Garrett.)

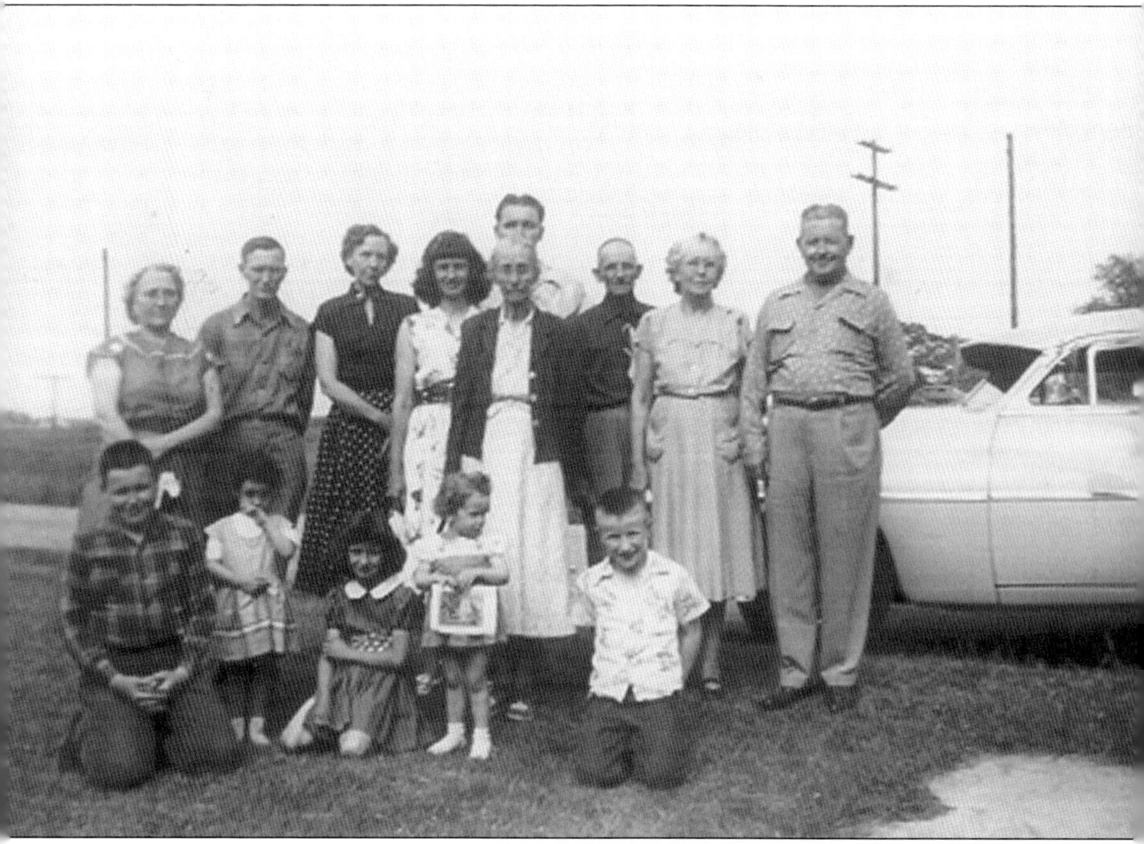

No military man or woman from the Argyle area lost his or her life in World War II. The list of those who served in the war is continued from the previous page: Morris C. Meadows, Joseph W. Payne, James Harvey Payne, Woodrow V. Pippin, Cecil E. Pippin, Cecil E. Pitt, Jessie Earl Smith, Melvin B. Smith, Vera W. Smith, Herman L. Smith, Carl Spencer, Eugene Spencer, Glenn Ray Stephenson, W.M. "Clyde" Stubblefield, Sam Stubblefield (POW), Walter H. Thompson, Perry Addison Wood, James M. Wood, Arthur C. Wynn, and Weldon W. Wynn. Above is a photograph of the Lynch and Wood families. Most of those in the picture were born, raised, and continued to live in Argyle. In the front row, from left to right, are J.L. Lynch, Clela Potts, Karyl Lynch, Marilyn Potts, and Johnny Lynch. Standing, from left to right, are Naomi Lynch, Leo Lynch, Thelma Lynch, Myrtle Lee Lynch, Wallace Lynch, Lee Lynch, Perry Wood, Clela Wood, and Herbert "Sid" Lynch. (Courtesy of Greta Garrett.)

This is a photograph of Bascomb William Meadows sitting in front of Meadows Store. Meadows was born in Selma, Alabama, on June 14, 1874. He came to Texas in 1891 to work on a farm and married Emma Allen Scott October 23, 1896. They had four children: Ovie Calloway, Lillian, William T., and Georgia Belle. On June 26, 1919, he was appointed Argyle postmaster. (Courtesy of Jackie Carpenter.)

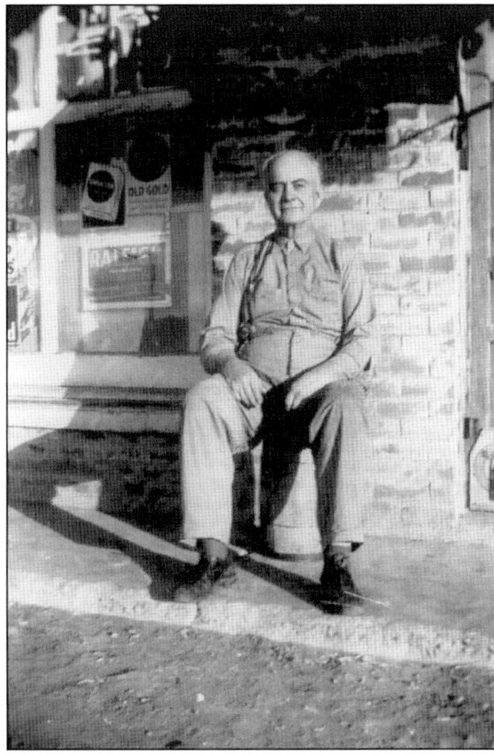

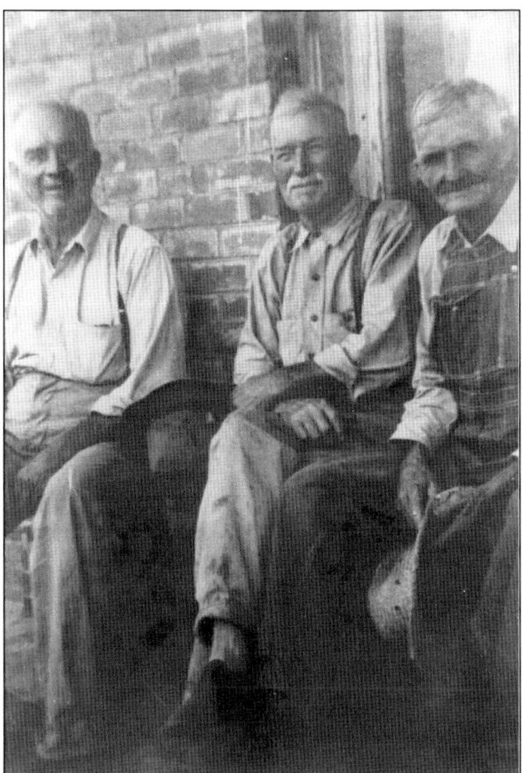

The two men at the left are B.W. Meadows (Yvonne A. Jenkins's grandfather, far left) and James Reed (Bill Carpenter's grandfather, center). When Larry Earl Smith was a boy living in Argyle on Denton Street, he met with his friends at Meadows Garage, and remembers seeing Reed walking from his home on Frenchtown Road to Meadows Store to sit on a bench and visit with friends. (Courtesy of Jackie Carpenter.)

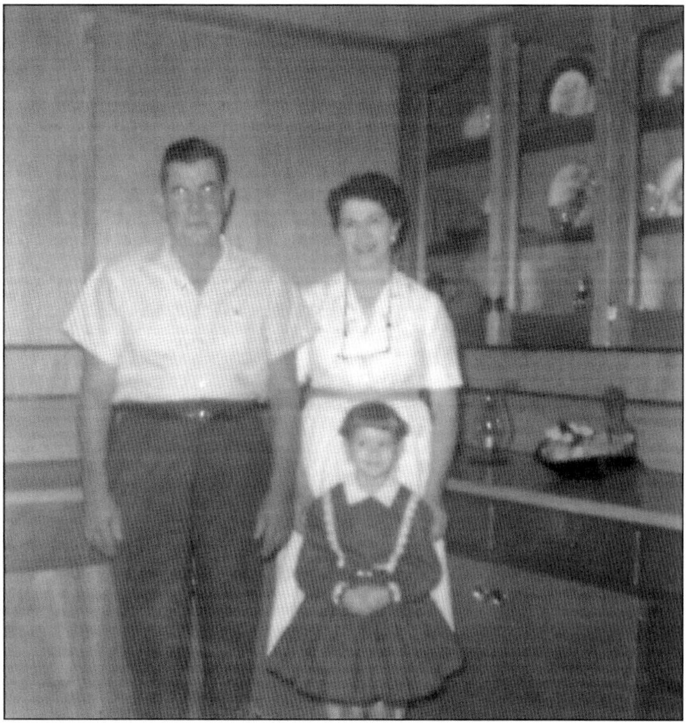

Kay Jenkins (Teer), Yvonne Allen Jenkins's daughter, is pictured with her grandparents Red Allen and Georgia Belle Meadows Allen on her birthday. In 1945, Georgia was appointed clerk and assistant postmaster. B.W. Meadows retired as postmaster on June 1, 1944, and his daughter Lillian Meadows Thompson became postmaster until she retired in 1968. (Courtesy of Kay Teer.)

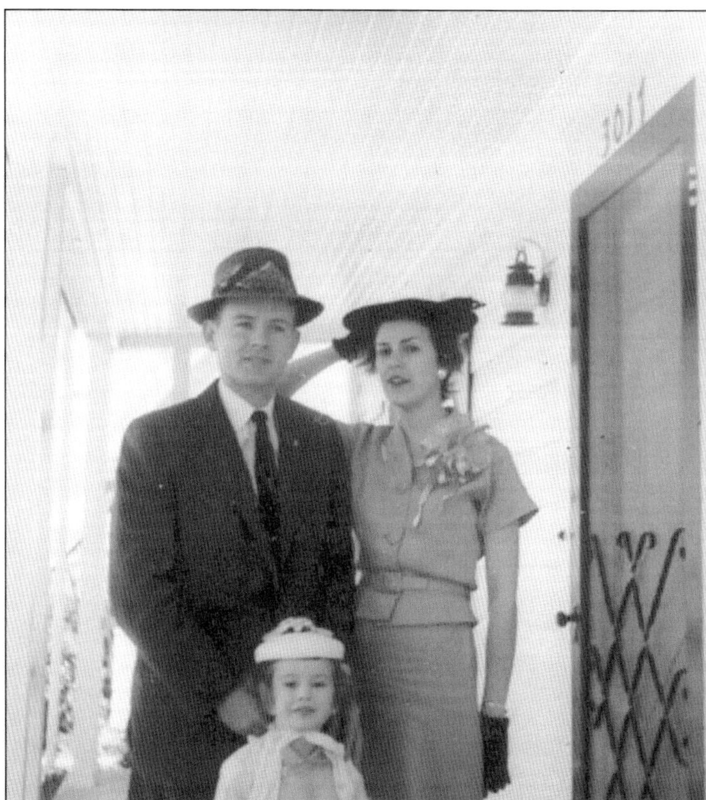

This 1958 Easter photograph is of Charles, Yvonne, and Kay Jenkins (Teer). Civic-minded Charles and Yvonne were actively involved in organizing the Argyle Volunteer Fire Department and forming the Argyle Water Supply Corporation where Charles served on the board of directors. Yvonne was elected mayor for a total of seven terms and Kay served on the Argyle City Council. (Courtesy of Kay Teer.)

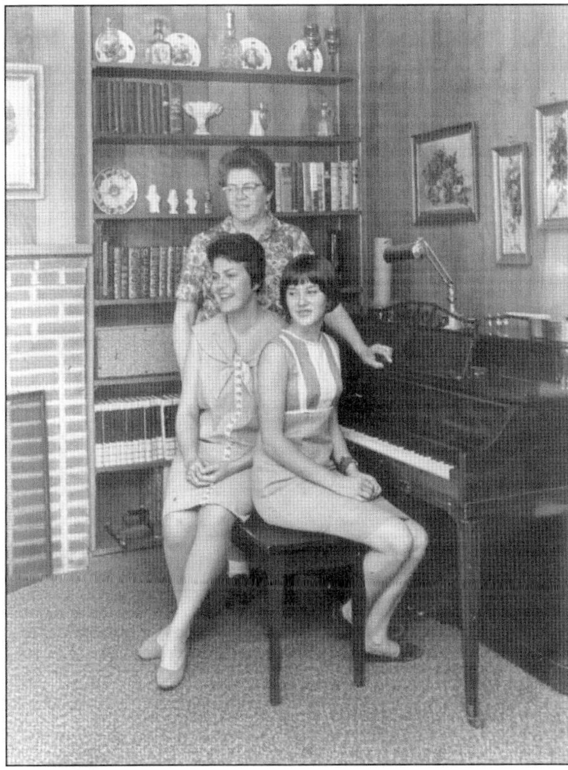

There are three generations in this 1968 photograph. Standing is Georgia Belle Meadows Allen and seated are Yvonne Allen Jenkins and Kay Jenkins (Teer). Jenkins was Argyle's mayor for two terms from 1981 until 1985, then she served five terms as mayor from 1991 until 2001. Under Mayor Jenkins's leadership, local citizens actively participated in civic projects and were enthusiastically involved in yearly parades and celebrations. (Courtesy of Kay Teer.)

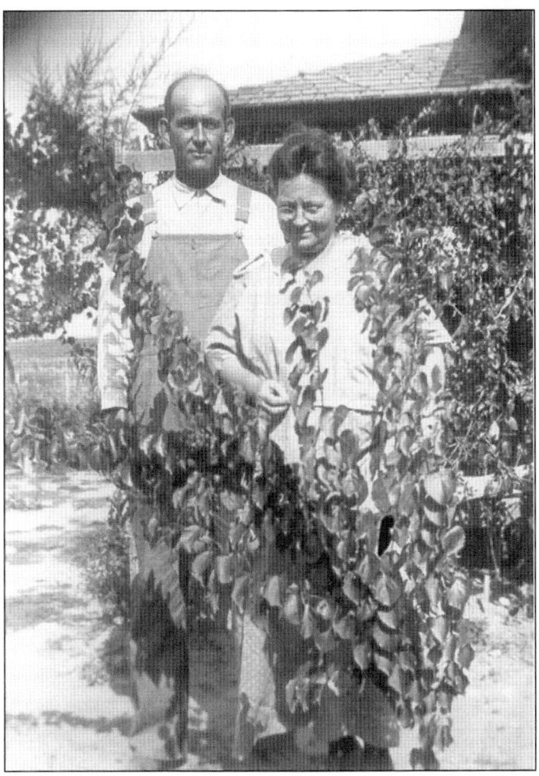

Seen here are William Walter Billingsley and Cynthia Davis Billingsley. W.W. Billingsley owned the Argyle Telephone Exchange until he sold it to Marion V. O'Kieff in 1933. Prior to General Telephone taking over the telephone service in the 1970s, independent telephone services were provided by different individuals. Before the modern practice of burying telephone cables, the telephone lines were strung along fence lines. (Courtesy of Mary Anne Carroll.)

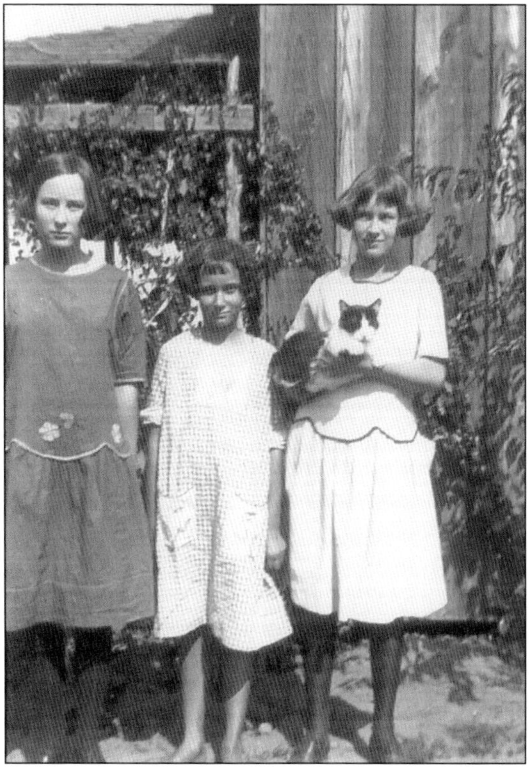

Pictured from left to right are Pearl Billingsley (White), Annie Billingsley (Boyles), and Mary George Billingsley (Sullivan). The girls' uncle Sam Davis was Argyle's first rural mail carrier. Since he and his wife, Trude Hayes Davis, did not have any children, Davis claimed the children on his mail route as his. The children fondly called him "Mr. Sam." Sam Davis Road is named for him. (Courtesy of Mary Anne Carroll.)

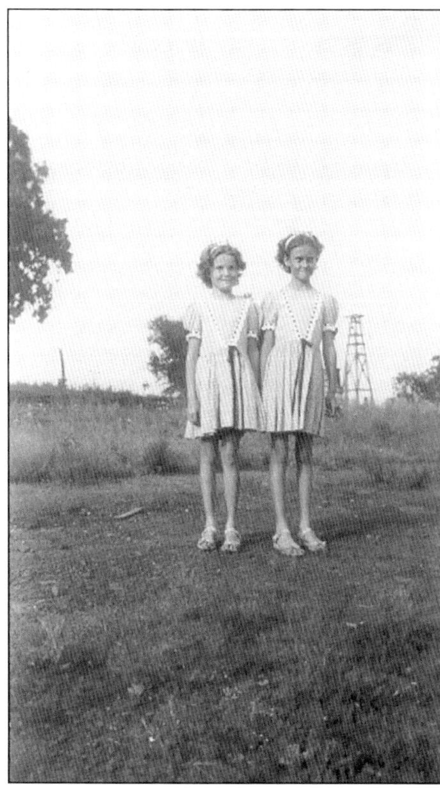

This is a photograph of Susie and Mary Anne Boyles (Carroll) taken in 1945 in the vicinity of the Argyle Baptist Church on Baptist Hill. The girls' mother, Annie Billingsley Boyles, was born and raised in Argyle, as was Mary Anne Carroll, who now lives next door to the house where she was born. (Courtesy of Mary Anne Carroll.)

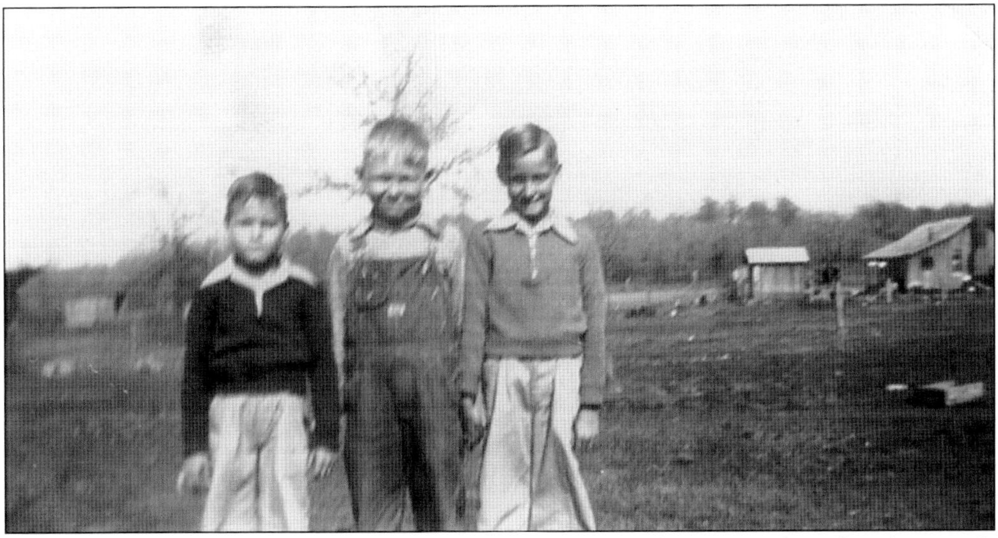

Pictured from left to right are Lewis Boyles, Johnny Smith, and Jimmy Boyles. This photograph was taken in the Boyles' side yard. The Smith-Choate house is visible at the far right. In the early 1980s and 1990s, Lewis was elected to the Argyle City Council. Jimmy Boyles was the mayor of Blue Mound, Texas, for a number of years. (Courtesy of Mary Anne Carroll.)

In this photograph, Pearl Boyles, the Boyles children's grandmother, is seen with her son Alton Boyles and her great-grandson Sam Carroll. Alton grew up in Argyle and married Annie Billingsley Boyles. He was the father of five children. His wife was the sister of Mary George Billingsley Sullivan, who lived by herself in Argyle until her death in 2011 at 102 years of age. (Courtesy of Mary Ann Carroll.)

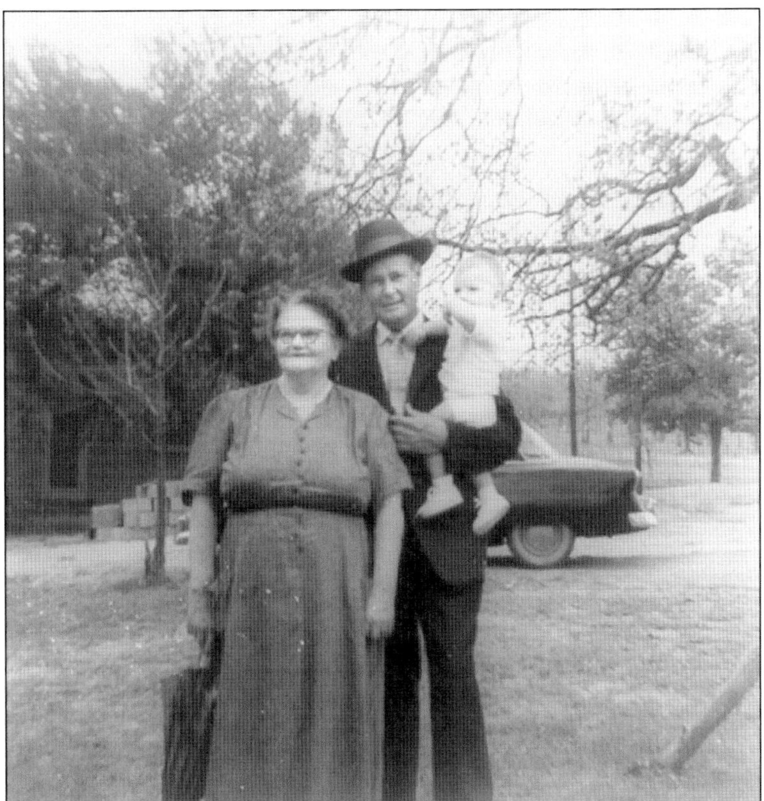

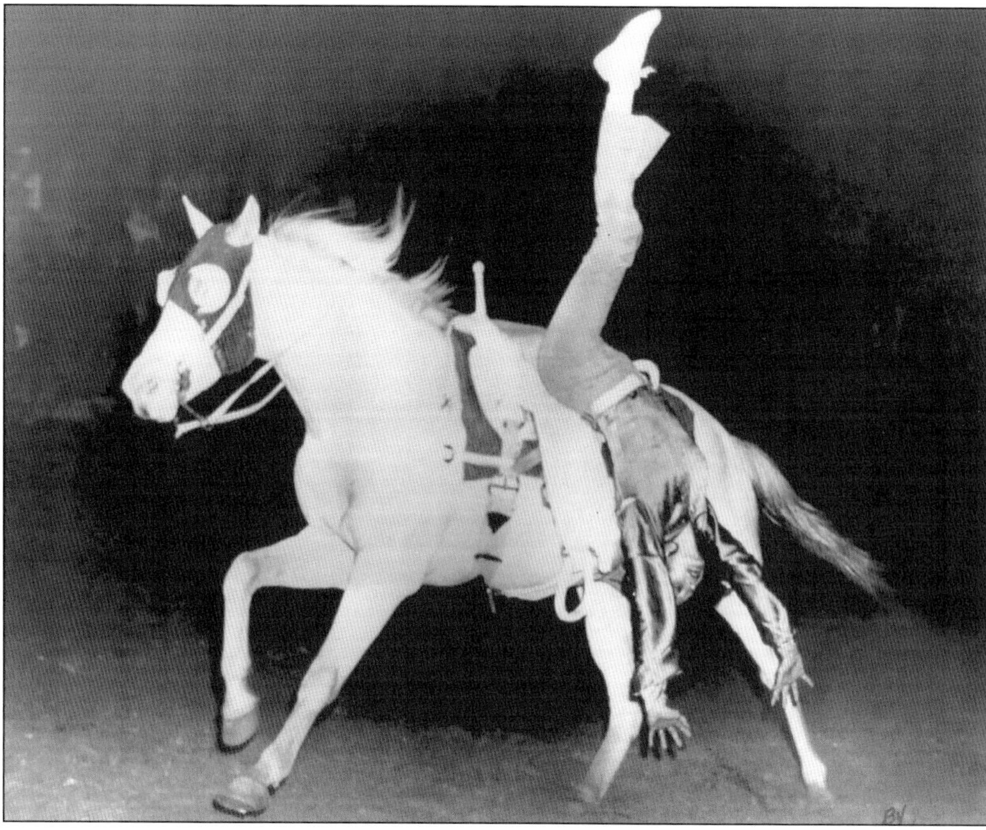

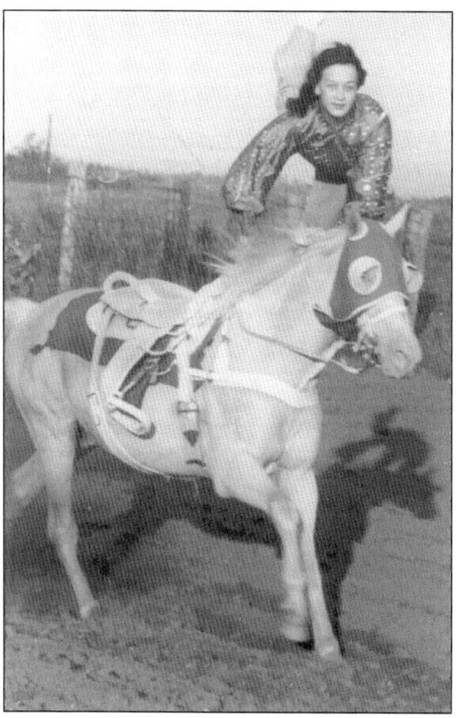

All the members of the L.F. Moon family participated in rodeos. L.F. did bull riding and saddle-bronc riding, Maureen Moon was a rodeo trick rider and did barrel racing. Their daughters Mary Ann and Lisa also did barrel racing. Maureen is pictured performing the "Russian Death Drag" at the Huntsville Texas Prison Rodeo. (Courtesy of Mary Ann DeBerry.)

Maureen Moon, sometimes referred to as "the ballerina on horseback," is seen doing the "one foot stand" on Little Joe, her all-white horse. Being a trick rider is a dangerous profession. The rider needs to have a keen understanding of horses and the poise of a dancer. During the 1950s and 1960s, Maureen Moon was on the rodeo circuit in Texas, Arkansas, Louisiana, and Oklahoma. (Courtesy of Mary Ann DeBerry.)

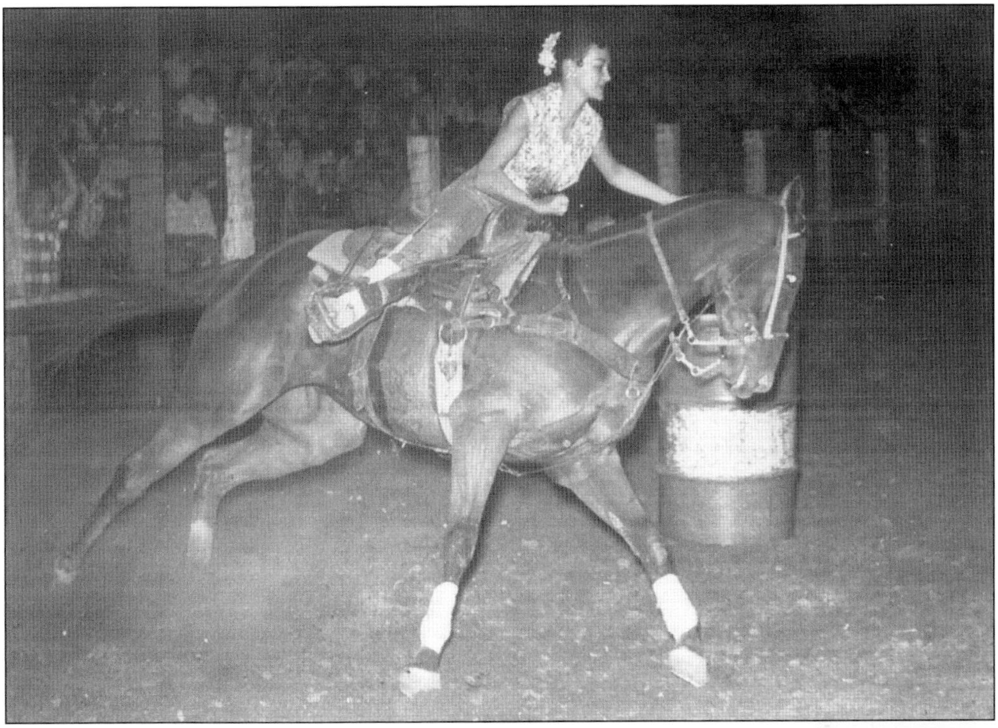

Maureen Moon took first place in barrel racing in Keller, Texas, on August 11, 1956. This was the first time her horse Red won. With the horse galloping at 25 to 35 miles per hour, the rider, such as Moon and her daughters, needed to have a lot of agility and a keen understanding of horses. (Courtesy of Mary Ann DeBerry.)

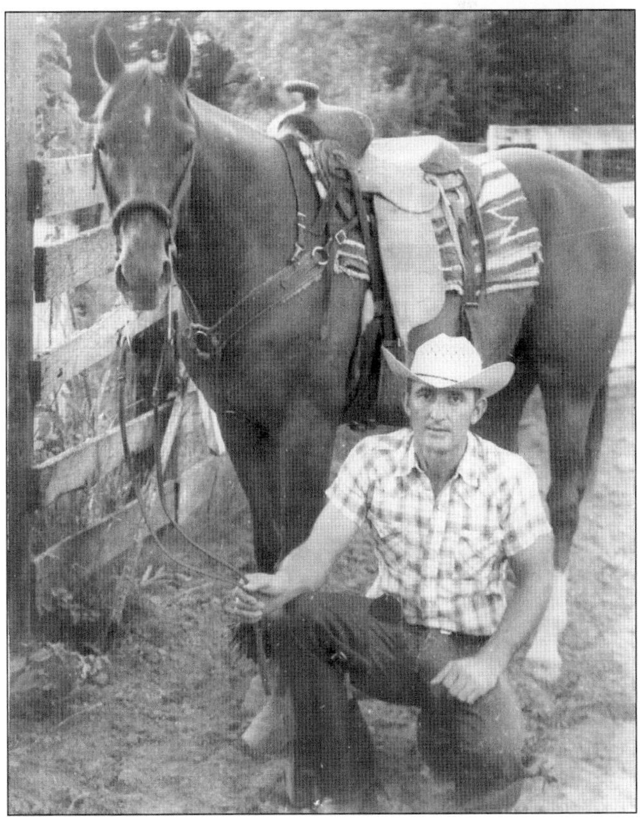

L.F. Moon is seen with Red at a bronc-riding practice in 1958. Moon owned a septic tank company in Argyle and was also a rodeo cowboy riding saddle bronc horses and bulls, and he was the best at breaking horses for riding. (Courtesy of Mary Ann DeBerry.)

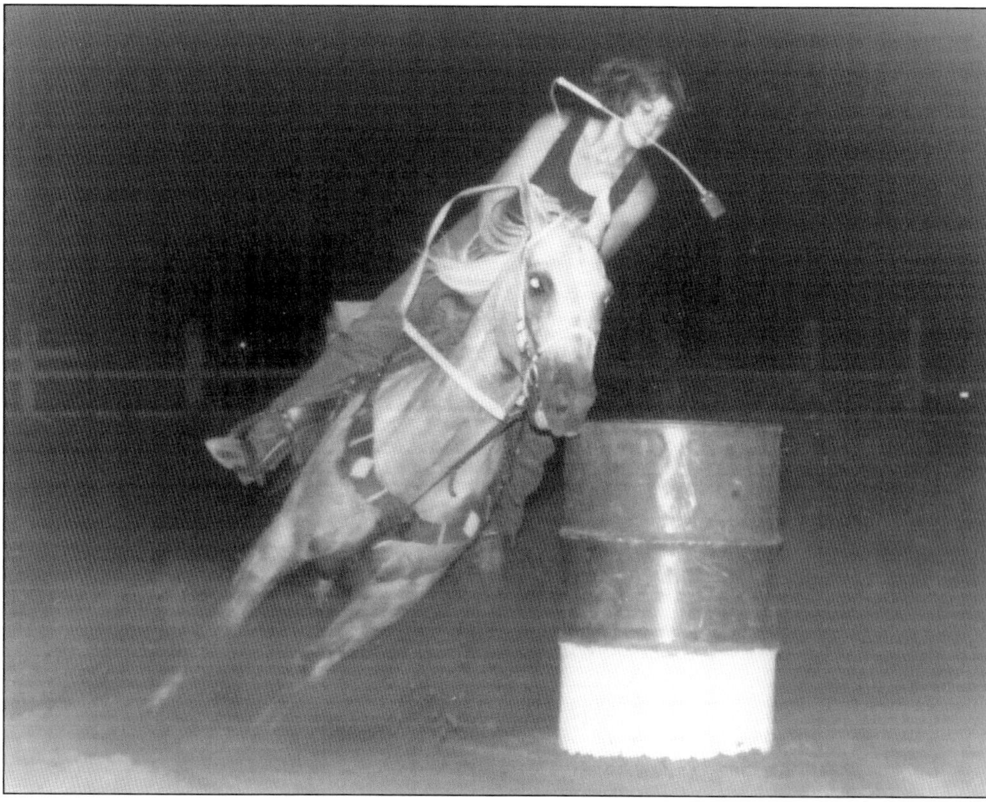

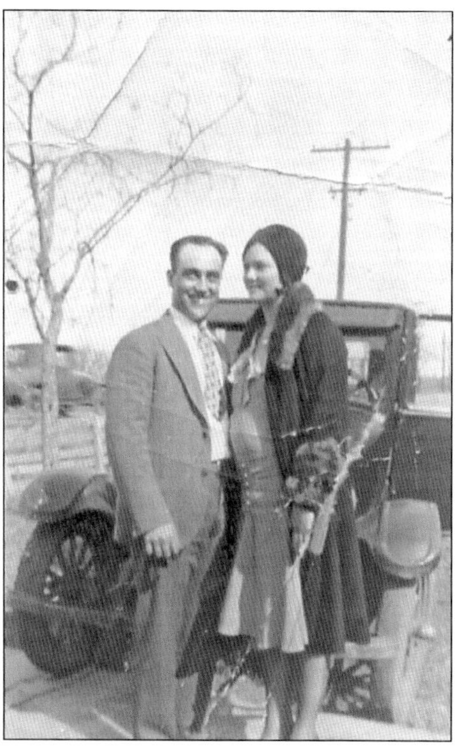

On August 23, 1985, Mary Ann Moon (DeBerry) won first place in the Steer Undecorating Event at the North Texas Fair Rodeo in Denton, Texas. Twenty-three female contestants removed a red ribbon fastened to the steer's back. Moon's winning time was 1.80 seconds. She was North Texas Rodeo Queen in 1975 and runner-up for the North Texas State Fair Queen in 1980. (Courtesy of Mary Ann DeBerry.)

William Presley Carpenter was born in Justin, Texas, on May 2, 1904. His wife, Oleta Gladys Reed Carpenter, was born on November 7, 1904, in Argyle. Bill Carpenter's profession was a carpenter and he built homes and barns. The couple married on September 16, 1933, making their home on West Front until they bought the railroad section foreman's house on US Highway 377. (Courtesy of Jackie Carpenter.)

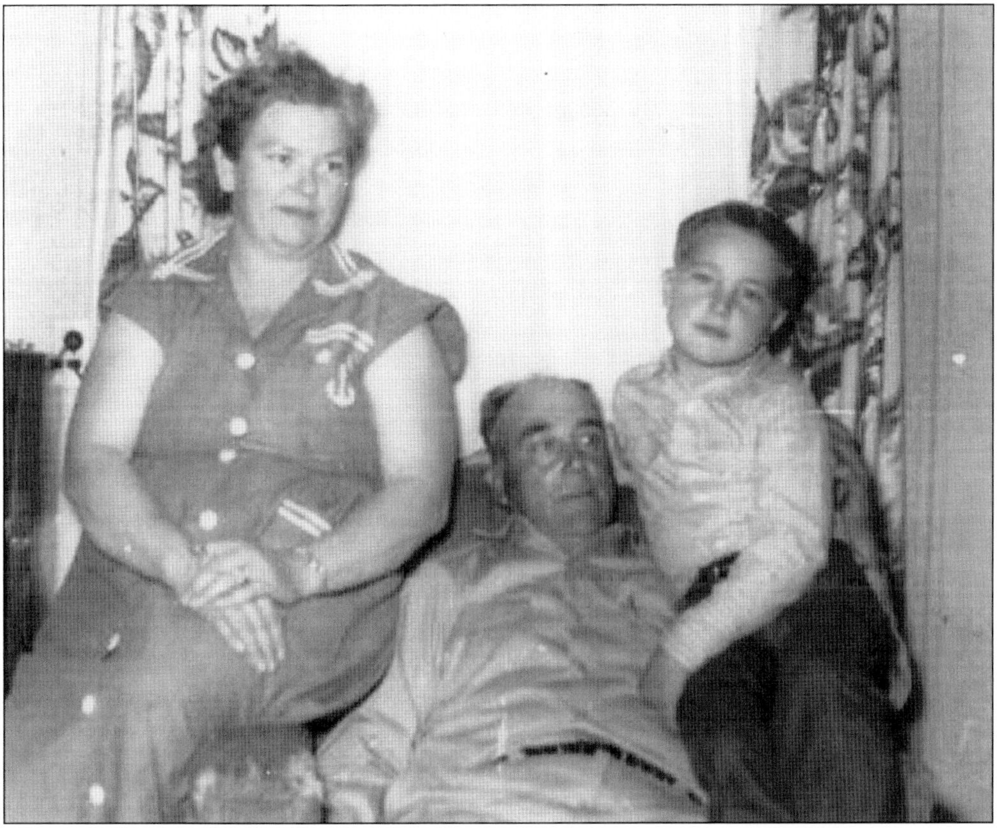

William "Bill" Presley Carpenter Jr. was born on June 29, 1946. He is seen here with his parents, Oleta and Bill Carpenter Sr. Bill grew up in Argyle, attending the Argyle School and graduating from Denton High School. He worked for Moore Business Forms as a pressman and ran their presses for 20 years. Then he went to work for Tetra Pak, where he retired from management. (Courtesy of Jackie Carpenter.)

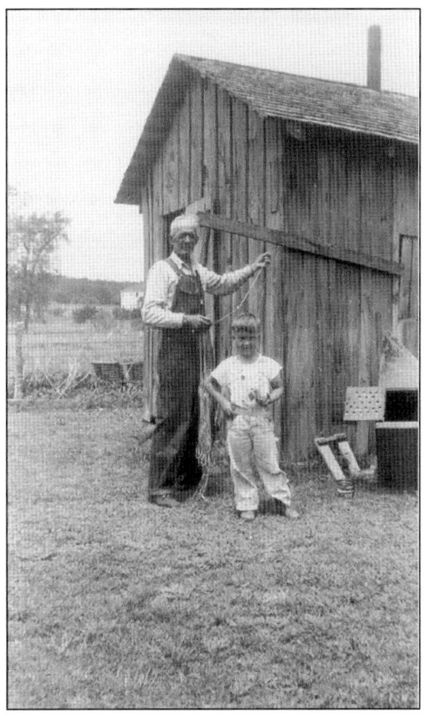

Bill Carpenter was five years old when this photograph was taken of him with Sam Foster. Sam was a neighbor of the Carpenters, also living on West Front Street, and young Bill often visited him. Cora Agnes Wood Foster, Sam's wife, was a cook in the lunchroom at the Argyle School. (Courtesy of Jackie Carpenter.)

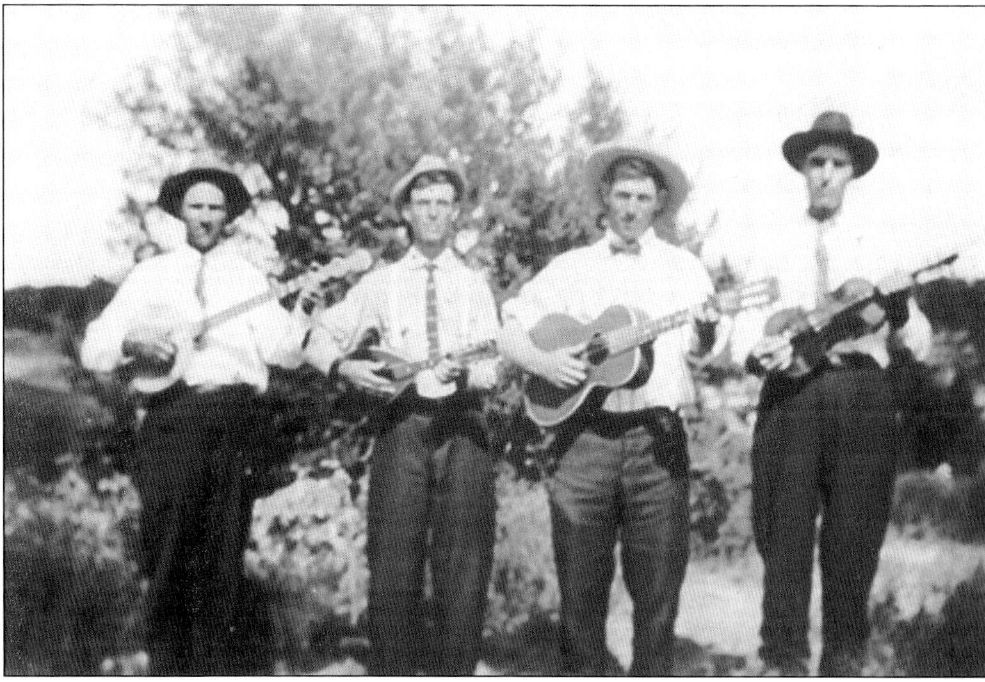

Bill Carpenter's grandmother Alma Gertrude Erwin was born on October 16, 1886 in Denton, Texas, and was buried in the Graham-Argyle Cemetery in 1912. From left to right, her brothers Lee, Alvin, Ralph, and Luther Erwin are pictured in 1916 playing their musical instruments. (Courtesy of Jackie Carpenter.)

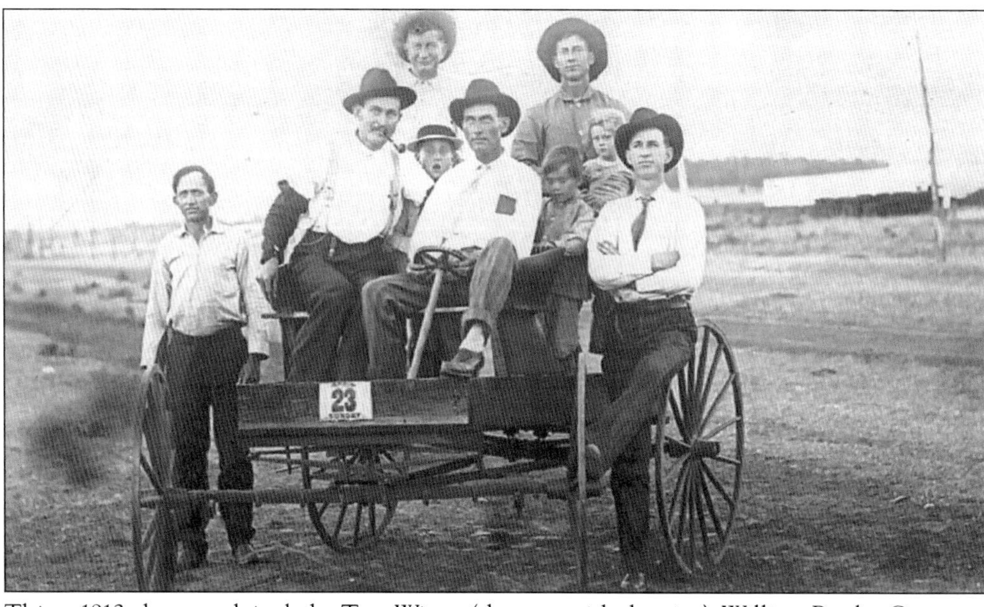

This c. 1912 photograph includes Tom Wingo (the man with the pipe), William Presley Carpenter (the boy wearing a hat), his brother Arthur Julius Carpenter (the other boy), and their sister Winifred Carpenter (the girl). The man behind the steering wheel is thought to be William Thomas Carpenter, the children's father. (Courtesy of Jackie Carpenter.)

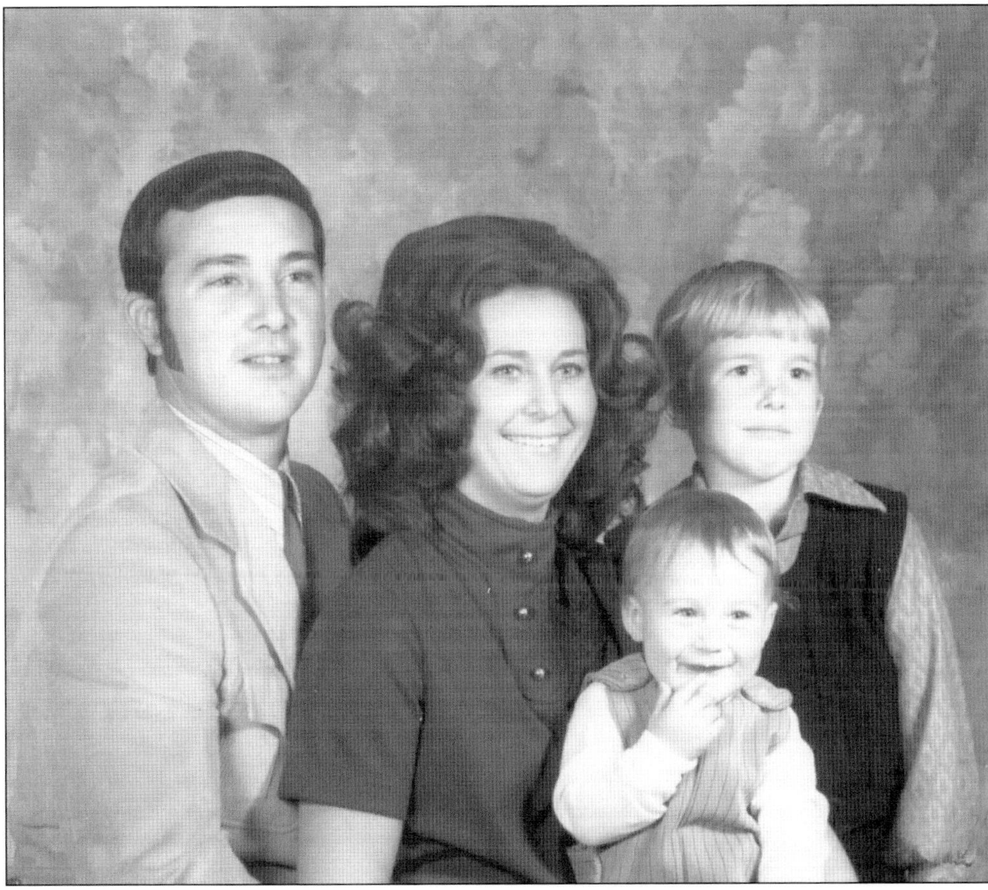

This is a photograph of William "Bill" Carpenter, Jackie Greener Carpenter, and their children Eric and Brent. Bill Carpenter served on the Argyle Centennial Committee and the Argyle City Council. Both he and his wife are officers on the Graham-Argyle Cemetery Committee. The Carpenters are well known for their cooking skills and willingness to help with community activities. (Courtesy of Jackie Carpenter.)

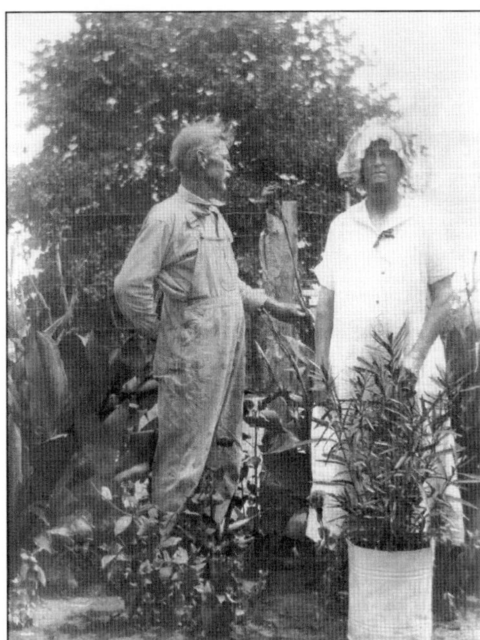

Bill Carpenter's grandparents were James Daniel Reed (born on July 1, 1870, and died on March 2, 1968) and Minnie Myrtle Frazier Reed (born on March 30, 1876, and died on June 2, 1942). Both are buried at Prairie Mound Cemetery. James Reed was a truck farmer. He grew and sold all kinds of produce, including watermelons, cantaloupes, peaches, and vegetables. (Courtesy of Jackie Carpenter.)

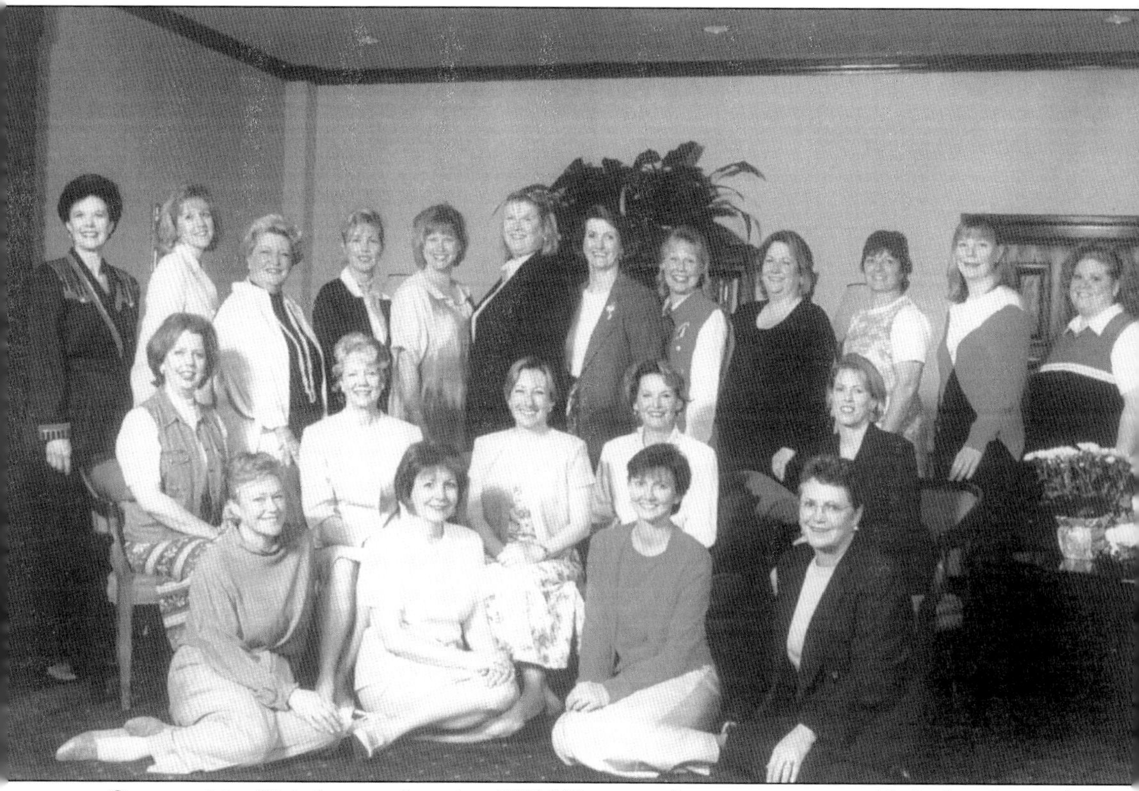

Communities Civic League, Inc., is a 501(c)(3) nonprofit organization established in September 1998 by Lynn Sheffield Simmons, Patti Smith, Sharon Draper, Emory Bishop (Brincks), and Vandi Brown, to raise funds for other nonprofit organizations in the Argyle area. In 2000, CCL, Inc., became the sponsors of the Argyle Angel Tree, buying clothes and Christmas presents for impoverished children. The following year, CCL, Inc., sponsored the "Back to School Program," buying school clothes for children in need. CCL, Inc., has benefited many children and local organizations. This is a photograph of its first-year membership taken in May 1999. Pictured from left to right are (first row) Mary Jean Donovan, Beverly Todd, unidentified, and Donna Kahney; (second row) cofounder and membership chairman Sharon Draper, founder and president Lynn Sheffield Simmons, cofounder and secretary Emory Bishop, Barbara Roberts, and Lynda Devine; (third row) Jody Bellinghausen, Barbara Gross, Kay T. Moore, cofounder and chairman of fundraising Vandi Brown), Judy Martin, Debbie Wuebbling, Ann Bixby, cofounder and treasurer Patti Smith, Sue Tipton, Alanna Summers, Carol Self, and unidentified. (Courtesy of Eagleton Photography.)

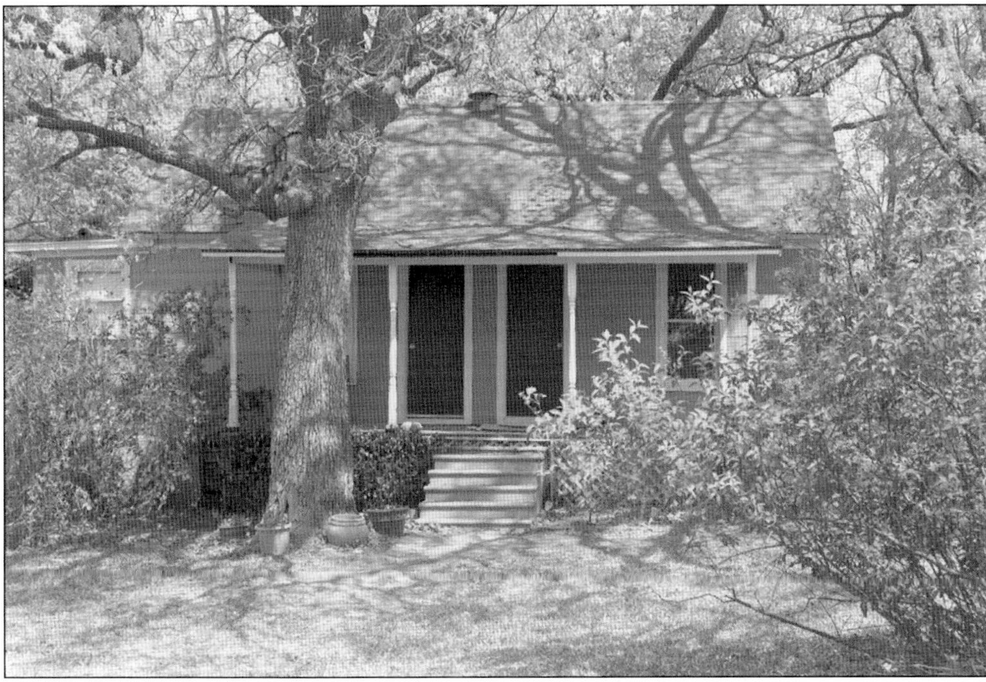

The newer Argyle houses have modern conveniences and are large brick or stone homes richly landscaped. The smaller, wood frame houses are older and less modern, but they have the distinction of being the homes of family members for many generations. This house is where Wallace Lynch was born. Today, his grandson Mayor Matthew Smith lives here. (Courtesy of Denise Remfert.)

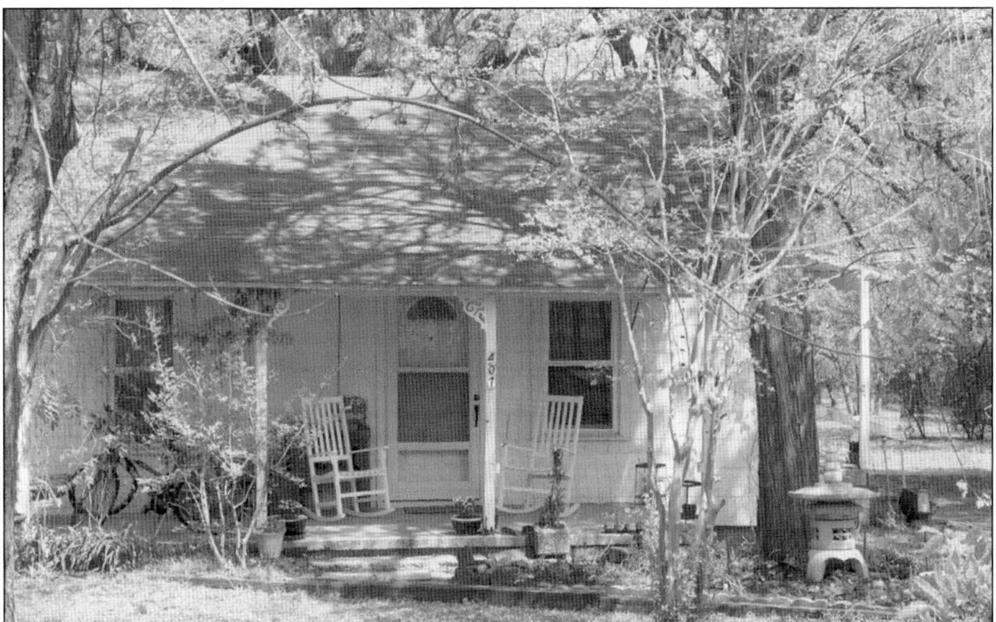

This quaint house takes one back to yesteryear. It is the house where Mary Anne Boyles Carroll and her four brothers and sisters were born. Today, her daughter Cindy Carroll Kelley lives in the house with her daughter Sarah Hill. (Courtesy of Denise Remfert.)

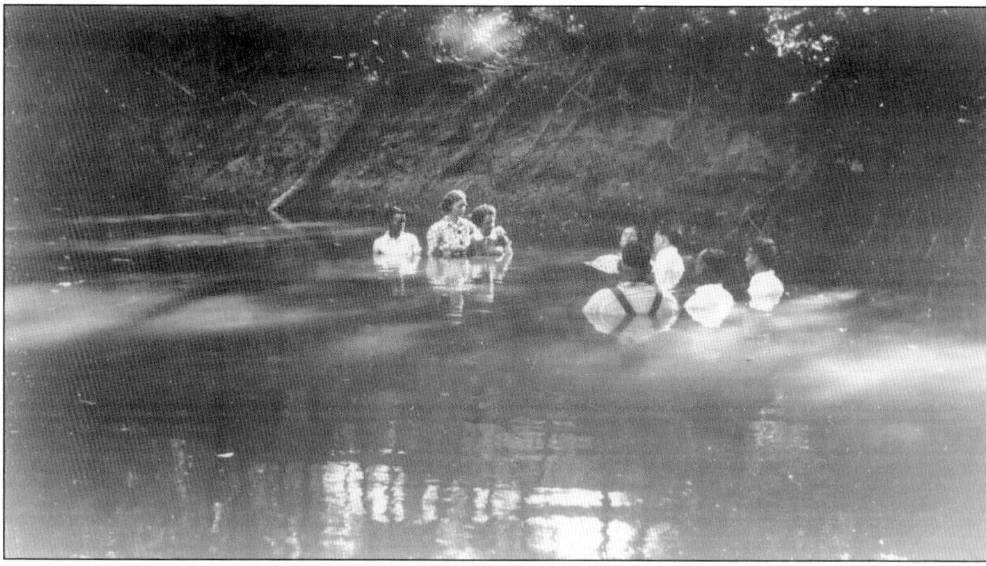

This photograph was taken in the 1930s of an Argyle Baptist Church baptism in Hickory Creek at Old Alton. "The old Baptist church on 'Baptist Hill' at Dallas and Mesquite Streets didn't have a baptistery, so we used creeks and ponds. I was baptized in the Webb family stock tank (pond) on Hickory Hill," said longtime Argyle resident Wallace Lynch. (Courtesy of Jackie Carpenter.)

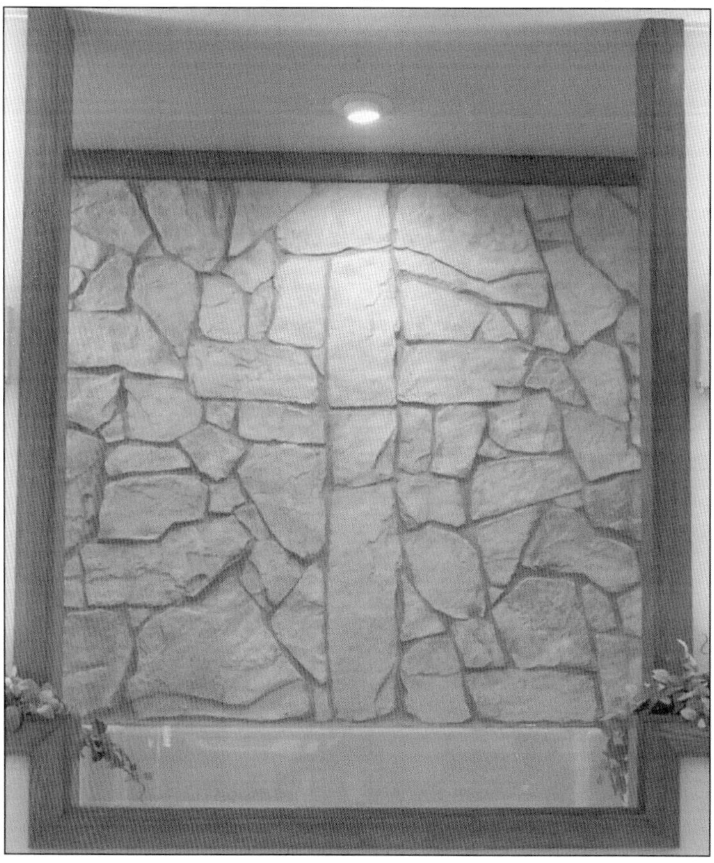

Many improvements have been made to the church buildings in Argyle. Most of the churches are made of brick or stone and they have all the modern conveniences. The First Baptist Church of Argyle no longer has to use creeks or ponds for baptisms. This photograph shows the baptistery at the First Baptist Church of Argyle. (Courtesy of Denise Remfert.)

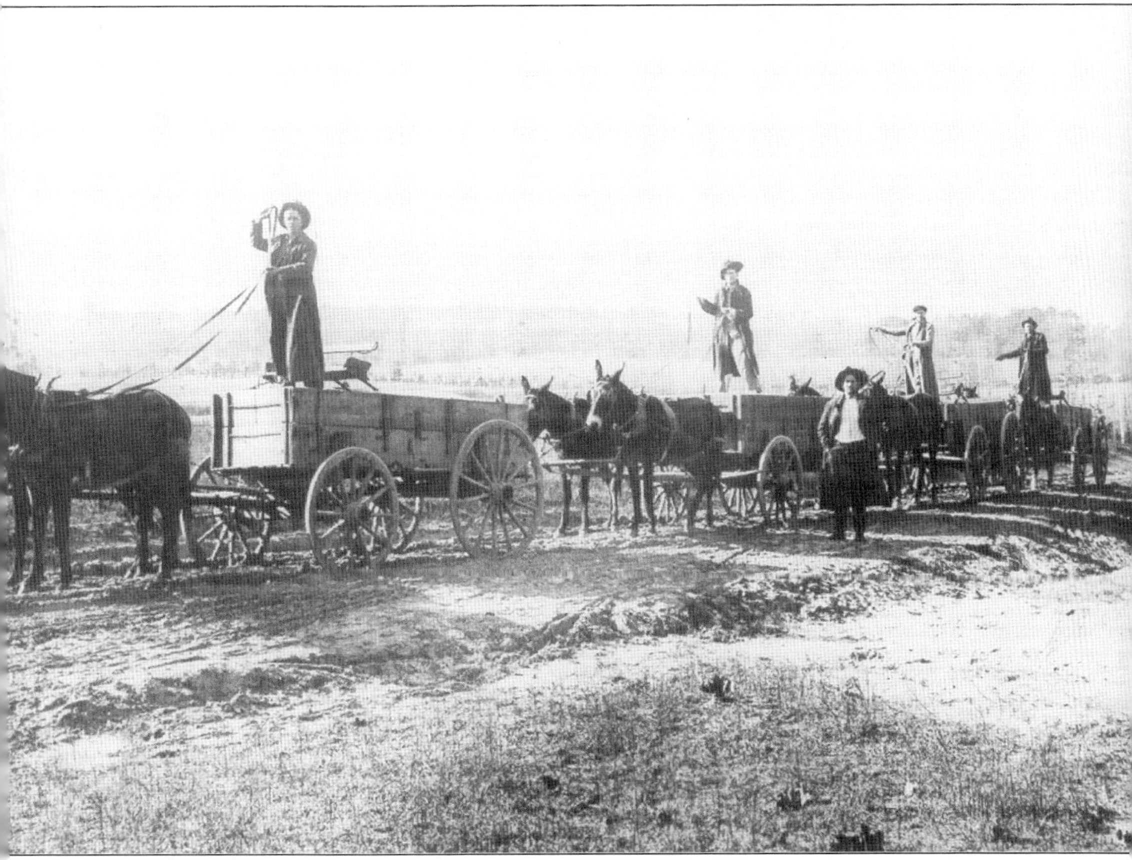

In 1881, when Argyle became a town, farming was the main occupation. Farmers used wagons pulled by horses or mules to transport their crops. Today, Argyle's farming days are long gone, but for people wanting to live in a rural atmosphere while working in the metropolitan area, Argyle has become a commuter's paradise. (Courtesy of Wallace Lynch.)

THE PLACE IS ARGYLE
by Lynn Sheffield Simmons

The place is Argyle,
where the tree lined hills,
have drawn us to dwell,
Where family gardens and farming,
once did very well.

Now it's to the cities,
to work and sell,
but returning to Argyle,
where unfolds a magic spell,
The place is Argyle.

www.arcadiapublishing.com

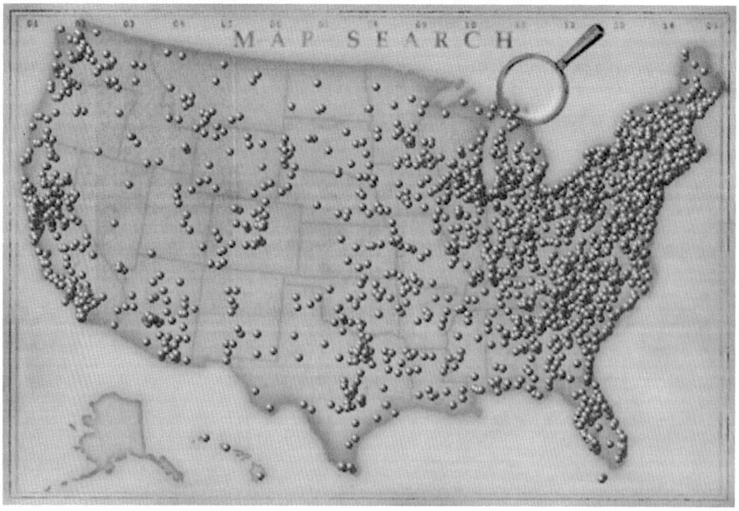

Discover books about the town where you grew up, the cities where your friends and families live, the town where your parents met, or even that retirement spot you've been dreaming about. Our Web site provides history lovers with exclusive deals, advanced notification about new titles, e-mail alerts of author events, and much more.

MADE IN THE USA

Arcadia Publishing, the leading local history publisher in the United States, is committed to making history accessible and meaningful through publishing books that celebrate and preserve the heritage of America's people and places. Consistent with our mission to preserve history on a local level, this book was printed in South Carolina on American-made paper and manufactured entirely in the United States.

This book carries the accredited Forest Stewardship Council (FSC) label and is printed on 100 percent FSC-certified paper. Products carrying the FSC label are independently certified to assure consumers that they come from forests that are managed to meet the social, economic, and ecological needs of present and future generations.

FSC
Mixed Sources
Product group from well-managed forests and other controlled sources

Cert no. SW-COC-001530
www.fsc.org
© 1996 Forest Stewardship Council

Find Your Place in History.